LINDA McQUAIG

THE QUICK AND THE DEAD

Brian Mulroney, Big Business and the Seduction of Canada

VIKING

VIKING
Published by the Penguin Group
Penguin Books Canada Ltd, 10 Alcorn Avenue, Toronto, Ontario,
 Canada M4V 3B2
Penguin Books Ltd, 27 Wrights Lane, London W8 5TZ, England
Viking Penguin, a division of Penguin Books USA Inc., 375 Hudson Street,
New York, New York 10014, USA
Penguin Books Australia Ltd, Ringwood, Victoria, Australia
Penguin Books (NZ) Ltd, 182-190 Wairau Road, Auckland 10, New Zealand

Penguin Books Ltd, Registered Offices: Harmondsworth, Middlesex, England

First published 1991

10 9 8 7 6 5 4 3 2 1

Printed and bound in Canada on acid free paper ⊗

Canadian Cataloguing in Publication Data
McQuaig, Linda, 1951–
 The quick and the dead
Includes index.
ISBN 0-670-83305-3

1. Business and politics – Canada. 2. International business enterprises –
Canada – Political activity. 3. Canada – Economic policy – 1971-   .*
I. Title.
HD3616.C22M3 1991   322'.2'0971   C91-095041-5

To Fred Fedorsen,
husband, soul mate, editor

Acknowledgements

I am indebted to a number of people for generously offering their time, advice and ideas in the long process of honing this vast subject into a book. In particular, I would like to thank: Mel Watkins, Rick Salutin, Daniel Drache, Marjorie Cohen, Geoff Meggs, Linda Diebel, Dennis Howlett, John Dillon, Rod Mickleburgh and Tom Walkom. (They are, of course, in no way responsible for any errors or shortcomings.)

The crew at Penguin Books — Cynthia Good, Brad Martin, Lori Ledingham, Pat Cooper and Karen Cossar — was a real pleasure to work with. David Kilgour did his usual thorough and thoughtful editing, and managed to come up with the key word for the subtitle long after the rest of us had given up!

Linda Manzer proved that if she ever tires of being one of the world's finest guitar makers, she can have a back-up career as a researcher. She did an excellent job as the researcher for this book, tracking down material with imagination and enthusiasm.

I am particularly indebted to Neil Brooks, who teaches tax law at Osgoode Hall Law School, but who is far more than simply a tax expert. His strong sense of social justice and his keen analytical mind make him equally adept at deciphering the mysteries of other economic issues and he generously gave his time in helping me sharpen the ideas for this book. His broad vision of social and economic justice make him, along with Noam Chomsky, one of the key influences in shaping my way of thinking.

Finally, I want to thank my husband, Fred Fedorsen, who proved that his true calling is neither that of brilliant criminal lawyer, nor repressed tomato farmer — but editor. He spent countless hours going over the manuscript, tightening up the logic, weeding out the mixed metaphors, and generally seeking ways to make my writing — and my life — just a little bit more exciting.

Linda McQuaig
July 1991

CONTENTS

THE
QUICK
AND THE
DEAD

1 • CARROT TOP MEETS THE 800-POUND GORILLA

Carrot Top looked impassive. And that enraged Simon Reisman, who was sitting on the other side of the negotiating table. As everyone in the room knew, Reisman was not likely to control himself for long. After all, he could take only so much, and Carrot Top seemed to be really pushing it this time with his damned indifference, his shrugging low-key manner. Reisman had been so direct, so plain in his language. Didn't he at least deserve a response from the mousy little man with whom he was supposedly negotiating?

But Carrot Top only shrugged again. That was it. Everyone in the room knew it was now just a question of time before Reisman reached his snapping point and let out a fierce tirade, venting his rage at the team of American negotiators across the table.

Nobody in the room disliked Reisman's temper more than the red-haired chief U.S. negotiator Peter Murphy, a.k.a. Carrot Top. Indeed, Murphy had come to truly despise the volatile, flamboyant, short-fused chief Canadian negotiator — Canada's "800-pound gorilla," as one U.S. business figure described him. As he braced himself for the gorilla's attack, which was sure to be furious, Murphy reminded himself that, unpleasant as the

1

diatribe would be, it was necessary. Otherwise, the Canadians would want to continue with the next agenda item.

Over the long, unpleasant months of negotiations, this was one of the delaying tactics that Murphy had devised to avoid dealing with certain Canadian demands. The strategy was simple: keep repeating something that irritated Reisman — or, better still, persist in saying nothing when a response was clearly requested. In the face of such obstinance, there was a good chance that Reisman would explode and the rest of the afternoon would be taken up with an outpouring of rage, leaving no time to discuss the progress of the committee working on the question Canada desperately wanted addressed: a set of rules that would ensure Canada access to the U.S. market.

It was all part of a disingenuous game Murphy played that kept the two men constantly at loggerheads. It would be hard to imagine two more different styles. Reisman was up-front, talkative, effusive. He would lay Canada's demands out emphatically and clearly, and insist that the American negotiators reply. But Murphy would respond with a blank look, an evasiveness, an obscure answer, a non sequitur.

Reisman would challenge this response, and Murphy would deny that that was what he had said. Reisman would insist that that *was* what Murphy had said, and a fight would ensue over whether or not it was indeed what he had said. Frustrated and angry, Reisman would demand that the record be read back, and then the argument would continue over whether or not Murphy had said what he was alleged to have said, which — whether he said it or not — was not very crucial anyway, since he had only said it to be evasive.

Away from the bargaining table, things were equally acrimonious. When the two men went out for private dinners by themselves, as they did in an attempt to resolve the impasse, the meals turned into unpleasant confrontations. The next day Reisman would respond to a point Murphy had made the night before, and the two would be back fighting over just what had been said. Sometimes Reisman would phone Murphy at home as early as 6:00 a.m. For Reisman, whose every moment was caught up in finding a way to get a deal, no hour of the day or night seemed unreasonable. But for Murphy, the whole free trade exercise was more like — well — just a job. And 6 a.m. was not part of his workday. It was the only time he had to spend with his young daughter. He was damned if he was going to waste it listening to the shouts of a man he regarded as a bellicose bully.

In fact, Murphy was a bit of a bully himself. For all his low-key manner, he was a hardbitten negotiator who was not accustomed to compromise. His training had been in textile negotiations, where the U.S. was infamous for driving hard bargains. Textile-producing nations were mostly poor, low-wage countries with little economic clout, and their desperation to get their products into the huge U.S. market was written all over the faces of their negotiators. As a result, textile negotiations between the U.S. and these struggling little countries were a farce: the U.S. held all the cards.

As one U.S. textile negotiator explained it, "We go out to some little island which has a population of about two million and we beat them up. We say, 'You can bring this much into the U.S. If you don't like it, tough.' That's what the negotiation is. You go out, and you give them a number, you beat them around a bit. . . . But you come home, you bring their heads — their scalps — back and show them to the domestic industry. You say, 'I've been out, I have six scalps from six little countries, and here's the quotas they're going to get.' "

If textile negotiators were known for stinginess, Carrot Top was the stingiest of the lot. In negotiations he was a haggler who would offer some small country a quota of, say, 100,000 shirts. And when the country said that wasn't nearly enough, he would come back with an offer for *less*. "The next offer would be for 90,000 and then 80,000," said one negotiator familiar with Murphy's style.

Things were supposed to be different, of course, with Canada. Canada was not the Third World. And it was America's largest trading partner. In U.S. trade circles, Reisman was known as the hard-driving negotiator who had broken new trade ground with the Canada-U.S. auto pact, a deal that was seen as a good deal for Canada; indeed, some in the U.S. thought it was too good a deal for Canada. "How did a country with such a small population end up a major producer of cars?" asked one U.S. trade lawyer. "Would that have happened without the auto pact?"

And yet, this time, somehow things were different. Canada was perhaps just a little too keen for a deal, was behaving a bit too much like a shirt producer. All this strengthened Murphy's hand. Let them come to me, was his attitude, as he offered up more obfuscation.

Murphy's evasiveness enraged Reisman, but at the same time seemed to lure him in deeper and deeper, without granting him the one thing that he had demanded from the outset: a set of rules to govern trade between the two countries. Only with such a set of rules could Canada be assured it wouldn't suddenly find itself barred from a crucial U.S. market just because some American senator wanted to score points with his constituents by calling for tough U.S. trade laws to be applied against Canadian imports.

Carrot Top had never had any intention of agreeing to a common set of rules to govern trade. He had been characteristically evasive on the subject. Still, although he had never made any promises, he'd obliquely held open the possibility, agreeing to strike a committee to study the issue. The committee never seemed to make much progress, however. And whenever the issue came up on the negotiating agenda, something somehow intervened — a U.S. delay, a fight over what had been said, an outburst by Canada's 800-pound gorilla.

Years later, Reisman still raged at the memory of it all. As he paced his office in March 1991 — more than three years after the events — the battles still seemed fresh in his mind. His office, where he conducts his trade-consulting business with well-heeled business clients, is spacious and elegant, suggesting his years of government service have paid off handsomely. Yet still, for a man who loves the limelight, he seemed oddly out of the fray. There was a sense of emptiness in the large, uncluttered office. On this day, Reisman was waiting in anticipation for a call from the Prime Minister. When the phone finally rang, Reisman bounded across the room to get it, only to discover that it wasn't the PM. Brian Mulroney used to phone regularly. But that was in the days when the feisty chief negotiator seemed to be holding the fate of the country in his hands. Reisman hadn't heard from Mulroney in months.

It was all part of the ache of no longer occupying centre stage in the Canadian political drama. As Reisman recalled those heady days of September 1987 when the whole country watched as he stormed out of the free trade talks, the excitement and the pain of disappointment still seemed to sting.

"This could have been the crowning activity of my career," he said, looking out his office window as the Ottawa sky grew dark. "I was getting close to the end of it. I had done most things, and this was a great thing and I believed in it. It could have had a real, real wonderful closing phase. . . ."

He resumed pacing the room as he came to the most painful part. "Instead . . . I had to go to the Prime Minister at the critical time and say, 'Prime Minister, I'm sorry to have to say this to you. It's the most disappointing thing in my life, but I have to tell you, I cannot get an agreement at the table that I can recommend to you.'"

Ironically, what Reisman saw as the most disappointing moment in his life was in some ways an impressive moment in Canadian history — Canada was walking away from a deal with the U.S. because it couldn't get the terms it considered necessary. That was spunky. It was what followed — Mulroney's willingness, in the end, to settle for a deal that fell far short of Canada's stated goal — that was the tragedy for the country.

Still, for Reisman, who had worked his way up from the junior levels of the civil service to become one of the most powerful mandarins in Ottawa, it was devastating to have to inform the Prime Minister he hadn't achieved the goal. Mulroney accepted his advice and the free trade talks were broken off, but the two countries reconvened the talks the following week. And when they did, Reisman was no longer Canada's chief negotiator. He was just one of a number of key players gathered in the adjoining room as Derek Burney, Mulroney's chief of staff, and U.S. Treasury Secretary James Baker hammered out the final details of the deal just before the clock ran out on the midnight deadline.

What made it all the more painful for Reisman was the thought that he had been stymied by an inferior. Carrot Top.

The very name suggested a buffoon. But Peter Murphy, a man Reisman considered not his peer, had got in the way of Reisman and his dream.

"I don't want to talk about him," snapped Reisman, then immediately plunged in.

"There were two things wrong with Murphy. He was young and he was inexperienced."

Reisman wasn't content to leave it at that. "He didn't have much of a mandate. He didn't have control of his team. His team didn't accept him. . . . In the end, he was a complete failure, a complete disaster."

More than anything, Reisman faulted Murphy for a lack of vision. Reisman himself is a man of passion, a man of large ideas and dreams, who had dealt with high-powered U.S. negotiators across the table many times before. There were a small number of them whom he considered his equal — men of scope and vision with ideas "big enough to capture the imagination," as he put it. "I must have committed great sins in my life to have been stuck in that [free trade] process with nobody who had that kind of vision."

Instead, Reisman was stuck with a nit-picker. But Peter Murphy, it seems, was a cunning nit-picker. He did, after all, manage to achieve the main U.S. objectives in assuring Canada would be open to American investments. "Simon is missing the point if he thinks Peter was incompetent," says Bill Merkin, Murphy's deputy during the trade talks. "Peter's strategy from the start was clearly delay, delay — string the thing out as long as possible." Murphy thought it was silly to make concessions at the negotiating table, Merkin says, because these would ultimately have to be made at the political level, by senior politicians.

Ultimately, Canada did win a partial concession at the political level, from Treasury Secretary James Baker, who would later become George Bush's right-hand man in the Gulf War. But Canada failed to win the major concession it wanted — a common set of rules to govern trade between the two countries. Instead, it settled for its secondary goal — a dispute settlement mechanism, which Canada had sought as part of a package to enforce the common set of rules. Reisman considers that this was a significant breakthrough. But it wasn't the victory that he and Mulroney had hoped for — and promised the Canadian people.

Carrot Top's delaying tactics had succeeded in drawing Canada in for so long that, in the end, Mulroney didn't want just to walk away. Reisman concedes that, if he had known at the outset that the Americans would not agree to a common set of rules, he would never have gone through the whole exercise. "If they had said [at the beginning], 'There's no way we are going to do that,' I'd have thrown in the cards. I'd have gone to the Prime Minister and said, 'Get yourself another boy.' "

Carrot Top had won. The U.S. had largely achieved its agenda, getting a sweeping agreement that covered important ground in the new items it was pushing for in world trading agreements.

A Canadian scalp was offered up to the U.S. Congress, which eagerly approved the deal. In Canada, the agreement was much more controversial. Many opposed it, and pointed out that Canada had failed to win what it had insisted all along was its bottom line. But Mulroney and the Canadian business community supported the deal anyway. They did so because, when it came right down to it, the agreement was about a lot more than selling Canadian products in the United States. It was about changing Canada. And that was something business — on both sides of the border — was very keen to do.

IN THE MASSIVE dining hall of the Sheraton Centre Hotel in the heart of downtown Toronto, about 300 business executives sipped on vichyssoise, nibbled at lean veal and contemplated the future. It was March 1990, and the future decade stretched out blank before them. What better time to come and pay homage to a concept that had already become a buzz-word for the nineties? Globalization.

It had such a forward ring to it. The word positively resonated with the future. It sang of computers and supersonic telecommunications and far-flung corners of the world only the flip of a microchip away. It meant selling junk bonds in the middle of the night on some stock exchange half-way around the world, and with more ease than you could order out for pizza.

"A feudal mind-set has no place in a global economy," warned David G. Vice, the thunderous chairman of the Canadian Manufacturers' Association, just in case anyone in the crowd was contemplating a corporate reorganization along feudal lines. Vice was also vice-chairman of Northern Telecom, the highly successful telecommunications giant and one of the few Canadian firms with a serious chance of scoring big in overseas markets.

The conference on Globalization had attracted some of the biggest names in business and politics, but what was the fuss all about? What was this Globalization that had these senior executives so enthralled?

"It's hard to explain," said Mickey Cohen, the usually articulate CEO of Molson's. Not one to be caught tongue-tied, Cohen fumbled when he was approached after his speech by CBC Radio's Stuart McLean and asked to define Globalization. "It's one of those things that you feel. Going global is not doing something. It's being something. It's simply sitting up and saying to yourself, 'My own home market is somebody else's global market and maybe I can do business in his market.' It's an attitude. I'm not sure I can really put that into concrete terms. There's not sort of ten commandments of being international. You *feel* it."

If Globalization made some top-level CEOs sound almost giddy, it turned others into virtual piranhas. Vice, for instance. In his stirring speech to the conference, Vice painted a picture of an international jungle where the strong adapted and grew stronger still, while the weak fell like flies. "Those that can't adapt will *not* survive," he warned sternly. Then, quoting Globalization guru Peter Drucker, he added, "If you don't think globally, you deserve to be unemployed and you will be." In case the message of potential carnage wasn't clear, Vice went on, "The nineties will be a decade in a hurry; a nanosecond culture. There'll be only two kinds of managers: the quick and the dead."

At its most basic level, of course, Globalization really just boiled down to world trade. But the concept of world trade lacked spin. It was an old idea, about as marketable and forward-thinking as the wireless or a TV set where you had to get up and switch the channels by hand. Marco Polo was engaging in world trade in the thirteenth century. Christopher Columbus had it on his mind when he "discovered" America. The Indians who sold Manhattan for a string of beads were indulging in a form of world trade. But the concept lacked cachet in the nineties. Would anyone come to a conference with a non-video title like "World Trade"? Would Mickey Cohen wax mystical on the powers of world trade, be reduced to describing how it made him *feel*? Could world trade serve as a fearsome god of the future, with the power to sort us instantly into two camps: the quick and the dead?

But if the world marketplace mythologized in Globalization was not particularly new, neither was it particularly palatable. It was the international jungle, alluded to by Vice, where only the strongest survived. It was capitalism at its most primitive, with all the excesses of Dickensian England and more. Huge corporate titans wandered the jungle, staking out their territory and driving away — or devouring — any lesser competitors. Eventually there would be only a handful of each species, each controlling its own domain, with smaller carcasses strewn throughout the jungle. There were no rules to stop the carnage or control the fattened titans that emerged; there was only one law in the jungle: survival of the fittest.

In practical terms, this meant immense power for the small group of companies that had emerged as players on the world stage. They derived enormous clout from their ability to move their capital around the world at will, encouraging nations to engage in an international bidding war for their investment. Certainly there was no shortage of desperate countries willing to bid, offering these corporate giants low wages, weak pollution standards, no taxes. The global marketplace was full of exceedingly poor people who, in their hunger and misery, would settle for less . . . and less . . . and less. After a while, the multinational corporations didn't even have to threaten to go elsewhere. The threats were simply understood. They were part of the Globalization mind-set. You knew who held power; you knew who lacked power. You could *feel* it.

For an advanced western culture like that of Canada, where the population had enjoyed a more civilized way of life, this descent into brutishness had little appeal. Hence the need for some kind of sales job. But it wasn't going to be an easy sell. After all, when it came right down to it, the international marketplace was really nothing new. Certainly computers had brought dramatic changes; money and data could now move around the world much faster, allowing companies to centralize their operations to a far greater extent. But, interestingly, international capital flows were no bigger a proportion of Canada's gross domestic product in 1990 than they had been a century earlier. The world was always changing. There was nothing in the changes of the nineties that dictated a return to the jungle.

Enter Globalization, which gave the worn-out idea of world trade new spin. Businessmen could hold conferences about it and solemnly warn how the global marketplace was the inevitable wave of the future. It wasn't a question of wanting to go global, but knowing that you had to. No more could we languish comfortably behind the walls of our own country. We were now part of the rugged, take-no-prisoners global marketplace. We could be quick (to adjust) or we could be dead. The "choice" was ours.

In short, Globalization could be used to sell an idea. It could become a virtual marketing logo for an unpalatable agenda — an agenda that the business community wanted to put in place but was otherwise having trouble promoting.

Before we go any further, we should perhaps stop to deal with the word "agenda." To suggest that business has an "agenda" that it wants to put in place is roughly the equivalent, according to some people, of saying businessmen are intrinsically evil and are always secretly plotting ways to take advantage of the poor. Such notions of business are stereotyped, old-fashioned and biased, these people argue, and therefore anyone using the word "agenda" is clearly the victim of paranoid conspiracy fantasies that block rational analysis.

So, before I am exposed as harbouring such paranoid delusions, let me state clearly that I do not subscribe to the view that businessmen are intrinsically evil, nor do I think they are plotting secretly to take advantage of the poor. I do, however, use the word "agenda" without apology or shame, because it conveys an important concept — that what the business community has been advocating and the Mulroney government has been delivering is not a haphazard string of unconnected policies. Rather it is a coherent plan of action, a set of things to be done to achieve certain results — in other words, an agenda. To deny this is to ignore the mounds of material that the business community and the business press constantly produce in an effort to explain their vision of the way the world works and what the government must do to make Canada adapt to it.

In short, I am not accusing businessmen of being secret plotters. Rather, I am simply giving them their due. To deny that they have a coherent agenda is to assume that they are stumbling buffoons who advocate policies on a haphazard basis without a clear sense of what's in the best interests of the businesses they represent. I draw no such insulting conclusions. My impression of business leaders is that they are an intelligent lot who are capable of understanding the needs and desires of the business community and who are representing those interests in an able and articulate manner.

If this isn't enough to dispel the notion that those who indulge in the use of the word "agenda" are somehow crazed conspiracy theorists, I add one further point — that business and government leaders themselves employ the tainted word to describe the set of policies they want to see in place. Stanley Hartt, for instance, who straddles the world of big business and big government as president of Campeau Corp. and former chief of staff to Prime Minister Mulroney, used the word unabashedly in an interview to describe the set of policies that both business and government considered essential.

Furthermore, what is perhaps the most important policy document produced by the Mulroney government was titled nothing other than *An Agenda for Economic Renewal.* This key document, presented to the public by Finance Minister Michael Wilson in November 1984, was not a description of the behind-the-scenes manipulations of evil conspirators, but a blueprint for the coherent set of policies the government planned to implement. To a surprising extent, the government has stuck by that "agenda."

So, on the question of the existence of an "agenda," there really is no difference between government or business leaders and me. Where we do differ, however, is on the question of whether this agenda is necessary or desirable for Canada. Business and government leaders insist that it *is* necessary, that it is an essential part of equipping Canada for survival in the global marketplace. I say that this is nonsense, and that the new agenda amounts to little more than a massive transfer of power and wealth to those so ably promoting it: business.

THIS BOOK IS about the new business agenda. It is the story of how that agenda was put in place, why it was put in place and who is benefitting from it. It is the tale of how the Canadian public was seduced into accepting the unpopular new set of policies, in the belief that they were part of a compelling new global imperative. There are many items on the agenda — from free trade to tax reform to high interest rates to cuts in social programs. We will explore a number of them, some in more detail than others. But we will also look beyond the specifics to the broader pattern of what the new agenda is all about, for it represents a coherent plan for redesigning our country.

Perhaps the best place to start is with the way business and government leaders explain the need for the new agenda. Above all, they say there is a need for greater emphasis on the private marketplace, and reduced emphasis on government. This theory is expounded on in some detail in key business and government documents of the early and mid eighties, notably the Macdonald Royal Commission on the Economy, the reports of the Business Council on National Issues and the Mulroney government's pivotal *An Agenda for Economic Renewal*. It borrows heavily from political right-wing movements in the United States and Britain, where the ideology became known as "neoconservatism."

But, whereas the U.S. and Britain both underwent dramatic social and economic changes that partly explain the rise of this new form of conservatism, Canada experienced no similar upheaval. The Mulroney government came to power in 1984 not on any sweeping platform calling for a new neoconservative economic order, but mostly because Canadians were fed up with Pierre Trudeau's arrogance and patronage. Canadians only discovered much later that the Mulroney Conservatives they had elected subscribed to the "neoconservatism" of Ronald Reagan and Margaret Thatcher — a mean-spirited, imported ideology that didn't fit at all with the long-established tradition of Canadian conservatism. More on this later.

Central to the new business agenda, then, is the notion that the private sector should be expanded and given more power, and that the public sector should be reduced and its powers trimmed. The public sector has become too big and intrusive, say the advocates of the new agenda, and now gets in the way of the efficient running of the economy, thereby destroying the health of the country. The proof they present to back up their thesis — indeed the centrepiece of their argument — is the federal deficit.

The deficit — the annual shortfall in government revenue after taxes are collected — is portrayed as the ultimate evil, the cancer that threatens to destroy Canada. It is the evidence presented by business and government leaders that we are living beyond our means, that the public sector has been allowed to grow out of control. And on the surface, their case appears to be convincing. The government does appear to be spending about $30 billion more a year than it is collecting in taxes, making us seem like an irresponsible family that consistently spends more than it earns, and is thus constantly digging itself deeper into debt until it can barely pay the interest. Not a pretty picture. But also, in fairness, not a totally accurate one.

The deficit is a problem, but only one of many. Child poverty and the devastation of our environment easily rank as equal or more serious problems — problems that directly threaten our quality of life, and the quality of life of our children and grandchildren. And yet business and government have yet to try to mobilize a national campaign around these issues; indeed, the Mulroney government's February 1991 budget slashed spending on both poverty and the environment in the name of deficit reduction.

Business and government leaders have stressed the deficit above all else because it helps bolster their argument that the government sector has grown out of control and must now surrender power to the private sector. With this in mind, they have hyped the deficit to the point of near-hysteria. We will return to this important subject in more detail in Chapter 8, in an attempt to dispel some of the mysteries of the deficit bogey-man. We will raise, for instance, the intriguing question of whether the monstrous deficit may be at least partly an account-ing fiction. Neil Brooks, a tax and public finance expert at Osgoode Hall Law School in Toronto, argues that the deficit is to some extent the product of the unusual method of govern-ment bookkeeping that is at odds with private sector bookkeep-ing methods. Says Brooks, "If [the deficit] were accounted for properly, it would probably be close to zero."

Furthermore, debt is not always all bad. Is it necessarily foolish for a family to go into debt to buy a house, or for a business to take a loan to expand its plant and equipment? Similarly, is it foolish for a government to go into debt to build a highway, railway or canal so that goods can be transported to market, or to create a superior education system so that citizens can be equipped to deal with an advanced world? Debt can be a smart way of financing something needed for the future. The notion that all tax revenues simply end up paying civil servants' pensions or the travel allowances of senators is a convenient one for those trying to whip up public anger against government, but it bears little resemblance to what governments actually do with the bulk of the money they spend. If the problem is that our government is spending money on the wrong things, the answer is clearly to use our democratic power to force it to spend on the right things, or put in place a government that will. Surely the answer is not that the government should stop spending, that it should cease to invest in the future.

Even the specific evils that the government attributes to the deficit — that it discourages private savings and investment — don't seem to be true on closer scrutiny: Canada has enjoyed a relatively high rate of savings and investment despite its deficit. Indeed, as *Toronto Star* columnist Tom Walkom has noted, the Mulroney government has presented us with a highly suspect version of history, suggesting that everything was fine in the good old days before deficits came along in the mid seventies and ruined Canada. "There is no evidence for this remarkable assertion that Canada's economic well-being has been directly and uniquely related to the state of the federal deficit," argues Walkom, noting that the government has conveniently omitted from its history of economic malaise such significant factors as the oil crises of the seventies and the world recession of the early eighties.

Government and business leaders have distorted the historical record in calling for an all-out assault on the deficit. Even with the country in a full-scale recession by the winter of 1991, they continued to escalate their crusade. Perhaps most telling was the government's 1991 budget — a gruesome bit of business with nothing to offer the growing legions of unemployed but a plan for even more vigorous deficit reduction. Following a similar budget the year before, the '91 budget slashed spending in a way that will have dramatic consequences over time. Dr Michael Rachlis, a medical policy analyst based in Toronto, said that the combination of those two budgets and the Mulroney government's first budget in 1985, will "end medicare in Canada. . . . Unless the tide is reversed, medicare as Canadians have known it will be dead."

Indeed, the deficit-reduction measures taken by 1991 were so draconian that even the government's own numbers in the budget showed that the deficit would shrink on its own over time. Brooks argues that, with inflation and economic growth, the deficit "would remain at most a minor irritant."

None of this dampened the deficit-reduction enthusiasm of the truly committed, however. Fresh from his grim budget, Finance Minister Michael Wilson attended the inauguration of the "Deficit Clock" in Ottawa with all the solemnity of a general seeing his troops off to battle while foreign planes attacked from above. At the ceremony, children came forward to contribute money to the national deficit-reduction fund. One of them was a young boy who had organized a car wash in the hopes of saving the country.

But was there any reason for this frenzy, for scaring children into believing the proceeds of their car washes, lemonade stands and paper routes were needed to fight something that was perhaps little more than a weird method of accounting? Was it really responsible to create a Deficit Clock to dramatize the importance of the issue to the country's children, instead of perhaps a "Poverty Clock" marking the number of Canadian children who slip into poverty each day, or an "Environment Clock" showing the litres of contaminants that are poured into our lakes each hour?

What is it about the deficit that has so captivated business and government leaders? One way to look for the answer to this question is to examine how these same business and government leaders propose to tackle it — because they have a very specific plan. They are not willing, for instance, to scramble around in search of alternative methods of deficit reduction, weighing the pros and cons of each, asking the public what would be most palatable. No. On this matter, there can be no divergence. There is only one prescription: the deficit must be reduced, *and it must be reduced in the way business and government demand.*

This rigidity is interesting. If government and business leaders were simply concerned with the deficit, presumably they would be open to the full gamut of ideas about how it could be reduced — from any assortment of tax increases and spending reductions to children's car-wash brigades. But, while Wilson accepted any cheque willingly, he had in mind a very specific plan for deficit reduction: reduce public sector spending, most notably on Canada's major social programs of health, education and welfare. This fit neatly, of course, with the business idea of reducing the public sector in favour of a greater emphasis on the private marketplace. But gutting the country's social programs seems, to say the least, a very unfortunate way to begin tackling the problem, particularly when the government has simply ruled out an alternative that most Canadians would probably prefer, if anyone bothered to ask them.

That alternative — taxing the rich and the corporate elite — has been definitively ruled out of bounds by those advocating deficit reduction. This is a curious omission, since it might seem logical for a government short of funds to look to those who have an ample supply. Merely closing off the tax breaks that favour the rich could save the Canadian treasury some $8 billion a year. And annual wealth taxes — similar to those that exist in most western industrialized countries — could raise another $3 billion. To put this in perspective, the total amount the government plans to save as a result of its nation-wide cuts in health and education spending outlined in its February '91 budget amount to $2.3 billion over the next five years. More on all this later.

At this point, it is enough to note that, in all the shrill calls for deficit reduction emanating from business and government sources, there has been not a single mention of wealth taxes or closing tax breaks enjoyed by the rich — even though Canada has one of the highest rates of wealth concentration in the western world, including the highest per capita accumulation of billionaires in any country. Such items are simply off the agenda, something not to be discussed, an example of incorrect thought.

The reason all this is not to be tampered with, according to government and business leaders, is that the rich will leave. Capital will flow out of the country. This age-old threat from the rich — that they will pack up their playthings and leave the sandbox if they don't get their way — is said to be far more real today in this age of Globalization, when money can fly from one corner of the globe to the other with nothing more than the flick of a computer button. So taxing the rich is deemed to be out of bounds. Indeed, if anything, the rich must be coddled and pampered in the hopes that they'll stay and, maybe, invest their money. Here then is one of the most basic rules advanced by those proposing the new agenda, who often happen to be rich: don't even talk about taxing the rich. It's out of the question.

With the rich off the hook, the rest of the country can logically be offered up for the task of deficit reduction. And so the government has enacted a regressive tax reform, which, among other things, has transferred $4 billion a year from the backs of corporations to the backs of consumers through the introduction of the GST. And it has begun slashing social programs, which, although available to everyone, are far more important to the lives of Canada's middle and lower classes. The essence of the new agenda in many ways could be neatly summed up: indulgence for the rich, austerity for the rest.

AS THE GOVERNMENT'S hype over the deficit reached a fever pitch in winter of 1991, almost all Canadians in some way felt the pinch of Ottawa's lean, mean austerity drive. Except, that is, for a small group of Canadian families. These were the richest families in the country — not just the well-paid professionals, but the truly rich who counted their fortunes in the millions and tens of millions of dollars. They were so rich that they had long ago set up private trusts to enable the transfer of massive family fortunes from one generation to the next tax-free.

Meanwhile, back in the Department of Finance, where the budget was being prepared in the winter of 1991, things were looking bleak indeed. Officials had scrounged in almost every corner for extra funds to contribute to the cause of deficit reduction. Yet, after six years of Tory budgets, most of the fat had long ago been trimmed and taxes had already been increased to the breaking point. So, as the government prepared its budget, something much more fundamental was taking place. Officials were mapping out cuts that would seriously erode the level of funding for the most basic of Canada's social programs — health care, education and welfare.

The process had actually begun in the 1990 budget, which had imposed a two-year restraint on these programs. It had seemed at the time to be a temporary measure. Now the government was planning to impose much longer-term austerity in these areas; it was planning cuts that would fundamentally alter the nature of these programs by placing legislated limits on their funding. And, as if to show how much gall it really had, it was also taking money out of its environmental restoration program, and, in the midst of the bleakest recession since the thirties, it was actually cutting funds from social housing and job retraining, and planning to raise the unemployment insurance premiums, one of the most regressive forms of taxation.

As experts in the Department of Finance prepared this grim budget, they were also working on another document. This one was going to be as generous as the budget was mean-spirited. But its generosity was restricted to that tiny coterie of rich families who had created their own family trusts.

While the budget would be publicized loudly with Michael Wilson calling on the country to unite in a crusade against the deficit, the other document would slip quietly into the hands of a small group of tax lawyers and accountants who specialized in estate planning. There would be no accompanying sermon about the deficit. Indeed, as the lawyers and accountants would be well aware, the message in this other document would fly in the face of deficit reduction.

And so on February 11, with only two weeks to go before budget day, the Department of Finance quietly released the other document under the less-than-exciting title "Release No. 91-018." Although it was available to any member of the press or public who cared to pick it up, it was so dull and technical and seemingly unimportant that, as Finance officials well knew, it would go unnoticed by the general public. However, for the small group of tax lawyers, accountants and the rich clients they represented, the news behind the technical jargon in the release was anything but dull. In essence, it said that the government planned to change the laws in a way that would allow the richest families in the country to save billions of dollars that they owed in taxes. For some, the deficit scalpel was clearly blunter than for others.

The story behind Release No. 91-018 dated back to 1972, when the Liberal government of Pierre Trudeau introduced some major reforms to the tax system. One of the key changes was the removal of the federal inheritance tax — a little-publicized measure that resulted in a massive and ongoing windfall to some of the richest families in the country — leaving Canada as one of the few countries in the industrialized world without such a tax. To help offset this loss of revenue, the Liberal government introduced a partial tax on capital gains, a key source of income for the rich.

Up until 1972, capital gains — that is, profits made from the sale of stocks, bonds, jewelry or real estate — had been tax-free. The Royal Commission on Taxation had recommended in the sixties that, in the interests of fairness, capital gains be taxed at the same rate as other income. But the Liberal government had been reluctant to do this, and instead opted to tax capital gains at only half the rate applied to other income.

The other special treatment capital gains were to receive was that they would only be taxed when an asset was sold. This would have meant that wealthy families could pass stocks from generation to generation without paying tax. So the government specified that any increase in an individual's capital property would be taxed at his or her death, whether it was sold or not. The rich would still be able to get around this by placing their assets in a private trust, which never died. So in order to limit just how long the rich could avoid facing the tax department, the Trudeau government placed a twenty-one-year time limit on tax deferrals for assets held in private trusts. At the twenty-one-year mark, any increase in their value would be subject to tax as capital gains.

With tens of billions of dollars of assets in these private trusts, the approach of the twenty-one-year mark in January 1993 seemed fortuitous: it meant that a large amount of tax revenue — in the billions of dollars — was due to come into the national treasury just as the government was hitting a peak of desperation about the deficit. This money — like the proceeds of paper routes and lemonade stands around the country — could obviously be used to help reduce the deficit or to allow the government to make its spending cuts less harsh, by for instance foregoing cuts in social housing, or job retraining, or loosening up funds for provincial transfer payments to cover social expenditures like food banks.

But, instead of collecting the money from the rich as scheduled, the Mulroney government decided to allow the rich to hold on to it. To accomplish this, the government proposed to create a new loophole that would allow family trusts to put off the tax payment date well beyond 1993. As outlined in Release No. 91-018, the loophole allows a wealthy family, in almost every case, to choose to put off payment until its youngest child dies, delaying taxes for another generation or more. This deferral amounts to a virtual tax exemption, because any amount that escapes taxation now can be invested so that it multiplies in value in the intervening years before it is due. It is a rule of thumb among tax experts that a dollar of tax deferred is a dollar of tax saved. And Release No. 91-018 quietly informed the rich that they would be saving billions — all without any embarrassing publicity.

The Department of Finance offered up some specious arguments in the release to defend what amounted to a massive giveaway. Its main argument was that the twenty-one-year rule might interfere with trusts established by parents for the benefit of a disabled child. This sounds at first glance like a caring approach for the government to take, but let's think it through for a moment. Anyone wanting to provide benefits for a disabled child would structure a trust so that it provided an ongoing income to the recipient, rather than a lump-sum payment receivable at some distant point in the future. And how many of Canada's ultra-wealthy families happen to have disabled children? Perhaps one or two, perhaps none. And yet the government is willing to forgo billions of dollars of desperately needed revenue for the sake of a child who might not even exist!

It would certainly be far more cost-efficient simply to put all wealthy disabled children on generous government pensions for the rest of their lives. But then this might seem like favouritism. After all, the government provides only the most minimal support for ordinary disabled people, relegating them generally to a life of semi-poverty. Indeed, the government's massive cutbacks in the areas of health care, education, welfare, social housing and job retraining will undoubtedly do more to hurt the disabled — that is, the non-wealthy disabled — than this twenty-one-year rule ever could. Of course, there is always the possibility that the government wasn't really thinking of the disabled at all when it decided to change the rule, but rather concocted the bogus argument about disabled children in case anyone questioned why it was altering the rule in a way that favoured the rich.

The point in all this is not that the government was being hypocritical, although it is hard to think of a way to explain its actions without reference to some measure of hypocrisy. Still, the larger point is the pattern that clearly emerges. While the Mulroney government has shown itself to be tough — almost to the point of ruthlessness — when it comes to demanding sacrifices from ordinary Canadians, it treats the rich with a gentleness and kindness that is striking.

AS THE BUSINESS agenda becomes less and less appealing the more we examine it, we begin to see the importance of the

Globalization argument. Without it, business and government leaders would be stuck in the tight jam of trying to popularize an agenda that offers almost nothing to non-rich Canadians. But with the invocation of Globalization, the picture changes. Business and government leaders can call for what amounts to a redesign of Canada, without ever really having to sell their positions to a skeptical public. If questions get too pointed or the austerity gets too bleak, they can simply resort to chanting the mantra of Globalization: we have no choice, we must compete in the global marketplace . . . we have no choice, we must compete in the global marketplace. . . .

Globalization does it all so cleanly — no probing questions, no wrenching moral dilemmas, just the cold reality of the brutal international marketplace. Indeed, there is no need for a national debate on the subject of changing the country, since the key decisions about the country's future are now to be made in boardrooms well outside the political process, even outside the country. Herein lies the true appeal of Globalization to its advocates: it takes decision making out of the hands of the national government, over which the public ultimately has at least some potential control, and hands it over to a faceless creature called the international marketplace, over which the public has absolutely no control.

Of course, the faceless creatures of the marketplace are not really faceless at all. Although, in the mythology of the marketplace, decisions are made by the anonymous forces of supply and demand, in reality they are, of course, made by real people. In handing over decision making to the marketplace, we are not handing it over to some neutral force that will arbitrate fairly in the interests of greater efficiency. We are handing it over to the small group of individuals who control the capital of the large corporations that dominate the market. What is being called for is nothing short of a major transfer of power from society as a whole to a small group of private interests.

The implications of this were clear from the start to those who pushed the new business agenda. One of the most articulate expressions of the business agenda can be found in the report of the Royal Commission on the Economic Union and Development Prospects for Canada, headed by former Liberal cabinet minister Donald S. Macdonald and heavily influenced by the business groups that made detailed presentations to its hearings. The Macdonald Commission, whose advocacy of a free trade deal with the United States in 1984 was a key catalyst in the government's move towards free trade, made no secret of the purpose of such a deal. The real impetus for free trade, according to the Commission, was not increased access to the U.S. market — although this was certainly desirable — but a need to redesign Canada, to strip away the nation's flab and submit Canadians, naked, to the discipline of the international marketplace.

The Commission said as much in its opening volume: "The explicit premise behind our free-trade proposals is that the Canadian economy must be made more competitive and that adjustment-retarding policies must be replaced with adjustment-facilitating strategies." The "adjustment-retarding" policies that were so repugnant to the Commission were those, such as unemployment insurance and regional development programs, that shielded workers from having to adjust to the brutalities of the marketplace — policies that were central to the Canadian way of life.

The Commission made no secret of the fact that one of the key aspects of this redesigned version of Canada was the transfer of power from government to private hands. But it is also clear that the private hands that the commissioners had in mind were not those of ordinary people, but those of the economic elite. They argued that it was necessary to strip government of power in order to guarantee political freedom, "by providing a realm of autonomy, outside the detailed reach of the state, to which individuals can retreat when they are out of favour with political authorities."

The individuals referred to here were clearly not run-of-the-mill Canadians, who do not have the luxury of retreating into a private business realm where they enjoy autonomy. Perhaps a select few — a Conrad Black or a Paul Desmarais — could sulk off to the comfort of their private business realms after, say, having a tiff with the Prime Minister. Most Canadians have no more power or autonomy in their work lives than they do in the political arena; indeed, they probably have less, since they don't even have the right to vote in their work lives. The transfer of power to the private sector, as advocated by the Macdonald Commission, would do nothing for these ordinary people.

But if there's any doubt about the Commission's intentions, let's hear more of what it has to say about transferring power to the private sector. It notes with some concern that when it was holding hearings "powerful economic actors, whose fortunes depended on government discretion, were afraid to voice in public their opinions of government policies for fear of the consequences." Clearly, the Commission was moved by the plight of these "powerful economic actors" whose "fortunes" were based on government largesse, and who thus had to keep their mouths closed lest they risk nipping the hand that feeds them so lavishly.

This focus on what would seem like a minor problem for the rich is particularly striking in view of the Commission's apparent indifference to the problems of the less powerful. Little is said about the plight and the problems faced by the millions of power*less* economic actors — like how to find a job or feed their families as the government ignores their situation. Indeed, there is no attempt on the part of the business-oriented Macdonald Commission to explain how transferring power to the private sector will help these ordinary people one bit. Evidently an oversight.

What business is calling for with its new agenda is nothing more complicated than a major transfer of power and wealth to itself. And yet this remarkable request is sparking precious little debate. Instead, we simply have business and government leaders lecturing us on the necessity of accepting the changes prescribed. After all, what is the point of debating the changes if they are inevitable, part of the imperative of the global marketplace? The debate about this fundamental redesigning of the country is being sidestepped, rendered mute and irrelevant by the invocation of Globalization, with all its mysterious powers.

In the rough-and-tumble world of the global marketplace we apparently no longer have to concern ourselves with questions of fairness — questions that have been fundamental to our political life in the past. Such questions are deemed irrelevant in the new international jungleplace, where survival is the only thing that counts. There is no use any more asking: Is it *right* for a small handful of companies to control the economy? Is it *fair* that large corporations should increasingly shift the tax burden onto those at the low end of the economic ladder? Is it *just* that Canadian workers should face a choice of lower wages or unemployment? These questions, compelling as they might be for a grade six class in public affairs, are seen as no longer relevant in the real world. To business, all these probing self-examinations are out of date. What matters in the new quick-or-dead world of international business is simply adapting for survival.

"The global changes we're seeing are fundamental," David Vice told the Globalization conference. "They are permanent rather than cyclical. We may never completely understand what caused them. Nevertheless we have to *act.* "

Here, then, is Vice's answer: Don't think; just act. Don't waste time pondering what's happening to our country or where the changes might take us. Just change, adapt, go with the flow. Let others — presumably the "powerful economic actors" championed by the Macdonald Commission — make the decisions for you.

Perhaps the best response to Globalization, however, is not to let it terrorize us. We are being told that, more and more, we will have to let the market make the decisions. Perhaps our best answer is: Thank you very much, but we'd rather make those decisions ourselves. While this may sound flip, the truth is that anything else amounts to a surrender of what little control we've managed to gain over our lives.

If business wants to change society, fine. But let's demand that it stop hiding behind the excuse of Globalization. Let's insist that it make the case for the changes it wants, not simply chant something about having no choice because of international competition. Let us hear the argument why it is *fair* that the rich should be indulged while austerity is imposed on the rest of the country. If there's a good reason why our tax system should be altered so that the burden is transferred from corporations to consumers, let's hear it. If it's *right* that the powerful economic actors should make the important decisions in our lives, then let's hear somebody explain why. Otherwise, we are simply giving in to the bully on the block — the powerful private interests that dominate the international marketplace.

The real danger in the nineties — one that looms as large as the tyranny of oppressive governments — is the tyranny of the marketplace.

IT WAS THE spring of 1990, and President Carlos Salinas de Gortari of Mexico had shocked Mexicans — as well as Canadians — with an announcement that his government intended to pursue a free trade deal with the United States. With much of the Mexican bureaucracy still reeling from the impact of that announcement and the changes that lay ahead, some senior officials at Mexico's central bank were surprised by the sudden arrival on their doorstep of a group from the New York office of American Express.

The visit was really just a courtesy call, but it was followed over the next year by a steady flow of senior American Express officials coming to talk about free trade. None of this would have surprised the Mexican banking officials had they followed developments in Canada's free trade deal with the U.S. — the deal that theirs was likely to be modelled on. American Express had played a pivotal role in bringing about the Canadian-U.S. deal. Indeed, the American Express chairman, James D. Robinson III, probably did more to bring about the deal than any other single person in Canada or the United States. It wasn't that he was particularly interested in this sprawling country to the north. But the ambitious Robinson was intensely interested in expanding the world empire of the massive corporate giant he oversaw. And that would bring two otherwise incidental nations — Canada and Mexico — into the cross-hairs.

2 · JIMMY THREE STICKS HAD A DREAM

4₂₂ . . . 423 . . . 424 . . . 425 . . . 426 . . .

The agony and the ecstasy. The agony was obvious — the sheer pain as the muscles strained, drawing the body upright yet another time from an outstretched position on the floor. No matter how often you did this ritual, after a certain point — about now — those muscles started to feel like they were in a vice grip, and the vice grip was tightening.

But the ecstasy was there too. It was more subtle, yet no less real. It was the joy of doing it, of feeling the muscles in your stomach turn to steel, of knowing you could do something almost no one else could do. Indeed, right now, it seemed almost no one else could even keep his eyes open, let alone throw his body around on a mat as if it were a thick, lean steak being flipped on a grill.

It was not yet 6:00 in the morning, and James D. Robinson III was more than half-way through his 800 sit-ups — part of the daily ritual that had turned his body into a sleek collection of bulges. Becoming such a fine physical specimen had not been easy. It had meant getting up at 5:40 sharp every weekday morning and going through a grinding exercise routine at his elegant Manhattan apartment, as well as spending hours on weekends in his "muscle room," while other men were content to atrophy in front of a ball game on TV. The muscle room — strategically located on his rambling thirty-six-acre country estate in Connecticut — was a fully equipped gym where Robinson lifted weights, had private aerobics instruction or worked out alone with the exercise video *Buns of Steel*. After years of this regimen, Robinson could just as well have starred in the video.

But for him, the daily ritual of endurance was a tonic for the soul as well as the body, a reminder that hard work and discipline would get you where you wanted to go — even if that was a very long way. When his alarm went off at 5:40 every morning, Robinson never dallied, never snuggled down into the pillow for just a few more minutes of blissful repose. With the city still draped in darkness, he rose out of bed promptly and began pressing himself to the limits of endurance. The grinding daily routine not only strengthened the body, it invigorated the spirit. It was the same discipline that had gotten Robinson to the very top of the corporate ladder and to the innermost circles of political power.

489 . . . 490 . . . 491 . . . 492 . . . 493 . . . 494 . . .

A blue-blood by birth, Robinson had never been one to rest on his laurels. His family, although wealthy, had always been achievement-oriented. His father and grandfather had both served as chairmen of First National Bank of Atlanta — an intimidating image for a young boy growing up with the same name as theirs, and with the idea that he had a tradition to uphold. It would have been hard enough being James D. Robinson II, but James D. Robinson *III*. Only royalty had names like that.

But he knew he wasn't royalty. In the Robinson family, you had to earn your title — or, rather, your bank chairmanship. And Robinson had done just that. Through hard work and discipline, he had parlayed the advantages of his birth and breeding into an even more grandiose post than the prestigious regional one attained by the previous James D. Robinsons. He had made it from Atlanta to New York, catapulting himself into the chairmanship of one of the most venerable financial institutions in the U.S. — American Express — and all by the neophyte age of forty-one.

That was in 1977. By the mid eighties, Robinson was straining to achieve an even higher goal — to make American Express the dominant financial institution in the world, and in the process, perhaps, position himself for a bid at the top job in the world — the presidency of the United States.

It was a brash and heady dream. And it would require a lot of savvy, a lot of luck to pull it off. But above all, it would require qualities Robinson was steeped in — hard work and discipline, getting the jump on the other guy. Here in the darkness of early morning Manhattan, Robinson was getting that jump. While he strained at his exercises, the rest of the world slept.

And, although few Canadians realized it, Robinson's dream was going to alter the future of their country.

596 . . . 597 . . . 598 . . . 599 . . .

IF ROBINSON WAS well-positioned for his bold gambit, it was partly an accident.

To be sure, he had always been groomed for high office. After graduating with a Harvard MBA in 1961, he landed a job with Morgan Guaranty Trust, where he soon found himself close to the power centre of the firm, as assistant to chairman Thomas Gates. Robinson left to become a partner at the investment banking firm White, Weld & Co. and after two years there — at the age of only thirty-five — was wooed to American Express as executive vice-president, in charge of the American Express International Banking Corporation.

Eugene Black, a Robinson family friend, sat on the Amex board, and proposed young Jim for the position. Robinson had already proved himself to be promising: Gates had considered him CEO material from the beginning. And he fit perfectly in many ways with the blue-blood, old-money atmosphere of American Express. Poised and confident, Robinson had the charm of a southern gentleman. But, not only did he have the demeanour necessary for a senior Amex executive, he worked like one. From the outset, he regularly put in twelve-hour days at American Express, showing himself eager for the top job that many observers felt he had been selected for from the start.

That opportunity landed in his lap in April 1977, with the early retirement of Amex chairman Howard L. Clark. Robinson was left to manage a corporate empire with over $10 billion in assets. It was a daunting task. American Express was an American institution, a company that had practically grown up with the country. It had developed from a delivery service in 1850, when the trip between Buffalo and Albany was a four-day venture by rail and stagecoach, to its modern incarnation as a travel services giant.

The challenge for the ambitious young Robinson was to keep up the company's phenomenal history of growth, known within Amex as "the Record." For the previous three decades, Amex's booming traveller's cheque and charge card business had kept the firm's profits continuously rising. Annual revenues — which stood at $4 billion — had steadily increased under Clark's stint as CEO, and profits of $300 million were thirty times what they had been when he took over seventeen years earlier. Although Robinson came from a long line of top-notch bankers, there were many on Wall Street who doubted the young man had what it took to keep the Record intact. His youthful looks made him seem all the more like a dauphin ascending prematurely to the throne. To catty Wall Street insiders, James D. Robinson III became known as Jimmy Three Sticks.

But Robinson was hampered by more than his own inexperience. By the late seventies, Amex was facing a potential profit squeeze — a squeeze that may have hastened Clark's retirement. The firm's international banking business was over-extended. Indeed, its thirty-one-nation international network included three offices in Bangladesh — a country not normally associated with banking and high finance. And the insurance company Amex owned, Fireman's Fund Insurance Company, although the seventh largest property and casualty insurer in the U.S., was performing erratically and contributing little to the maintenance of the Record.

More serious, the company's Travel-Related Services division, by far the most profitable part of the Amex empire, was increasingly facing competition in its lucrative traveller's cheque and card business. After years of market dominance by American Express, Bank of America and Citicorp had begun making inroads into the traveller's cheque business in the 1960s, just as the travel business was starting to boom. By the late seventies, American Express still held 50 percent of the market, but was losing ground to competitors, including the banks' new entrants, VISA and MasterCharge. Since most traveller's cheques were purchased at banks, and the banks had an obvious interest in selling their own cheques, Amex's place in a market it had dominated since the thirties appeared threatened.

That was a sobering thought indeed for Robinson as he took over the Amex helm. The traveller's cheque generated far more than the service charge on each transaction. Since most cheques were held by purchasers for up to two months, they provided the company with an enormous pool of money it could invest and earn interest from until the cheque was cashed. With an average balance of $1.5 billion worth of cheques outstanding at any moment, Amex had a huge fund of cash for short-term investments, generating tens of millions of dollars in profits.

Even more lucrative was the American Express card, which the company introduced in 1958. Originally targetted at an elite crowd — paying with plastic at restaurants and hotels around the world was a joy largely confined to the international jet set in the late fifties — the card had been successfully marketed to eight million consumers by the late seventies. But some in the company wondered just how much more of an elite there was out there.

As it turned out, there were millions more in the elite, or the would-be elite. By the late eighties, Amex was still convincing consumers in droves that they needed the prestige of an American Express card, even though the Amex card required an annual fee while other cards that did the same thing were available for free. The secret appeared to be Amex's scrupulously maintained image of elitism, reinforced through an extensive advertising campaign based on the slogan, "Membership has its privileges" and featuring portraits of rich and famous stars along with dates of when they had joined the Amex club. The ads encouraged the notion that Amex cardholders would somehow be better treated in restaurants and stores than those paying with mere VISA or MasterCard — an unlikely scenario since Amex demanded a larger cut on each sale from retail establishments than competing cards. Still, the magic whiff of elitism in Amex ads somehow worked. Consumers happily signed up for the privilege of belonging to the club, even though it had no clubhouse, no facilities, just 34 million other members who were generally neither rich nor famous.

In the late seventies it appeared to many that the Amex card, which was producing net profits of $70 million a year, was heading into a congested market. Skepticism about Amex's most lucrative arm was reflected on Wall Street. Amex stock was unpopular, and analysts were expressing doubts about the company under Jimmy Three Sticks. What was needed, it seemed to Robinson and his top advisor, Roger Morley, was an aggressive new thrust. American Express was brimming with assets, assets that provided its new chief executive officer with a chance to strut his stuff on the Wall Street stage and shed the Jimmy Three Sticks image. There was always of course the option of starting a new business. Amex's last new business had been the card. But that was a tough act to follow; far too risky for the new kid on the block. Robinson settled for a safer way to prove himself — a corporate takeover.

In fact, this safer route proved to be fraught with perils. Although Robinson personally studied the financial data of potential takeover targets in great detail, his initial overtures — to Philadelphia Life Insurance Company and Walt Disney — were spurned. The business press, in typical knee-jerk fashion, treated the failed attempts as evidence to support earlier suspicions that Robinson lacked the guts to run American Express, whatever that meant.

Robinson's next move — at the lucrative publishing house McGraw-Hill — proved to be even more of a public relations disaster. The feisty chairman, Harold McGraw, it turned out, did not want to sell the family-run business, and fought back in a lively battle that grabbed Wall Street's attention. McGraw-Hill took out advertisements in major newspapers posing such embarrassing questions as whether it was appropriate for American Express to own *Business Week*, a McGraw-Hill publication, when American Express was often the subject of business articles. More upsetting from Robinson's point of view, however, were some of the other questions posed in the ads. For example, one ad disputed the morality of American Express traveller's cheques, on the grounds that the company did not pay interest on the money that it received from those buying the cheques. That hit a little close to the jugular. In the end, Robinson backed off from the McGraw-Hill takeover and the whole episode was regarded on Wall Street as a fiasco. Morley left American Express shortly afterwards, and many expected Robinson to follow.

But Robinson stayed put, and even persisted in his pursuit of a corporate acquisition. His next move proved to be a turning point, both for the company and for himself. Whereas his previous acquisition targets had had only the loosest connections to Amex's existing businesses — in the case of Walt Disney it was hard to see any connection beyond perhaps a potential ad slogan: "Mickey Mouse, cardholder since 1953" — this time the object of his aim fit neatly into the American Express cupboard. Indeed, it seemed to offer the possibility of finding new ways to market existing wares.

The new target, Shearson Loeb Rhoades, was an aggressive Wall Street brokerage house that had gobbled up smaller financially troubled firms at bargain prices throughout the seventies. While much of Wall Street struggled in the seventies, Shearson had expanded through carefully orchestrated moves that showed pluck and bravado. By the beginning of the eighties, Shearson was the second largest brokerage house in the U.S., boasting truly impressive profits, a huge client list and a reputation for being one of the most smartly run firms on Wall Street. Although Shearson was in many ways the exact opposite of stodgy, blue-blood, bureaucratic American Express, Robinson was intrigued by its lean, street-smart ways.

What was particularly intriguing to Robinson was the potential fit between the two companies. One of Amex's great assets was its client base — millions of affluent, high-spending cardholders whose names and addresses were, of course, all recorded in the company's computers. Wouldn't they like to buy some stocks from time to time? And what about Shearson's extensive client list, collected from years of picking up the clients of firms it had digested? Wouldn't these stock-buying customers, who obviously had some disposable cash, want to sign up for an

American Express card to assist them in spending their money? How about some American Express traveller's cheques next time they contemplated a vacation? And American Express was also in the business of selling life insurance through its subsidiary, American Express Life. Wasn't there clearly a need for life insurance among Shearson clients?

The possibility of pairing up customers and products within an expanded Amex empire was dizzying. It conjured up images of a dream store where well-heeled customers could gorge themselves on an endless array of junk bonds and pork futures, indulging in a virtual orgy of financial services.

As Robinson toyed with the idea of Amex as the giant of financial services, he was beaten to the punch. In March 1981, the mammoth Prudential Insurance Company bought up the large securities firm Bache Halsey Stuart Shields and was suddenly able to offer a full range of products — insurance, stocks, bonds, mutual funds. The news had Wall Street agog. In one fell swoop, Prudential had ushered in the eighties and set off alarm bells that the financial markets were soon to be dominated by huge corporate monoliths. The signals were coming partly from Washington, where the freshly elected Reagan regime was clearly intent on loosening regulatory restrictions governing who could own what financial institution, and turning a blind eye to greater corporate concentration. The small, dignified Wall Street firm seemed destined to become a thing of the past, to be swept aside by the one-stop financial supermarkets that would replace them just as surely as McDonald's had replaced the hand-made hamburger.

Jarred by the Prudential move, Robinson swung into action. Within five weeks, he had negotiated a $1 billion takeover of Shearson, whose executives were also spooked by Prudential's aggression and fears of a new age of corporate giants on Wall Street. With Shearson in its empire, Amex was well on its way to becoming the General Motors of the financial sector — a plan Robinson had stumbled on almost by accident when his earlier takeover targets eluded him.

Robinson became obsessed with the idea of Amex as a financial services giant. He became convinced that the company's best growth prospects for the future lay in cross-marketing its financial services, a form of cross-fertilization that would produce richer results in all parts of the corporate empire. For Robinson, the plan took on the force of a driving idea, a neat prescription for growth. Robinson was fond of neat, succinct ideas that could emanate from his office and filter down into the mind-set of Amex's 70,000-odd employees. This was surely such an idea. "One Enterprise" he dubbed it, meaning that the various sections of the American Express empire were all really one big store, where customers would glide with their shopping carts from aisle to aisle, running up a big bill to be paid at the check-out counter with their American Express cards. The idea became Robinson's pet concept, the stamp he was determined to put on the company, and he offered hefty bonuses for Amex executives who came up with ways to implement the One Enterprise idea.

Robinson also moved to expand the products offered at the big American Express supermarket, putting together a bizarre assortment of companies in the process. Amex acquired the prestigious Trade Development Bank, a Swiss-based investment bank that attracted a discreet international clientele of the super-rich, largely through the personalized service of its owner, the legendary Lebanese financier, Edmond Safra. But no sooner had Robinson paid half a billion dollars in this bid to bring the global jet set into the Amex supermarket, than he turned around and paid $725 million for Investors Diversified Services, a humdrum Minneapolis-based financial firm best known for selling insurance and securities across kitchen tables throughout the Midwest.

Shearson meanwhile continued to round out its own mini-financial empire within the larger Amex orb. With its rough edges and street-fighting credo, Shearson stunned the financial world in 1984 in its presumptuous move of buying up one of the most established investment houses on Wall Street, Lehman Brothers. Lehman's history dated back to the 1850s, and the firm exuded the grace and quiet power of an old-monied aristocracy. Original Rembrandts, Renoirs and Picassos hung on the office walls, and its private panelled dining room served only the finest wines and culinary delicacies prepared by a former chef from Le Pavillon in Paris. Nevertheless, in the free-for-all of the eighties financial scene, Lehman Brothers was to become absorbed into the motorcycle club atmosphere of Shearson. In the end, Shearson Lehman became a mixture of both worlds, with the old Shearson management keenly adapting to the opulent requirements of serving an upscale clientele. In only a few short years, the American Express empire seemed poised to corner the financial market at both ends, to be simultaneously Safeway and Saks.

Although Robinson had stumbled into this strategy almost by accident, by the mid eighties, it was starting to look like a stroke of genius. The business press now hailed him for creating a state-of-the-art financial services empire. A cover story in *Business Week* praised him for transforming American Express into "the unrivalled colossus of financial services" by carrying out "what is widely considered the most successful financial services diversification drive of the 1980s." It certainly looked brilliant. The demand for financial services was growing and American Express had got an early jump in a market that was increasingly attracting some of the largest corporations. Indeed, some of the best-known giants — General Motors, Ford, General Electric and Sears Roebuck — were all branching out further and further from their traditional base of selling manufactured products, into selling financial services.

General Motors, for instance, the largest car maker in the world, had originally entered the financial market by offering loans for car purchases. But over time, GM came to offer an ever-broader list of financial services, including some that had little or nothing to do with cars. By the mid eighties, GM subsidiaries were offering a wide range of loans, mortgages, credit cards and insurance policies to millions of customers. And, like American Express, GM was attempting to exploit cross-selling within its empire. For instance, GMAC, GM's financing arm, offered its mortgage customers a $500 discount if they bought a Cadillac through GMAC financing. With more than 200 finance offices located around the U.S., GMAC had quietly become the fifth largest bank in the country.

Similarly, General Electric made its original foray into the financial business by providing loans for consumers to buy GE products. But, by the mid eighties, the financing arm of the GE empire was accounting for almost one-quarter of GE's massive annual earnings. Indeed, GE Capital Corporation had expanded its loan and real estate financing to the point that it rivalled the size of the Toronto Dominion Bank. It had also issued some 50 million credit cards — second in the U.S. only to Sears Roebuck, which had more than 80 million in circulation.

Like the others, Sears had also entered the financial business through consumer finance. As the largest department store and mail order chain in the U.S., Sears had developed an "easy payment plan" for purchasing Sears merchandise and the plan evolved into the Sears credit card. Sears had also ventured at an early stage into insurance, establishing the highly lucrative Allstate Insurance back in the thirties. In 1981, Sears bought Dean Witter Reynolds, a large securities firm, as well as Coldwell Banker, a real estate broker. This paved the way for Sears to offer an impressive cross-section of financial treats. At 300 of the largest Sears department stores, customers could take a break from their shopping and wander into a Sears Financial Center, a financial supermarket that would make Jim Robinson's mouth water. Here they could purchase life insurance from Allstate, mutual funds from Dean Witter or line up a mortgage from Coldwell Banker.

Sears even introduced the Discover card in 1985. Although it functioned as a general purpose credit card, Discover was more than this. Its real purpose was to lure the consumer into doing all his or her financial dealings in one place by offering a credit card that could be used for all financial purposes. Accordingly, Discover cardholders received a monthly statement that noted their mortgage payments, their mutual funds and their savings account balance, as well as a record of their purchases. If that wasn't enough to make Jim Robinson twitchy, Discover also offered cardholders *travel* services, such as insurance and discounts on tour packages, and gave them access to cash through machines located in Sears department stores.

The financial supermarket — whether the Sears, GE or American Express brand — was, of course, promoted to the public as the ultimate in consumer convenience. No more trotting down to the bank every time you wanted to negotiate a mortgage, no more arduous trips to the securities firm to buy those mutual funds, no more lengthy visits with insurance agents every time you wanted more coverage. Just load them up in your shopping cart and put it all on your card. If there was considerable hype over the fast-food-style convenience of the new supermarket, the truth was that the one-brand option offered little real advantage to consumers, who generally don't buy insurance, negotiate mortgages or invest in mutual funds on a daily basis anyway. But if the benefits to the consumer were perhaps limited, the advantages for the companies involved were considerable. The breakdown of the old system — where banks, insurance companies, stock brokerages and trust companies all operated in largely separate, distinct markets — was paving the way for the emergence of financial titans.

Under the old system, each market was kept compartmentalized and tightly regulated, to ensure its financial stability and protect the interests of consumers who had bought insurance, mortgages or stocks, or placed money in bank or trust accounts. This tight regulation was considered necessary, since financial products, unlike manufactured goods, are largely intangible. Unlike a sofa or dining room set, financial products aren't things you can necessarily have delivered the next day. Life insurance purchased today, for instance, might not be delivered for another forty years.

Clearly, if such a system was to work, there had to be enormous trust and stability. Consumers had to know that their insurance company would be there forty years down the road, and that it would have set aside the assets to pay what was owed. As a result, a tight set of rules had been devised to govern each financial market, regulating the ownership and activities of all the players. But that tight set of rules, designed to keep financial markets separate and sound, also placed limits on the growth of the players. Over time, financial firms found loopholes in the regulations. Under the benign supervision of the Reagan administration, that process speeded up. More and more, a small number of financial giants seemed to be gaining control over an increasingly unregulated financial marketplace. And American Express — with assets of close to $100 billion — had emerged by the mid 1980s right up there at the front of the pack.

But as Amex and other giants surveyed the financial horizon looking for new terrain to control, some of the lushest pastures were offshore. The financial walls in Britain, Germany, France and Japan were also starting to crumble, opening up immense opportunities for the creation of global financial empires. Starting in the early eighties, a wave of takeovers swept across national borders, as giant banks and financial firms from the U.S., Japan and Europe bought up large stakes in each others' financial markets.

By the mid eighties, some of the largest financial institutions had far-flung global empires: American Express had 122 foreign affiliates, the U.S. bank Citicorp had operations in eighty-eight countries, France's Credit Lyonnais was operating in fifty-three countries, the Fuji Bank of Japan had expanded its network to twenty nations, the U.S.-based securities firm Merrill Lynch had affiliates in forty-eight countries, Nomura Securities of Japan was doing business in twenty-one, insurance giant Prudential of America had set up shop in sixty-seven. The global corporate concentration that had taken place in manufacturing and mining in the sixties and seventies was beginning to strike with a vengeance in the financial marketplace.

All this represented an immensely appealing world landscape for Jim Robinson. In his short time at the helm of American Express, he had transformed the stodgy old firm into a modern financial services giant. And he had put together that massive empire just as the financial services market was blossoming all over the world, offering unheard-of opportunities for growth. Never mind that his triumph had largely been an accident, that, if he'd succeeded in his original quest, he might have been spending his time instead managing a publishing empire or a children's fantasy garden. The point was that he was now in a position to get a jump on the rest of the world in the quest for dominance of the newly emerging global financial markets. Robinson, whose whole life had been geared to achievement, was well aware of the opportunities. And if he wasn't, his wife was.

A FEW YEARS earlier, when Robinson was successfully putting in place the key parts of his financial empire, he was having considerably greater difficulty putting together the key parts of his personal life. His marriage had broken up, and he was doing the predictable thing for a rich, handsome, powerful man nearing fifty — dating glamorous young women. He was publicly taking out stunning actress Morgan Fairchild, among others, and cut a dashing figure in New York's swanky restaurants and parties with his muscle-laden body tucked discreetly under fine, perfectly tailored suits. He seemed destined to live out his years as a kind of Hugh Hefner of the financial services world, a perennial favourite at the top of everyone's list of eligible New York bachelors, when an odd thing happened to him: he fell in love.

It was odd because high-powered, intense CEOs of big corporations don't normally have the time or inclination (or willingness to admit vulnerability) to fall in love. And what made it perhaps even odder was the target of his affections: not a windswept model or sultry actress with a string of fallen men in her past, but a no-nonsense go-getter who could outmanoeuvre men at their own games. Linda Gosden was quick and glib and intensely interested in the world of politics and business. She had a spark, a commanding self-assuredness, a grasp of the world. And a grasp of Jim Robinson. For the first time in his life, Jim Robinson felt truly at home with someone. He had found his soul mate.

Like Robinson, Gosden was born to wealth and prominence, but had still made her own way in the world through hard work and ability. Her father was the well-known radio actor, Freeman Gosden, who had played Amos in the popular forties radio show *Amos 'n' Andy*. The family belonged to that exclusive California milieu where politics and entertainment intersected; as a popular radio star Freeman Gosden mixed easily with well-known Republicans who enjoyed the company of celebrities. As a child, Linda heard the endless talk of Republican politics, and sometimes found family friends such as Ronald Reagan and Dwight Eisenhower at the dinner table.

Her father, seventeen years older than her mother, was the towering figure in her life. She had learned from him the values of the male world — competitiveness, toughness, the need to win. He had taught her to work hard and play hard, and to throw a baseball like a boy. After an unsuccessful two-year marriage to the son of a prominent West Coast industrialist, she went to Washington at the age of twenty-seven to work as deputy to James Lake, who was at that time press secretary for Reagan's 1980 presidential bid. Although Lake was later squeezed out, Linda survived, becoming an effective background player with the Republican National Committee. Her savvy and political smarts made an impression on Drew Lewis, an important businessman who was deputy chairman of the committee. When Lewis was appointed secretary of transportation in the Reagan administration, he chose Linda for his press secretary. She managed to guide him unscathed through the air-traffic controllers' strike as well as an unpopular gas tax increase, creating a reputation for herself in political circles as a smooth operator with a keen sense of "optics" — that is, how something looks to the public.

After a diet of glamour girls, Jim Robinson was mesmerized by the optics of Linda Gosden. He had found someone as highly driven and excited about her work world as he was about his. And the two worlds were not unconnected. As a top-ranking CEO, he played a prominent role in politically important business organizations. And many of the key players in Republican politics, such as Drew Lewis, were important figures in the business community. Lewis, in fact, had introduced Linda and Jim at a dinner party that combined the elites of both business and politics.

In no time at all, Robinson was smitten with the thirty-year-old dynamo. In the ruthless world of Wall Street, where executives left their backs unprotected at their own peril, Jim Robinson was unabashedly in love. He had it bad. He and Linda were seen wandering together through the halls of the American Express building, holding hands. After a whirlwind courtship, they were married in a quiet ceremony where Jim's touching speech brought everyone at the small family gathering to tears. When asked about her by journalists, he would use words like "love" and "caring" and talk about how she had opened him up to his own feelings. One reporter said that Robinson went teary-eyed when asked about her, volunteering that he couldn't stand to share her with a child — hardly the kind of revelation normally offered up by senior business figures in interviews.

And the reserve normally associated with the top echelons of the business world was suddenly lacking. Although Robinson remained cool and self-possessed, with his southern gentleman veneer intact, he was capable of being downright playful when Linda was around. He smiled adoringly when she gushed in public, "Isn't he cute?" and obligingly flexed his muscles when Linda suggested that a female reporter feel his biceps. He even dressed up as Superman for a costume ball they attended, which was perhaps only fitting: with his bulging biceps, Robinson always looked like he might duck into a phone booth at any moment. Indeed, if anyone came across as the sexpot in the relationship, it was probably body-beautiful Jim. When the Robinsons took a private cruise with a small group of friends off the coast of Turkey, Linda caught more attention with her strong swimming than her bathing attire, which was as conservative as her politics. But a semi-clad Jim turned a few heads. Recalls one of the women on the cruise, "He has muscles that I've never seen on a man."

While Linda Robinson was opening up her husband emotionally, she was also becoming his trusted business confidante. Much of the complex job of surviving as CEO of a top company involved delicate stickhandling with the board of directors, senior management, the rest of the business community, the press, the public. It involved "optics," how your actions look to those assessing your performance. And Robinson was convinced that Linda had an instinct for optics.

His conviction was confirmed when, within a few years of their marriage, she set up a New York public relations firm, and quickly became one of the leading PR gurus in a city where PR experts are as common as overpriced apartments. Although still in her mid thirties, she was charging $300 an hour for her advice and winning front-page acclaim in the *Wall Street Journal* as the most powerful woman on Wall Street. Her firm boasted an impressive array of clients, including Texaco and IBM. Competitors muttered resentfully that she was simply scooping her clients from her husband's business contacts.

Being married to one of the most powerful businessmen in the country certainly wasn't a drawback. It never hurt in the PR business to attend the most sophisticated parties in town on the arm of one of the most powerful men in the country. Certainly, the Robinsons cut a wide swath through Manhattan's social scene, counting among their close contacts top business figures as well as prominent people like Henry Kissinger (who sat on the American Express Board), Frank Sinatra, Tom Brokaw, Barbara Walters and Henry Kravis, the leveraged buy-out king of Wall Street. They attended the same New Year's Eve bash as the Reagans, as well as an almost constant string of lavish society events in Manhattan and Long Island. They kept residences in the most exclusive enclaves: Manhattan's Museum Tower, the Palm Beach Polo and Country Club in Wellington, Florida and the rolling hills of Litchfield, Connecticut, a weekend playground for the famous and well-to-do.

But the tall, willowy Linda Robinson had become a force of her own partly through her own connections, partly through her own personality and partly through her own hard work. Her contacts with the press were legendary in media circles. She knew how to win favour with journalists by dishing out juicy tidbits of information and flattering them with a familiarity that was unusual in the wife of one of America's leading CEOs. All this was of course no guarantee her clients would receive gentle treatment in the press. Yet, more often than not, it seemed that they did.

It seemed particularly true for the person everyone recognized to be her most important client: her husband. No longer Jimmy Three Sticks, Jim Robinson was now generally portrayed in the press as being a highly competent CEO, with any failings often shunted off onto others. And many observers suspected that Linda Robinson had a hand in creating and peddling the remodelled version of Jim Robinson.

Under Linda Robinson's tutelage, another change was taking place in Jim Robinson. By the mid eighties he seemed to be focussing his gaze more and more on Washington. Increasingly, he appeared to play the role of senior statesman for the business community, or sometimes just senior statesman. He travelled abroad making speeches about the importance of reopening international trade negotiations. He came up with a comprehensive plan to solve the Third World Debt Crisis. It was beginning to look like Jim Robinson had his eye on a top-level post in Washington. Perhaps Secretary of the Treasury. Perhaps something higher.

And if ever there was an issue that would aid the twin goals of helping American Express reap bigger profits and helping Jim Robinson make his mark among those who counted in business and politics, it was world trade . . . or, rather, Globalization.

JIM ROBINSON WAS only twelve when George C. Marshall made a speech to the Harvard graduating class that signalled the beginning of the American era. It was 1947, and Marshall, a wartime general who had become Secretary of State in the administration of Harry Truman, outlined a plan to rebuild devastated Europe with American money. Under the Marshall Plan, which became the centrepiece for the post-war economic boom, the ruined economies of western Europe were rebuilt, providing the already strong U.S. economy with markets for its exports. Indeed, although the plan benefitted both sides, the biggest winners were the emerging U.S. multinational corporations. With European business all but destroyed in the war, U.S. companies could easily penetrate the newly recovering European market, establishing themselves as the uncontested barons of world commerce. At the time, Jim Robinson paid no more attention to the Marshall Plan than any other American pre-teen did, but, years later, it was to become a central theme for him.

The Marshall Plan had a simple prescription for peace: a Pax Americana featuring U.S. military might and world economic prosperity. Although the military might was a familiar message, what was new about the Marshall Plan was the notion that economic prosperity was just as important. Jim Robinson liked that idea, and he took to repeating Marshall's dictum in speech after speech. "The underlying principle of the [Marshall] Plan was simple. It gave economic considerations parity with military might in defining national security," Robinson told a gathering in London to honor the fortieth anniversary of the

Plan. In invoking the spirit of the Plan — and Robinson rarely let a speech go by without paying tribute to the "statesman" George Marshall — he was invoking the spirit of peace through prosperity. It had a nice unwarlike ring to it. It sounded friendly and world-embracing. And it stirred memories of a time of unquestioned U.S. dominance.

Indeed, the prosperity realized in the Marshall Plan was a prosperity based very much on the capitalist model. The communist and socialist movements that had been gaining ground in western Europe in the wake of wartime fascism were firmly marginalized as Marshall Plan money — equivalent to $73 billion today — rebuilt economies along capitalist lines. The Plan, implemented by conservative governments in Europe, had the effect of propping up the old orders of Europe, leaving untouched the tremendous inequalities of wealth that had been the breeding ground of western Europe's strong socialist and communist movements.

Above all, the Plan created European markets open for U.S. exports, ushering in an age in which U.S. business flourished on a scale unrivalled in the history of the world. Within a few years, one-third of American exports were finding their way into countries subsidized by the Marshall Plan. Some, like the oil companies, reaped particularly large bonanzas. In the first three years of the Plan, the five largest U.S. oil companies sold more than $2 billion worth of oil to European countries, with Marshall Plan funds financing the bulk of the purchases. Essentially, the U.S. government was using U.S. taxpayers' money to create prosperity — a prosperity that was based on the growth and dominance of U.S. corporations.

Washington also ensured that moves to set up a new international trading order in the wake of the war would serve U.S. business interests. When fifty-four countries met in Havana in 1947 to draft a charter for the proposed International Trade Organization, there were strong elements of collectivist and even socialist thinking around the table, particularly among the delegates from the United Kingdom, Australia and New Zealand. The draft charter of the new trade organization reflected some of this thinking, including rules obliging member countries to promote full employment and guarantee labour standards and to allow them to expropriate the assets of foreign companies — and pay compensation in local currency. These kinds of provisions were anathema to U.S. business interests, and Washington effectively scuttled the new trade organization by declining even to present the charter to the U.S. Congress for approval.

Instead, the U.S. manoeuvred to put in place a new international trade body, the General Agreement on Tariffs and Trade — or GATT — which lacked the irritating collectivist provisions of the earlier organization. GATT concentrated on lowering tariff barriers, thereby opening up world markets for the goods pouring out of the buoyant U.S. factories. In the hospitable atmosphere created by the Marshall Plan and GATT, large U.S. corporations thrived over the decades that followed, branching out to control markets all over the world. By the mid eighties, there were some 600 manufacturing and mining giants with annual revenues each exceeding $1 billion. This "billion-dollar club," as the United Nations called it in a 1988 report, was still heavily dominated by U.S. corporations, despite the entry of major Japanese and European players.

The U.S. giants remained committed to the same ideology that had shaped the Marshall Plan: open markets. Only by keeping markets open everywhere could the dominant multinational firms continue to expand and prosper. The enemy for these "global" corporations was anything that prevented them from moving goods freely around the world to conduct business in the most profitable manner, regardless of borders. (Of course, while these U.S. giants pushed for open borders around the world, the U.S. Congress was often promoting protectionism at home in order to protect domestic jobs from cheap competing imports in areas such as textiles.)

But, as other countries had slowly rebuilt their economies after the war, it had become clear in many parts of the world that the economic order ushered in by the Marshall Plan and GATT was very much geared to U.S. business interests. Many countries, particularly in the Third World, began erecting tariff walls in an attempt to foster and encourage their own domestic production rather than rely on American imports. This protectionism only increased with the punishing recession of 1981–82, and desperate governments increasingly began to impose barriers such as controls over foreign investment and limitations on foreign ownership.

For Jim Robinson, now a leading U.S. business figure as the chairman of American Express, this protectionism was a dangerous sign. At a May 1984 speech to a business group in Paris called the Executive Club, he referred to "the virus of protectionism" and the "dangerous contagion of protectionism." Apparently not satisfied that he had stated his case against protectionism strongly enough, he went on to call it "economic heroin." Said Robinson: "An injection brings a sense of temporary well-being. But in the end, it undermines the whole system."

The system that Robinson wanted to preserve was, of course, the same open-market system that U.S. firms had thrived on since the days of the Marshall Plan. But Robinson had a particular reason for wanting to see it revived and revitalized. For years, it had favoured the growth and prosperity of multinationals in manufacturing and mining, such world-wide colossuses as IBM, Exxon, General Motors, DuPont, Dow Chemical, Mobil and Texaco. But now, empires of the same breadth and magnitude seemed possible in a whole new corner of the marketplace — the one occupied by services, particularly financial services. With breakthroughs in technology that made possible the instant world-wide transmission of data, and growing markets in financial services around the world, the prospects for international growth for a financial services giant — like American Express — suddenly loomed large and inviting.

But nowhere was the problem of protectionism — the "heroin" of the system — more pronounced than in financial services, which lie at the heart of a country's economic infrastructure. Financial services involve the most basic questions of how an economy functions — how money is raised for investment, how the assets of corporations and individuals are protected and spent, how the value of a country's currency is maintained. These are sensitive areas, central to the economic development of a country, and national governments have traditionally been unwilling to surrender them to some swaggering foreigner.

Indeed, this sensitivity had kept these items largely off the world trade agenda. In the more traditional areas of manufacturing and mining, countries around the world had largely gone along with the U.S. demand for an international set of rules that kept their markets open for the trade of goods, as formalized in the GATT agreement. For decades GATT had served as a kind of international police force and court of appeal to prevent the rise of protectionism. But GATT only covered trade in goods. There were no GATT clauses to enforce international trade in services, no rules aimed at keeping world financial markets open. This would involve far too great a sacrifice of national sovereignty, and few countries would stand for it.

That, at least, was the situation in the early eighties, when American business — and American Express in particular — set out to change things, to put services on the world trade agenda. In fact, there had been an earlier U.S. push to get services on the world trade agenda back in 1974, with a campaign spearheaded by a few major corporations, including Pan American Airways and the American International Group (AIG), the U.S. insurance company with the largest international business. As a result, U.S. trade negotiators at the Tokyo Round of GATT negotiations in the seventies had tried to get services on the agenda, but had failed when they came up against strong resistance from other countries. With services taking on increasing importance as a growth industry for the U.S. in the eighties, the issue was to surface again. And this new thrust was to be championed by American Express and its ambitious chairman.

American Express had long had an international orientation, with its world-wide travel empire. But by the early eighties, the company was approaching the subject of international trade with new gusto. To some extent, this development, like the transformation of American Express into a financial services giant, was partly an accident.

It came about largely through Harry Freeman, who was the company's executive vice-president. Indeed, Freeman, a lawyer who had also worked for Bechtel Corp., became one of Robinson's most trusted advisors. Freeman was also a good friend of Geza Feketekuty, a high-ranking official at the office of the U.S.

Trade Representative, or USTR, the branch of the U.S. government that oversaw international trade for the White House. Feketekuty's area of specialty was services, and he had been one of the key trade officials trying to get services addressed in the Tokyo Round in the late seventies. Feketekuty and Freeman had become friends in the late sixties, when they both worked for the federal government in Washington. Feketekuty managed to interest Freeman in the issue of international trade in services, helping Freeman see the importance of the issue to American Express. "Harry then got Jim Robinson interested," recalls Feketekuty.

Robinson, like many top CEOs, was always searching for a broad vision, something inspiring that would put his personal stamp on the company's overall strategy. The Globalization of financial services had just such a ring. So in 1981, when Feketekuty was setting up a private sector advisory committee to help the USTR formulate policy on the services issue and give it a higher profile in business and political circles, Robinson seemed like the perfect guy to serve as chairman. He accepted.

Robinson's chairmanship of that committee defined him from the early eighties as a leader on the services issue. He became convinced that international trade in financial services represented a vital new thrust for American Express, and for American business in general. Once Robinson was sold on an idea, he promoted it tirelessly, making countless speeches on the subject and using his considerable lobbying skills and connections to give it a higher profile. Inside his company, he elevated it to a top priority, and gave Freeman a free hand — and endless resources — to push it. Freeman hired Joan Spero, a political science professor at Columbia University who had served as U.S. Ambassador to the UN Economic and Social Council. She was made vice-president of international corporate affairs at American Express, and worked closely with Freeman and Robinson on the issue.

Robinson's chairmanship of the USTR committee positioned him nicely to play an influential role in formulating U.S. trade policy. Although the USTR was a branch of government run by bureaucrats, its policies were heavily shaped by the business people who served as advisors on its many private sector committees. Certainly Robinson's interest in the services issue meshed nicely with that of William Brock, who was appointed U.S. Trade Representative by the Reagan administration in 1981. Brock had developed a strong interest in services — particularly financial services — when he'd served as a member of the Banking Committee of the U.S. Senate.

Robinson went on to become a central player among the USTR's private sector advisors, serving on the blue-ribbon panel at the very top of the pyramid of all the USTR's private sector committees, the Advisory Committee for Trade Negotiations. Indeed, in 1987, Robinson was appointed by Reagan to chair that top committee, reflecting the status he enjoyed at the most senior levels of government as a business advisor on trade.

Robinson also became an outspoken trade advocate within the top echelons of the business community. Not only was he chairman of a leading U.S. corporation, but he headed up the influential international trade committee of the Business Roundtable, an exclusive organization of CEOs of some of the biggest U.S. companies.

Poised at the top of the business and political world, Robinson was in a unique position to push for a new trade agenda that put services at the very centre. Cedric Ritchie, chairman of the Bank of Nova Scotia and one who watched from Canada as the services issue became more prominent in the U.S., recalls Robinson and American Express playing a leading role from the early eighties. "That's part of the American Express strategy," said Ritchie in an interview in his elegant Toronto office. Ritchie, who knows Robinson personally, describes him as a "superb lobbier" who was highly successful at pushing services to the forefront of the U.S. trade agenda.

Much of the legwork for Robinson was done by Harry Freeman, whom Robinson came to view as a brilliant strategic thinker. Although Robinson hadn't hired Freeman, he promoted him within the company, creating for him the prestigious post of executive vice-president, attached to the chairman's office. The two men also became personal friends. With Robinson's encouragement, Freeman devoted himself to the task of getting services on the U.S. trade agenda.

Part of the problem was a lack of attention to the issue within the U.S. administration. As we've seen, it had traditionally focussed on knocking down barriers that kept U.S. *goods* out of foreign markets. But American Express, as it tried to expand its empire around the world, was constantly encountering barriers to *services*. No one at American Express was more aware of this problem than Freeman, whose job made him essentially the company's "foreign minister," with responsibility for ensuring that Amex could gain entry to new markets. "We were running into problems around the world," he recalls, "and there was nowhere to go to ask for help in the U.S. government."

By 1981, American Express had become the leading company pushing the services issue, with Freeman spearheading the drive. Freeman, who left American Express in 1989 and is now a Washington consultant, recalls that a small group of companies, including AIG, Citicorp, Arthur Anderson and Peat Marwick, joined forces with American Express and a few officials, like Feketekuty, to form an activist group that became known in trade circles as the "services mafia." The group became the leading protagonist pushing to get services on the U.S. trade agenda in the early eighties and to get another GATT round started, with the ambitious goal of revising GATT rules to include services. This led to a massive campaign, with the "mafia" applying pressure on countries around the world, on business groups and on the Organization for Economic Co-operation and Development (OECD), as well as on the U.S. government.

The "mafia" met often to map out strategy and come up with ideas for promoting its cause. One of the main aims of its campaign, Freeman notes, was getting changes made in U.S. trade laws. Its efforts paid off handsomely on this front in October 1984, when a U.S. trade bill included some key changes that elevated "services" to the same status as "goods" as a trade priority for the government. This gave the President clear authority to retaliate if a U.S. company was discriminated against when trying to sell its services in an overseas market.

The "mafia" had also pushed for the new trade bill to include provisions for the U.S. to enter into bilateral free trade agreements with individual countries — agreements that could serve as models for later multi-country GATT negotiations. Once again, the "mafia" was successful: the new trade bill specifically authorized negotiations to establish free trade agreements — covering both goods and services — with Canada and Israel. In fact, an Israeli deal was already in the works. Freeman, who had been instrumental in bringing about the changes in the trade bill, was delighted with its encouragement of these bilateral trade deals. As he told the *New York Times* in October 1984, "Over the next three years we'll see more bilateral agreements with services, as with Israel."

Freeman's words were prophetic: a deal with Israel was soon completed. Its significance was limited, however, since trade between the two countries was on a small scale. More important were developments on the Canadian front. Brian Mulroney had come to power the month before the passage of the U.S. trade bill which authorized Washington to enter into negotiations for a free trade deal with Canada. Freeman recalls American Express being very interested from the outset in the prospect of such a deal with Canada. While the Israeli deal had "no real impact," Freeman notes that Canadian-U.S. trade was "the largest trading relationship in the world." Getting a comprehensive deal on services with Canada would clearly advance the cause of pushing GATT to incorporate services into its rules. Feketekuty refers to negotiations with Canada and Israel on services as "dress rehearsals" for the vital GATT negotiations to follow.

In fact, services was only one of three new items that was to alter the U.S. trade agenda dramatically in the eighties. The guiding principle of the new agenda was the same as the old Marshall gospel of open markets. And the enemy was still the familiar Satan-worshipping, heroin-ingesting contagion of protectionism. The primary means of achieving the new agenda was familiar too — the world forum of GATT. But added to the old list of rules aimed at keeping markets open was a new set of demands. As Robinson spelled out clearly in speeches to business and financial groups, what was needed was a set of GATT rules to govern three new areas: services, investment and intellectual property.

The three new agenda items reflected the priorities of U.S. business in the eighties. The services sector, championed so well by Robinson, was a sector that promised tremendous growth for U.S. business. The international market for services, particularly financial services, was a rapidly growing segment of world trade, accounting for some $600 billion a year. Not only was it big, but, for the U.S., it seemed ripe for the picking. While the U.S. was being eclipsed by Japanese and European competitors in so many manufacturing fields, the U.S. remained clearly dominant in the services sector.

Cedric Ritchie notes that the U.S. started pushing hard to get services on the trade agenda in the early eighties, when it "saw that the growth in [its] multinational [corporations] was going to be on the services side" — which included data processing, banking, insurance, advertising, engineering and telecommunications. Roughly one-quarter of American Express's business, for instance, was done abroad, and foreign markets also promised the greatest growth potential for the company. But, despite the growing importance of services, particularly financial services, the lack of international rules governing their trade made expansion prospects uncertain.

Investment was another area that U.S. business wanted addressed as part of a new set of trade rules. The investment issue — which involved questions about the rights of foreigners to invest in the economy of another country — had been considered largely outside the GATT realm. This whole area was seen by many countries as crucial to their prospects for growth and independence. But U.S. business increasingly saw foreign restrictions in this area as interfering with the freedom to operate world-wide empires.

An excellent example of such interference was Canada's National Energy Program (NEP), which was aimed at increasing the level of Canadian ownership in the oil industry and raising the federal government's share of oil revenues. The imposition of the NEP by the Liberal government of Pierre Trudeau in 1980 had outraged U.S. business and soured relations between the U.S. and Canadian governments. The NEP was just the sort of nationalist policy that the U.S. wanted to see outlawed in a new set of international trading rules.

The demand for rules in the third area — intellectual property — reflected the desire of U.S. multinationals to maintain their dominance in areas where their superior research and technology gave them an advantage. The concept of intellectual property was based on the notion that a product invented or developed, often after costly research, was owned by the company that had invented it, and that company exclusively should reap the rewards from its sale. This meant that other companies, even in foreign countries, could not manufacture cheap copies of the product — which could be anything from pharmaceutical drugs to electronic systems. The issue was highly contentious because it meant that advanced U.S. companies could essentially corner a market in a vital product — such as a life-saving drug — and charge outrageously high prices for it. It also meant that companies in the Third World, which lacked the resources of giant U.S. firms, were unable to piggyback on U.S. research in order to try to catch up.

It is interesting to note that the intellectual property issue had nothing really to do with trade. Rather, it was a question of getting foreign governments to respect U.S. patent laws, and it smacked of protectionism — that is, protecting U.S. "property" — rather than free trade and open markets. Still, the U.S. was highly committed to getting it on the new world trade agenda, in part because of the enormous influence of Ed Pratt, chairman of the pharmaceutical giant Pfizer. Just as Robinson had played a key role in getting services on the new trade agenda, Pratt had been the driving force behind getting intellectual property on the agenda. Like Robinson, Pratt had been a key player at the USTR, serving just prior to Robinson as chairman of the top private sector committee there.

These three new agenda items were aggressively put forward by the U.S. at two high-level international meetings in the mid eighties to discuss the future direction of GATT. Robinson was a member of the U.S. delegation at both of these top-level meetings and he kept the focus of the U.S. negotiators fixed on the three new issues, reminding them that these were crucial to maintaining the support of U.S. businesss. "A critical test for companies like mine," Robinson told an international conference in New York sponsored by the National Foreign Trade Council, "will be how successfully U.S. negotiators can forge a GATT agreement on the 'new issues.'"

When it came right down to it, the "new issues" amounted to more than just an attempt to expand the scope of GATT to cover new areas of world trade. As the intellectual property issue illustrated, the focus of some of these new demands went well beyond the traditional notion of free trade and open markets. The push for the new issues was really a push for a new world economic order — an economic order that was more suited to the needs of global corporations in the eighties and nineties. Whereas the focus of U.S. business in the past had been to guarantee free trade in world goods, it was now to redefine what free trade was all about. Through international trade negotiations U.S. business sought to achieve a world system that would guarantee the rights of business, that would impose laissez-faire, free-market economics on a global scale, eliminating any meaningful interventionist role for government that could threaten its own interests.

This amounted to a bold new version of George Marshall's Pax Americana. And, increasingly, Jim Robinson seemed to be the man to bring this vision into reality, to lead America into this glorious new realm where it would once again dominate the world economy. Robinson's dream was to be the father of a plan that was as all-encompassing and as good for America — at least for American business — as the Marshall Plan. He waxed lyrical when talking about it. "What is needed is a new and comprehensive grand design in the spirit of the Marshall Plan . . . a grand design, a shared vision . . . ," he told a Japanese business gathering in Tokyo in February 1986. Although Robinson said he couldn't think of what to call the new design, it soon became known, perhaps not to his chagrin, as the "Robinson Plan."

The plan ostensibly revolved around a solution to the world debt crisis. But it was more than this. At the heart of Robinson's proposed debt solution was the establishment of an international body that would effectively use the Third World's debt as a lever to destroy forever the demon of protectionism, to force these debtor nations to open their markets to foreign business interests, by accepting the three crucial new items the U.S. had placed on the GATT agenda. Robinson explained to the Japanese business group that debt relief "might particularly be made available to those countries who open their markets and adopt constructive postures in the upcoming GATT round."

Just as Marshall had used the lever of war devastation to secure markets for U.S. business after the war, Robinson was proposing to use the Third World's debt devastation to force these economies to allow still deeper penetration by U.S. business, into areas that had previously been out-of-bounds for foreigners. And if the proposal turned out to be a winner like the Marshall Plan it aped, both Robinson and American Express would evolve to a higher plane.

BEFORE BRIAN MULRONEY had even been elected Prime Minister, Jim Robinson had been contemplating the possibilities of a Canada–U.S. free trade deal. His trusted advisor, Harry Freeman, had begun to push the idea of free trade agreements with Canada and Israel in the early eighties, with his efforts culminating in the October '84 passage of the U.S. trade bill authorizing such deals — only a month after the Mulroney government took office. For Freeman, as well as for Robinson, such deals offered the opportunity to establish precedents. As Robinson later said in a 1987 speech in Washington, a free trade agreement with Canada could set a precedent that would have an impact "on trade agreements around the world — particularly GATT."

So when the newly elected Mulroney government began to show an interest in a free trade agreement with the United States, it was a subject that interested Robinson. On first glance it didn't seem like much of a fit. The three trade items that most interested him — services, investment and intellectual property — didn't particularly interest the Canadians. The Canadian agenda was straightforward. It contained really only one item: obtaining secure access for Canadian goods and natural resources to the American market. Robinson's three items appeared nowhere on the Canadian agenda. But then the three items didn't appear on the Third World agenda either, and that hadn't stopped him from devising a plan to change minds in those countries. Robinson was not a man easily discouraged. He knew the importance of leverage.

Up on the fifty-first floor of the American Express tower in the World Financial Center, Robinson looked out over New York harbour and beyond that to the open sea. From his elegant suite, he could summon in a moment the best in the world — a caviar snack, a glass of rare wine, the sharpest minds on Wall Street.

Canada . . . Interesting . . .

On the large antique globe in Robinson's office, Canada's massive bulk stretched seemingly forever across the northern hemisphere.

Canada . . . Hmmm . . .

It could just turn out to be a stepping stone to his real goal: the world.

3 · BILLY LOEWEN HAD A NIGHTMARE

If Jim Robinson had grown up feeling there was a big world out there to conquer, Bill Loewen had grown up almost completely unaware of anything beyond the town limits of Elkhorn.

Loewen was born in 1930 in the small northern Manitoba town, located near the Saskatchewan border. It had a population of only 300, and back in the thirties and early forties when he was growing up, there were not more than twenty cars in the whole town. Loewen's family was not one of the lucky ones that could afford a car, and Loewen was fifteen before he made it to the nearest big city — Brandon, Manitoba (population 25,000) — which was only 120 kilometres away. Indeed, the trip to Brandon was a fluke. Elkhorn's grocer, one of the town's more prosperous citizens, took his family every year to the spectacular Brandon fall fair. And when he happened to have an extra space in his car one year, Bill Loewen got his first glimpse of the outside world.

Despite the isolation, Loewen never felt particularly deprived growing up in Elkhorn. People didn't need to travel; everything was right there within walking distance. Besides, expectations were much lower in the thirties than they are now. Indeed, in Depression-era Elkhorn, anyone with a steady job was doing fine. Loewen's father John, who had dropped out of school after grade ten, was steadily employed as a grain elevator operator. And his mother Ada, in addition to having seven children, was a registered nurse who filled in whenever the town doctor was feeling "under the weather," which was frequently the case. So the Loewen family lived relatively well, if modestly. Although for years they were all crowded together in a small two-bedroom house, they eventually moved to more spacious quarters, switching homes with the local butcher who, by Elkhorn standards, had lived in grand style.

Life in Elkhorn abounded with simple, small-town virtues. There was always an activity, whether it was Elkhorn's hockey team taking on the team from the nearby town of Moosomin, or the local Saturday night dance that young and old attended together. In addition to the constant round of socializing, the Loewen parents spent long hours in public service activities around the town, teaching their children a sense of responsibility to the community. John Loewen, a second-generation Manitoban, served as a town councillor and school trustee, and put in many hours of volunteer labour, along with the other local men, building the town hall. Ada Loewen led the local choir, and also came to function as the main health-care-provider in the area, tending to the sick in town or going by horse and buggy or sleigh to neighbouring farms, often in the dead of night.

Above all, the Loewens exemplified the self-sufficiency of those who lived in northern Manitoba during the Depression. Ada Loewen had grown up in the picturesque southern Ontario town of Elora where, according to family legend, the family had once owned the local mill. But she readily adapted to the hardier life of northern Manitoba, learning how to feed her family with home-grown vegetables, which she preserved and served all winter. And when her husband went off to war, she managed her brood alone and still found time to play an active role in the British Empire Service League, a group of Elkhorn women who knitted socks to send to the troops overseas.

It was hard not to have a sense of community growing up in Elkhorn. Everyone in the town knew everybody else, and in the long, cold Prairie winters, they felt tied together in their semi-isolation from the world. Occasionally, an Elkhornite would make a trip to Winnipeg (340 kilometres away) and come home and regale the others with tales of the tall buildings and the fast-paced life there. Nobody ever seemed to make it any farther than Winnipeg. Certainly the U.S. was a mysterious, faraway place, full of Americans who were perceived to talk too much and too loudly.

But if Elkhorn had its simple pleasures, Bill Loewen knew he would eventually leave to complete his education. So after graduating from Elkhorn High in 1948, he headed for the tall buildings of Winnipeg. There he trained as a chartered accountant. For the next fourteen years, he worked as an accountant and a company comptroller in Regina and Edmonton before returning to Winnipeg. By 1968, the whole world of computers was opening up and Loewen, with his accounting and administration background, sensed an opportunity in the burgeoning field.

He came up with the idea of specializing in corporate payrolls. In the past, corporations had largely done their payrolls by hand, using a long and laborious method whereby each employee's cheque and earnings record was handwritten on a carbonized form. By the late sixties, very large companies were doing this work by computer. But firms with fewer than 500 employees generally didn't want to invest in their own computers, which were still large and expensive. Loewen teamed up with a small Winnipeg trust company, which gave him space in the back of its office. For $59 a month, he rented a key-punch machine from IBM and computer time from the University of Manitoba, and was soon running the first Canadian company to specialize in payroll services.

The following year, the Royal Bank and the Bank of Commerce entered the field. With their branch networks and reputations for reliability, the banks quickly gobbled up much of the market. Still, Loewen's firm, Comcheq, was able to carve out a considerable niche for itself by serving companies with more complicated payroll requirements, such as those in the construction or hotel business. Furthermore, Comcheq was able to capitalize on situations where the banks, with their slow-moving bureaucracies, were slow to adapt. For instance, when the federal government introduced changes to the unemployment insurance system in the late seventies, the banks told their payroll customers that they were unable to process the complex new employee work forms that were now required. But Comcheq devised a way to process the forms for its customers, sparing them and their employees a major nuisance. Indeed, the federal and provincial governments were constantly making small changes that complicated the payroll process — and provided Comcheq with an opportunity to outperform the sluggish banks.

Comcheq's growth record would have impressed Jim Robinson. The company grew steadily, only once dipping below 20 percent annual growth — down to a low of 17 percent — in the recession of the early eighties. And its success was based on competitiveness, on constantly seeking out ways to provide a little more service, a little more convenience, a little better price than the larger competitors in the field. By 1990, Comcheq boasted annual revenues of $24 million and employed 475 people in eighteen offices across the country, from Halifax to Victoria.

With his modest, soft-spoken manner, Loewen may not have fit readily into most people's image of success. He had a folksy charm that made him look, even in a well-tailored business suit, as if he would actually be happier out tossing hay. When asked about his success, he shrugged modestly, "We're in a growth industry."

Yet he was a successful businessman. Indeed, he was more than simply a successful businessman. He was that elusive character much mythologized in business culture: the entrepreneur, the risk-taker, the self-made man — someone who had created his own business from scratch and built it into a thriving little empire, largely by offering more service at a better price. It was a mark of distinction that put Loewen in a special class among businessmen — a class to which not even Jim Robinson could claim to belong.

IRONICALLY, THE TECHNOLOGY that had made Loewen's business possible had also enabled the transformation of American

Express into a financial services giant. Both grew out of the immense new range of possibilities spawned by the computer revolution. As computer technology, developed largely for military purposes during World War II, was adapted for commercial use, it promised to alter dramatically the whole infrastructure of the industrial world. Some were describing it as a development as important as the Industrial Revolution.

It certainly seemed to go hand in hand with Globalization. The dominance of multinational corporations in the world marketplace was enhanced by the new technologies, which allowed for instant processing and transmission of information around the world. To a greater extent than ever before, decision making could be centralized in one place — a place that could be located far from the scene of the business transaction or workplace. A 1985 report by the office of the U.S. Trade Representative summed up the impact of the new computer technologies: "The implications are staggering." The global manager could now truly govern a far-flung empire from New York.

For multinational corporations, the new technology offered the possibility of streamlining their massive world-wide operations. What data processing really boiled down to was the transformation of bits of information — such as a corporation's inventory, sales, profits, markets and products — into a form in which they could be usefully analysed for corporate decision making. In the past, companies had generally compiled this sort of information locally, and local managers had used it as the basis for making local decisions. This was more efficient than sending it back to head office where it would have taken longer for the company to react to quickly changing local market conditions.

But computers changed all this. To begin with, far more information could now be processed quickly and presented in digestible bits for analysis. Furthermore, information was transmittable anywhere. So in the retail industry, for instance, an item-by-item breakdown of every cash register receipt from every store in a national or international chain could be fed back to head office. Once processed there, the data could be used for corporate analysis of buying patterns, measurement of the effectiveness of a sales campaign or assessment of which kind of products sold well in which markets. It could also help head office answer exotic questions such as whether a particular toothpaste tube would appeal to Italians, or whether Latin Americans would prefer a soft drink if advertisements showed it being sipped by a woman with dark hair rather than blond hair.

The new technology also allowed for greater flexibility. With instant world-wide communications, corporations could alter production at any stage in response to a rise or decline in demand in some far-off corner of the globe. Furthermore, the various components of a product could be produced in many different locations all over the world, depending on where labour was cheapest, tax breaks most generous and government subsidies most available. And the assembly of the components could then take place in yet another location, again determined by which country offered the most lucrative benefits and lowest labour rates. It was all enormously beneficial to corporations, as struggling foreign governments, hoping for jobs and foreign currency, outbid each other in a desperate attempt to lure rich multinationals to their shores. It was all part of an international bidding war for the rich.

In less than a generation, the new technology had permeated the international business scene, transforming it dramatically in the process. Fully 94 percent of 380 global corporations surveyed by the Rome-based Intergovernmental Bureau of Informatics in 1983 were using or planning to use computer-to-computer links across national borders. And, as American companies lost much of their competitive advantage to the surging manufacturing industries of the Far East and West Germany, computer techonology remained one of the few areas where the U.S. remained in the lead.

While the impact of computerization on all types of industry was significant, it was most noticeable in the service sector, particularly financial services. Whether an office was down the street or around the world made little difference if the service it offered could be reached through a computer terminal. More than 80 percent of job growth in the U.S. in the sixties and seventies was in the service sector, and virtually all of the twenty highest-growth occupations forecast by the U.S. Bureau of

Labor Statistics involved the handling of information. By 1980, the U.S. service industry, which had formerly been confined largely to domestic markets, was exporting some $60 billion worth of services, making it one of the bright spots on the U.S. trade horizon.

Increasingly, U.S. business interests were becoming dependent on the unfettered flow of data around the world. The issue was taken up by prominent U.S. business interests, with American Express at the front of the pack. The aim of Amex and other American multinationals was to prevent foreign governments from creating laws and regulations that would restrict the free flow of data across national borders. This was a small but important part of the larger issue of creating international rules to govern trade in services — the issue that Robinson was to champion as part of the new GATT agenda.

As early as April 1978, American Express proposed a code of conduct for multinationals, under which they would regulate their own behaviour in transborder data flows. The ostensible purpose of Amex's proposed code was to prevent possible abuses, such as the transmission of confidential information about individuals. But the Amex code was also a way to try to head off governments from imposing regulations restricting data flows in general. American Express was arguing that such regulations were not necessary; business could regulate itself.

The issue was also championed by the Business Roundtable, largely at the instigation of Robinson, who headed up the Roundtable's international trade committee. Noting that the free flow of data had "transformed the way in which companies, manufacturing or service, do business internationally," the Roundtable, the bastion of U.S. multinationals, called for strong action to keep national borders open. In 1985, in a forty-page statement entitled "International Information Flow: A Plan for Action," the Roundtable made clear the priority it gave to the issue: "The U.S. approaches this area from the premise that the 'free flow of information' should be foremost, and that any exceptions to this principle for other overriding public policy interests should be limited and narrowly drawn."

The Roundtable even attempted to put a high-minded gloss on the goal of keeping borders open for international business communications. Not only did it advance the national and world economy, according to the Roundtable, but the "free flow of information internationally *advances the human condition.*" This appeared to be stretching things. Would humankind really be worse off if business failed to transmit its inventory and sales figures, the numbers from its cash register receipts? Perhaps Italians would be left with little choice but to buy toothpaste in tubes they found unappealing, or Latin Americans would see advertisements of blondes drinking soft drinks when they preferred to see brunettes. But the human condition?

If the right to transmit data internationally became a freedom cry for U.S. business, it set off alarm bells in national capitals around the world. Not only did governments fear that free data flows would wipe out infant domestic industries struggling to get started in the data processing field, they also feared a drain of jobs to the U.S. in existing industries, as foreign-owned multinationals increasingly centralized their operations back home. The "staggering" implications of the new technology that so excited U.S. business were no less staggering to those who suspected they would end up on the losing end of the stick. In addition to potential job losses, there was the less tangible, yet potent, fear that the free flow of data would increasingly allow decisions about countries' economic futures to be made by forces outside the country. With such concerns mounting, more and more countries were working on establishing rules to control the international flow of data across their borders.

By the early eighties, U.S. business was starting to feel the pinch of these restrictions. A survey by the U.S. Conference Board found that roughly a quarter of 238 multinationals had already encountered serious obstacles or restrictions to international data flows in more than thirty countries. And 86 percent of the companies reported "serious concern" about the impact possible future regulations of this sort could have on their international operations. Alarmed by the possibilities, the U.S. government pushed in 1982 for the signing of an international "Data Declaration." The declaration, drawn up in Washington, was aimed at preventing the erection of national barriers that might impede the international flow of business data.

U.S. business figured it was important to establish an international set of rules before too many countries imposed restrictions that might be treated as precedents by other countries. "Preventative action is essential to ensure that this rapidly growing area of international commerce remains open," warned the Business Roundtable. Indeed, guaranteeing the free flow of data became a key part of the business demand for a new international GATT agreement covering services.

Business, for instance, wanted to establish new rights that went by names like "national treatment" and the "right of establishment." Basically, these would guarantee that a corporation had the right to establish itself in a foreign country and be granted the same rights and privileges as local businesses. But in the area of services, business also wanted something more: the "right of *non*-establishment" — that is, the right to be granted the same privileges as local businesses of a country, without the requirement of actually operating a business in that country. American Express, for instance, criticized a Canadian law that prevented a financial company from selling its services in Canada unless it established a subsidiary in Canada. "American Express believes that U.S. firms should have the right to offer their services either from within Canada or from across the border," said Harry Freeman in a 1987 speech to the Brookings Institution in Washington. In the era of instant round-the-world data transmission, business was demanding a free hand to position its operations exactly where it wanted, without losing market access.

Essentially, business leaders were seeking to get rid of any notion that business owed anything to a foreign country in exchange for the right to do business in that country. Thus they sought to kill the spectre of "performance requirements" — requirements that foreign firms create jobs or buy local products — in order to gain access to the local market. The Business Roundtable found such requirements to be a nuisance, and out of sync with the global marketplace. "A particular danger that must be avoided in the creation of any rights of presence [in a foreign country]," the Business Roundtable warned in January 1985, "is that they be linked to a series of performance requirements." The Roundtable wanted business to have the exclusive right to determine how many — or how few — jobs would be created. It was particularly concerned by a growing interest in many world capitals in imposing requirements that local data be processed and stored within the country where it was produced, as a way of keeping jobs in the country.

Such a requirement would clearly impede the ability of a multinational to manage its empire on a global basis, transmitting data freely between the many parts of its world-wide operations. The Roundtable therefore argued that what was needed was a "right of presence" that would be free of any performance requirements. This, the Roundtable explained, would guarantee a foreign corporation the right to transmit its data freely across a nation's borders, and process and store that data *outside* the nation's borders, if it chose to do so.

As the U.S. became more aggressive in its campaign for open borders, other countries dug in their heels. The developing world was highly suspicious of the U.S. moves, and feared that free data flows would lead to even greater foreign domination of their economies. But the fear was by no means confined to the Third World. Sensing the potential for U.S. dominance, the Europeans — particularly the leading powers, France and West Germany — were reluctant to cede much ground to the U.S.

While neither France nor West Germany banned transborder data flows, they threw up impediments that made it difficult for foreign multinationals to ship data easily for processing elsewhere. So, for instance, while France provided excellent telephone links to other countries, its international data transmission lines were poor, and the French government showed no great interest in improving them. Similarly, the West Germans vigorously protected their government monopoly over international data links and made it difficult and expensive to move data out of the country. U.S. efforts — spearheaded by American Express — to gain permission for private companies to set up their own international data transmission lines were vigorously opposed by the West German government.

As the U.S. stepped up its lobbying for new international agreements guaranteeing free information flows, more and more countries seemed to be lining up against Washington.

Michael Blumenthal, chairman of the large U.S. multinational, Burroughs Corp., summed up the situation tersely in 1981: "It's largely an issue of the U.S. versus the world." While the U.S. had a great deal to win, many countries felt they had a great deal to lose.

Yet, ironically, the U.S. was soon to get support from one of the countries with the most to lose.

FOR THE AUDIENCE at the Montreal conference, the prediction was a little startling. It was September 1978, and the subject of international data flows was still a relatively new one, even for the sophisticated audience of academics and bureaucrats who had gathered at the Four Seasons Hotel for a special conference on the subject. And now they were discovering that, behind the computer lingo and high-tech imagery of the exciting new information age, there lay some real dangers: Canada stood to lose thousands of jobs in the computer service industry, and that was just "the tip of the iceberg of the potential economic impact on Canada." If the prediction sounded ominous, it was more so because of who was making it: not some wacky futurist or scare-mongering politician, but a vice-president of the Royal Bank.

"The control of the actual process, manufacturing of the widgets if you wish, could very well remain local. But the higher type of job opportunities, the challenges, could be carried out at a remote distance," said Jim Grant, the Royal Bank's vice-president for technology. "It is mandatory to protect national and individual interests, both economic and social, by retaining business functions in this country. . . . The implications of this are far-reaching and may require legislative intervention to protect national and individual interests."

Such a tone of alarm is rare in the speech of bank executives, particularly executives of the staid Royal Bank. But Grant, the bank's leading expert on computer systems, clearly saw the situation as threatening to Canada. His mood was echoed at the conference by Peter Robinson, a policy advisor in the federal Department of Communications. Robinson revealed that preliminary investigations by his department had found that some

$300 to $350 million worth of processing of Canadian data was being done outside the country that year, and he predicted the figure could soon be five times that amount. But it was hard to know the full scope of the problem. His department had only twigged to the situation after a flurry of inquiries from U.S. multinationals asking if there were any Canadian restrictions on shipping data back to the U.S. for processing. The department quickly discovered there were none.

As the conference wore on, it seemed that what was really at stake was the eventual transformation of Canada from a branch plant economy into something far worse: a warehouse economy. With most corporate functions performed outside the country, Canadians would graduate from being hewers of wood and drawers of water to being little more than sales clerks in an international storeroom. Bernard Ostry, former Deputy Minister of Communications, tried to illustrate the problem once to a U.S. business gathering by telling a parable of a man who entrusted his brains to his neighbour for safekeeping, only to discover that his neighbour wasn't necessarily home when he needed them. The Americans, it seemed, were only too happy to keep our brains for us; indeed, they didn't particularly see the need for us to have brains at all.

With growing concern in the federal bureaucracy — and even apparently in the Royal Bank — the Liberal government appointed a special committee shortly after the Montreal conference to investigate what potential dangers the new computer technology posed to Canada. The committee, headed by B.C. judge J. V. Clyne, was not to be a rambling, unfocussed exploration of the new information age. Rather, it was given a mandate to move quickly — in the name of urgency — and report to the government within three months about how Canadian sovereignty could better be protected in light of the computer-communications revolution. Although the subject was somewhat technical, a number of the eight members of the Committee — such as *Toronto Star* publisher Beland Honderich, *Saturday Night* editor Robert Fulford and economist Carl Beigie — were not computer experts, but were apparently chosen for their ability to look at the problem as wise, concerned Canadians.

But if the government wanted urgency and strong medicine, the Committee went beyond even those expectations. With speed uncharacteristic of government-appointed committees, the Clyne Committee sifted through dozens of written and oral briefs and produced a stinging, 100-page brief in only three months. "We believe this report will make the urgency clear," it said in its opening chapter. The theme of the document, which came bounding off the first page, was that Canada had only so much time. The new computer techonolgies were transforming society and setting the terms of life for the twenty-first century. "There is an opportunity today, which will not last long, for Canada to exploit the informatics revolution to its own best advantage, and we believe that policies and actions must begin at once."

The Clyne Report was unabashedly nationalist in its stance, and had little patience for the market-oriented solutions being advanced south of the border. "Telecommunications, as the foundation of the future society, cannot always be left to the vagaries of the market," it said. "If we wish to control our economy then we will require a sophisticated telecommunications sector developed and owned in Canada to meet specific Canadian requirements." And the report made clear that, ultimately, it came down to a question of jobs. "We believe few people understand how devastating that impact might be on jobs for Canadians and trade for Canada," the committee argued. In broadcasting, another field dramatically affected by the advances of computer communications, the committee saw growing threats to Canadian cultural sovereignty. It urged the preservation and strengthening of the CBC, tougher Canadian content requirements for private broadcasters, and the redirection of some of the enormous revenues of cable TV into the production of Canadian programs and films.

What the Clyne Committee was calling for was a strong interventionist stance on the part of government. It argued that nothing short of this would prevent the crucial information industry of the future from falling into foreign hands. And it warned that, while countries all over the world risked such a fate, Canada was particularly vulnerable. "The close proximity of Canada to the United States and the increasing flow of data across the border make the sovereignty of Canada in this whole field strikingly more vulnerable than is the case in many other countries." To stop that southward flow of data, and the procession of key jobs that would inevitably follow, the committee recommended what seemed like a simple and harmless solution: that businesses operating in Canada be required to have their data processed here.

But, if the Clyne Committee wanted to take Canada in a strongly nationalist direction, elements in the Canadian business community had other ideas. Beland Honderich recalls that most of the industry representatives who appeared before the Clyne Committee "weren't very concerned" about the issue of Canadian sovereignty. Canadian firms with global operations were increasingly coming to share the view of their U.S. counterparts that nationalistic restrictions only impeded their worldwide growth. Ironically, the first Canadian multinational to publicly push for free information flows was the same one that had sounded the alarm only a few years earlier: the Royal Bank. Only this time, the push wasn't coming from just a high-ranking bank executive. It was coming from the chairman himself.

Rowland C. Frazee, the chairman and chief executive officer of the Royal Bank, actually knew next to nothing about computers; his background was exclusively in banking. He had first joined the Royal in the local branch of his childhood home town, St. Stephen, New Brunswick, and had worked his way through the ranks until he was named chief executive in 1979. But if Frazee knew nothing about the new computer technology or "informatics," as it was often called, one of his board members, high-powered Montreal lawyer Frank Common, had developed a keen interest in the subject.

Common, a senior partner at the prominent Montreal firm Ogilvy, Renault (also, incidentally, Brian Mulroney's law firm) was steeped in the world of international business. His father, a successful Montreal corporate lawyer with impressive international business connections, had sat on the board of Swiss pharmaceutical giant CIBA-GEIGY and was once invited to become a partner of the powerful U.S. investment banking house Dillon, Read. (The invitation had come from

James Forestall, one-time Assistant Secretary of the U.S. Navy.)

Common had followed in his father's footsteps, joining the same Montreal firm, specializing in international corporate law and developing a keen interest in international business. Indeed, almost all Common's clients were U.S. or British firms seeking incorporation in Canada. Common ended up on the boards of many of these foreign-owned subsidaries, as well as the U.S. boards of some of the parent companies, including the candy conglomerate Cadbury-Schweppes. It's not surprising, then, that Common's interest in computers, which dated from the late seventies, came mostly from the perspective of facilitating international data flows for global corporations.

Certainly the warnings of the Clyne Committee were not uppermost in Common's mind. "It was very nationalistic," Common recalled of the committee's report, over lunch recently at his reserved table in Montreal's pricey Beaver Club. Common was an internationalist — an internationalist with a strong connection to multinational corporations. This, of course, was also the orientation of the Royal Bank, which had operations in fifty countries and counted major multinationals among its clients. So when Common spoke to Frazee about the new age of computers and what it meant for the Royal Bank, it was not to raise the concerns expressed in the Clyne Report.

It happened over dinner one night at Common's house. Frazee had barely heard the word "informatics" before it came up that night. But before the evening was over, Common had given Frazee an earful and piqued the bank chairman's interest in a subject he later became convinced was crucial to the bank's future.*

That conviction was furthered when the bank's Austrian branch appeared to be running afoul of regulations that placed

---

* Common went on to establish the Atwater Institute, a Montreal-based think tank funded by business, which was largely devoted to the goal of opening up borders for international data flows. With his connections, the charming Montreal lawyer raised $1.3 million from Canadian and U.S. companies, including $25,000 from American Express in 1986. "Harry Freeman put up $25,000 on the condition that I would convince [Royal Bank chairman] Allan Taylor to support free trade," Common recalled.

some restrictions on the processing of data outside the country. The matter was quickly cleared up — it turned out that the bank was operating within national guidelines — but it left authorities back at Royal Bank headquarters in Montreal wondering just how treacherous this new information field could become if countries started adopting nationalistic policies along the lines recommended by the Clyne Report.

Furthermore, the bank had made a strategic decision to invest heavily in automatic teller machines (ATMs), a costly computerized technology that promised to revolutionize consumer banking and virtually eliminate the local branch. But, like other aspects of the new computer technology, ATMs could end up subjected to restrictions. The whole area was so new and uncharted, it was hard to know where it would lead and what actions governments might take if the systems moved across national boundaries. With the bank investing hundreds of millions of dollars in the new systems, it was definitely preferable to ensure now that there wouldn't be problems down the road.

For Frazee there was another motive for pushing for free data flows. As chairman of Canada's largest and most established bank, Frazee was virtually a diplomat for Canadian business. And, in his constant travel on bank business in the early eighties, he was shocked to discover how agitated U.S. business had become over some of the nationalistic policies of the Trudeau administration, most notably the National Energy Program and the Foreign Investment Review Agency (FIRA). Frazee came to feel that there had been a serious deterioration in the relationship between the U.S. and Canada. One bank official who worked with him at the time recalled Frazee returning from a trip to the U.S. surprised by the anger of American businessmen: "I remember him saying, 'My God, they think we're a bunch of socialists!' " The bank official said that Frazee was very interested in coming up with "something positive, instead of all the bickering . . . something governments could grab on to."

Free trade in informatics — that is, the free flow of data across borders — seemed like the perfect thing. It was something U.S. business was keen for, and Frazee had been convinced that it was important to the bank's future as well. "Our whole life was based on the transfer of information; we were an international bank," recalls Frazee. "There were no real rules of the road. We were quite vulnerable."

To tackle the problem, Frazee called in his team of trouble-shooters — a group of five young, up-and-coming bank employees who were on special assignment to the chairman. They were a somewhat eclectic group for banking circles, including specialists in political science, law and economics as well as a woman who had written a Ph.D. thesis on the work of Ezra Pound. The team had been assembled to deal with difficult problems of particular interest to the chairman. They had previously been assigned, for instance, to figure out a way to move much of the Royal Bank's head office out of Montreal without antagonizing Quebec sensibilities. The assignment this time was equally delicate: to get a grasp of the complex field of informatics and how it affected the bank — and then explain it all in lay language to Frazee (or Mr. Frazee, as they called him).

By assigning his young foot-soldiers to tackle the issue, Frazee was giving it a high priority within the bank. Since they were on special assignment to him, the team members were given full access to all parts of the bank's operations; top managers couldn't simply brush them aside. Their special status was reflected by the large amounts of time they got to spend with the chairman. Members of the team also travelled to Ottawa and Washington in 1982 to check out the attitudes of officials on the subject. Once the groundwork was prepared, the chairman was briefed well enough to make forays to the national capitals, to discuss the issue with trade officials in Washington and Ottawa. While the Reagan administration was interested in Frazee's proposals for freer trade in informatics, the Trudeau government was wary, with Trudeau himself noting in a letter to Frazee that the issue raised serious concerns about Canadian sovereignty.

For Frazee, the important thing was to get both governments onside before the general public became alarmed about the issue. In a speech to a U.S. business audience in Los Angeles in March 1983, he emphasized the potential of the issue to inflame nationalist sentiments. It was an odd speech in some respects, in that it appeared to be making a case for the nationalist cause: he illustrated in some detail how the free flow of information had already had a negative effect on Canada. He described, for instance, how a U.S. airline had closed its Canadian operation, moved its computer facilities and employees to the U.S. and now handled the Canadian market by telephone. He also described another situation in which a Swedish city had bought a computer-based fire protection service from a U.S. company. The data base, which contained crucial information about the location of buildings, fire hydrants and dangerous chemicals in the Swedish city, was accessible by computer in Sweden, but was located in Connecticut.

"It is . . . newsworthy items like those that fuel protectionist fires," Frazee told his audience. "They raise concerns over jobs, privacy, national security, economic, political and technological dependence. They worry Canadians. In fact, they worry most of the world's nations, developed and developing alike." Frazee seemed to be making the case for the implementation of the Clyne Report, hardly what this U.S. business audience wanted to hear. "[B]ecause of clear American domination of the information business," he continued, "if the borders were simply left open, if we had no rules at all, many nations, including Canada, feel that they would be giving the world's best runner a head start. They not only don't want that — they will *not* allow it to happen." Had Frazee forgotten where he was? Did he think he was addressing a student rally on the dangers of U.S. imperialism?

But, if the audience was starting to wonder if Canadians really were a bunch of socialists, Frazee soon made it clear that he was simply alerting the business crowd to the emotional potential of the issue, and the need for corporate behaviour to defuse rather than inflame nationalist sentiments.

Frazee noted that the danger of nationalism was even to be feared in the U.S. So far, American dominance in informatics and the flow of jobs to the U.S. had prevented nationalist concerns from arising among Americans. But Frazee warned that, "Sooner or later, because of growing sophistication and capacity elsewhere, U.S. citizens will have reason to share Canadian concerns about privacy and jobs and sovereignty."

The answer, according to Frazee, was to put in place a Canada-U.S. agreement on free information flows — even though such an agreement was bound to encourage the kinds of situations that he identified as fuelling nationalism. But then, once both governments had signed such an agreement, there would be little likelihood of nationalist protest. The issue would have been decided, the transborder facilities already in place. Nationalism would have been frozen in its tracks. As Frazee said, "These kinds of agreements will prevent them [nationalist concerns] from arising."

Frazee had no trouble convincing American business, which had long espoused the glory of open borders. But on the Canadian side, a feisty Elkhornite was gearing up to take on some huge hombres on both sides of the border, with all the force of a farmer waving a pitchfork at a low-flying bomber.

THINGS IN THE real world never seemed to make sense the way they had in Elkhorn.

One of the things that made little sense to Loewen in his post-Elkhorn life was the behaviour of the Canadian oil industry. In the fifties and early sixties, Loewen had worked on the periphery of the oil industry as an accountant with an oil equipment manufacturing firm in Edmonton. In those days, there were virtually hundreds of small, prosperous Canadian-owned exploration companies, and a few larger ones too. Canadian Oil Companies, for instance, was a highly successful Canadian firm with a well-established distribution system — a system that made it attractive to Shell Oil, which eventually bought it. Similarly, North Star Oil, a Winnipeg-based company, with gas stations all across the West, was acquired by Shell in 1960.

Loewen watched as, one after another, these Canadian-owned companies were sold to larger U.S. oil interests when the opportunity came along. Indeed, in his early days as an accountant in Winnipeg, Loewen had worked on the audit of Bailey Sellburn, a Canadian firm with oil production facilities in Alberta. The company's Winnipeg owners had done well with the company, but decided to sell it in the mid-fifties for $5 million — a handsome sum. Yet in the early sixties, with the same management running the company, Bailey Sellburn was transformed into Pacific Petroleum and bought by PetroCanada in 1979 for $13 billion. Canadian taxpayers, through federally owned PetroCan, were paying billions to buy Canadian control of an industry that, less than a generation earlier, had started out in Canadian hands.

But Loewen only came truly to realize the scope of the problem when he saw the same pattern repeat itself in the computer industry years later. In the late sixties and seventies, Canada had a thriving computer service industry, with hundreds of firms springing up across the country to take advantage of the possibilities offered by the new technology. The industry was almost entirely Canadian-owned and seemed determined to remain that way. Industry associations — such as the Canadian Association of Data and Professional Service Organizations and the Canadian Business Equipment Manufacturers Association — expressed a strong interest in keeping the business Canadian.

But by the late eighties, many of those early entrepreneurs had reaped their private profits and sold their companies to U.S. interests. Once-prominent Canadian firms had come under foreign ownership, leaving the industry almost 85 percent foreign-owned. And the industry associations that had once seemed so nationalistic had shifted to a continentalist stance. A small offshoot group, the Canadian Independent Computer Services Association, with some sixty Canadian-owned firms, alone remained committed to an independent industry. Loewen was its president.

Operating out of Comcheq's Winnipeg office, the association waged a meagrely funded but spirited campaign throughout the eighties to keep the computer industry Canadian and to keep computer-related jobs in Canada. Loewen produced brief after brief for government hearings, made speeches to any business association that would listen (some wouldn't), and met and corresponded with countless government officials on the subject. The association carried out its own studies that showed the potential job loss would be above 350,000 — and challenged authorities to prove its numbers wrong. But there was no response. What was the matter with these people? Had they never read the Clyne Report? Couldn't they see the sense of urgency that had led those eight committee members — including some very prominent Canadians — to write, "With all the force at our command, we urge the Government of Canada to take immediate action to alert the people of Canada to the perilous position of their collective sovereignty that has resulted from the new technologies of telecommunications and informatics."

The sense of urgency generated by the Clyne Committee had all but evaporated once the report was handed in. The government had done little to publicize Clyne's dramatic findings. Indeed, it seemed to have lost all enthusiasm for the subject of the new information revolution, relegating it to a slow-moving interdepartmental task force that would take a more technical approach to the issue.

What was most galling for Loewen was to watch the government stand idly by as the industry became more Americanized and the flow of data became increasingly southward-bound. Between 1982 and 1984, the Canadian Radio-television and Telecommunications Commission (CRTC) — the federal body that regulated telecommunications — approved a series of applications to install cross-border data facilities at Montreal, Toronto, Sarnia, Ontario, and Blaine, British Columbia, thereby linking computer facilities in eighty-two Canadian centres with ninety-three U.S. centres. With these approvals, the CRTC was actively facilitating the north-south flow of data, undermining decades of Canadian government policy that sought to direct transportation and communication links in an east-west, cross-Canada direction. Loewen charged that the CRTC was giving U.S. companies better access to the Canadian market than Canadian companies had. But CRTC officials shrugged off his entreaties. In the absence of federal government policy to the contrary, they said, the CRTC had no choice but to approve the applications.

But what was preventing the government from acting? As Loewen pointed out in his briefs, there was no legal regulation compelling Canada to facilitate these north-south links. There was nothing in GATT or other international agreements that required countries to keep their borders open to international information flows — although the U.S. was pushing hard to get a new GATT agreement along these lines. Rather, the driving force behind Canada's willingness to facilitate the free flow of data seemed to be the same notion that was cropping up with greater and greater frequency — the notion that Canada could no longer hide from the world; that she had to go naked into the global marketplace, and survive as best she could.

For Loewen, this was empty and foolish bravado. He noted that so many of the Canadian efforts to penetrate the U.S. market had been dismal failures, as companies dramatically over-extended themselves only to discover that Americans do exactly what Canadians don't: they tend to buy from their own nationals. "Canadians should forget their obsession with the U.S. market and concentrate on doing a good job at home," argued Loewen in a 1984 brief, adding that there were other foreign markets far more hospitable to Canadians than the U.S. Rather than chasing the mirage of riches in the U.S. market, Canadians should see the potential for a lucrative self-sufficiency in their own market, with additional sales in other markets around the world. "We should strike such bombastic phrases as 'world leaders,' 'world class companies' and 'world product mandate' from our vocabulary. We are a small but wealthy country in economic terms. Unfortunately our wealth is squandered on ill-conceived ventures and policies that owe more to bravado than good business sense."

Loewen even took to quoting the folk wisdom of Canadian poet William Henry Drummond:

> De win' can blow lak' hurricane,
> An' s'pose she blow some more
> You can't get drown on Lac St. Pierre
> So long you stay on shore.

The point was not that Canadians couldn't venture forth on Lac St. Pierre — or in the world, as it were — but that they shouldn't necessarily do so in the midst of a hurricane. A little common sense would keep them rooted on the ground and prevent their country from being needlessly swamped by a tidal wave coming from a country ten times its size.

This was a theme Loewen was to push throughout the eighties — and still pushes in the nineties — as the idea of free trade in informatics evolved into the idea of free trade in everything. Yet it was a message that much of the business community seemed to want to shut out, settling instead for chest-thumping cries about how we could compete with the best in the world, anywhere, anytime. From Loewen's viewpoint, this was simply poor business judgement; these businessmen were allowing their thinking to be clouded by the power of positive thinking, by the notion that if you repeat often enough that you are the best in the world you can count on being the best.

As the free trade debate hit its full fury in the fall of 1988, Loewen tried unsuccessfully to convince the Manitoba branch of the Canadian Manufacturers' Association to allow him to speak to its members, so that he could present an alternative view to the pro-free trade stance relentlessly advocated by the association. But, with only months to go before the November '88 election that was to decide the free trade issue, the association declined Loewen's speaking offer, explaining in a letter that "the time we could offer to your presentation would not adequately cover the topic." Better to have no presentation at all, it seemed.

There was a certain irony in this rejection. Loewen's credentials as a businessman were impressive. He was not merely someone who had studied business. He had actually built a business and developed it into a successful company. Comcheq was now the third largest payroll processor in the country, after the Royal Bank and the Bank of Commerce, and processed the payrolls of 1 million Canadians. But the Winnipeg business group had no time to hear — even from a successful businessman — about another vision of how to create prosperity in the country.

What Loewen wanted to tell them was that the Canadian market was a lucrative one and gaining access to it was a privilege that entailed responsibility. If foreign corporations wanted to sell in our market, they should be required to maintain levels of employment in Canada consistent with the volume of their sales here. Otherwise they were simply taking advantage of business opportunities and giving nothing back in return. Essentially Loewen was arguing for just the sort of "performance requirements" that so offended the U.S. Business Roundtable. The Roundtable rejected such requirements for the same reason Loewen advocated them: they forced business to take some responsibility for the country it operated in, as well as taking a profit.

For Loewen it really boiled down to self-sufficiency and responsibility to the community — values that had made sense in Elkhorn, but that seemed to have no place in the human jungle of the global marketplace.

IF THE VALUES of Elkhorn seemed to fit easily with the country that Loewen had grown up in, much of that had changed by the late eighties. It wasn't so much that Canadians had changed, but a new aggressiveness on the part of business had altered the political landscape. Canadian business had joined the push for the kind of trade agenda long advocated by the U.S. Business Roundtable. And with that came demands for dramatic changes in other parts of the economy — for cut-backs in social spending, deregulation, privatization, and a tax reform that pushed an increasing burden onto the middle class.

Most Canadians were hostile to this new business agenda — a fact that made the political task of putting it in place formidable. It would take someone who understood the importance, not of pleasing the public, but of pleasing those who really counted — and that was a lesson that one desperately ambitious politician had learned from a very early age.

4 • SINGING FOR THE COLONEL: BRIAN MULRONEY AND THE POWER TO PLEASE

Twenty years of Brian Mulroney's political dreams hung precariously in the balance in the Schefferville high-school gym.

It was February 1983, only weeks after Joe Clark had failed to win the 67 percent support he needed from the Conservative leadership review in Winnipeg to justify prolonging his embattled position at the helm of the party. A devastated Clark immediately called a leadership convention for June, throwing his own hat into the ring. Brian Mulroney once again had a shot at the goal he had been coveting for more than two decades.

But with the leadership race on in earnest, Mulroney's performance at the Schefferville high school suddenly loomed ominously before him. The media spotlight would certainly be fixed on him — the front runner making his first major public appearance since the announcement that the race was officially on. The appearance had all the makings of a disaster. There was little Mulroney could say to wiggle out of the jam he was in. He was president of the Iron Ore Company of Canada and his task was to explain the actions of his company in shutting down its operations in Schefferville, a northern Quebec town that had been created to serve the mine and that now faced extinction.

In many ways, it was no accident that he was in this particular bind. Mulroney had been chosen for the prestigious top job at Iron Ore back in 1976 largely because of his labour relations skills. At that time, Mulroney was a successful Montreal labour lawyer who had excelled at representing management in difficult labour negotiations. Iron Ore, which was controlled by Cleveland-based Hanna Mining Co., had been among Mulroney's clients, and Mulroney had been effective in representing the large mining conglomerate. As Hanna looked for a replacement for retiring Iron Ore president Bill Bennett, one of its major concerns was to find someone who could smoothly manage the significant staff cut-backs that were on the horizon at Iron Ore for the late seventies and early eighties. With 4,500 employees, many located in remote northern areas, the cut-backs were bound to cause considerable labour strife.

Mulroney had seemed like just the man to handle such a delicate situation. Not only was he skilled in labour relations, he also came from northern Quebec, where a large part of Iron Ore's operations was located. His father, an electrician, had moved to the northern town of Baie Comeau in its early days and lived a modest life there with his wife and six children — just as many of the Iron Ore workers had moved north to the new towns of Schefferville and Labrador City, where they lived modest, hard-working lives. Mulroney was a child of the North Shore; he understood the lives of the people there and could speak to them in their own language. He could present himself to the workers as one of their own, even as he took their jobs away: the perfect guy for a dirty job.

And he was handsomely rewarded for the task. He negotiated for himself a generous five-year contract with rich stock and pension benefits. In the meantime, there were immediate perks: a handsome salary, membership in the Mount Royal Club, a couple of company planes at his disposal, box seats behind the bench of the Montreal Canadiens at the Forum, a company fishing camp in Labrador. If Mulroney had to nurse his wounds from the defeat of his first bid for the Conservative leadership in 1976, he would at least do so in style. Furthermore, he was immediately catapulted into a position of enormous prestige in the Montreal business community — a good jumping-off post for another try at his political dream.

But now, in the winter of 1983, the dirtiness of his job was coming back to haunt him, just as he was finally poised to grab the Tory leadership. Throughout the late seventies, Mulroney had presided over lay-offs at Iron Ore's operations in Scheffer-ville and Sept-Iles, Quebec, and in Labrador City, Newfound-land. But the real crunch had come in 1982, when world markets for iron ore collapsed. With increasing competition for disappearing markets, Hanna was less interested in producing the expensive iron ore from Quebec's North Shore, particularly since the company also held major interests in Brazilian iron ore mines, where the ore was a higher grade and the wages were considerably lower. A special meeting of the Iron Ore Com-pany's board in Cleveland concluded in late October that there was no choice but to shut down Schefferville. Mulroney was dispatched to make the announcement on November 2, 1982.

It was not the kind of message would-be prime ministers like to deliver. The image was wrong and could prove hard to shake, especially for a young politician who was still unknown to many people in the country. Mulroney would come to public promi-nence as the man who had shut down a once-thriving town because a board of directors in Cleveland concluded it was no longer profitable for them to operate. His contribution to the Canadian scene would be a ghost town. He would be seen as the highly paid overseer for a group of faceless Yankee bosses.

But in his handling of the Schefferville shut-down, Mulroney showed the finesse that later brought him to power. Only a few days before Joe Clark's leadership was to be reviewed in Win-nipeg, Mulroney had announced a package settlement for more than 526 Schefferville workers that left them with close to $20,000 each in severance and relocation allowances. The deal was, in fact, subsidized by the federal and provincial govern-ments, which picked up more than 30 percent of the cost. But the political credit for what was seen as a generous setttlement went largely to Mulroney.

Still, he wasn't out of the woods yet. The Quebec govern-ment, in a show of concern over the shut-down of a town, was keeping the spotlight trained on the company and on Mulroney, scheduling three days of hearings to investigate the situation, and adding to the drama by holding them in the school gymnasium of the soon-to-be-deceased town. The event, which would attract a swarm of media to see the Tory front runner perform, was fraught with pitfalls. Mulroney plotted his moves carefully. For a week, he holed up in Florida preparing his defence, as company officials descended with boxes of data to bolster the company's case that world markets had left it little choice.

Mulroney's task had been made more difficult by revelations in the press, only days after he announced the Schefferville shut-down, that Iron Ore had paid out $225 million in dividends to its shareholders — which included Hanna as well as a number of large U.S. steel companies — during the two years prior to the shut-down announcement. Mulroney's initial response had been to deny the press reports vigorously, but after careful preparation of the company's case, he confirmed them.

A master tactician, Mulroney worked the numbers into a tight case, and in the packed Schefferville gymnasium left the audience overwhelmed by his presentation of graphs and charts. His message was that the company had done a great deal for the town, and that the dividends paid out to shareholders represented a small return on investment. Besides, the company was now doing a great deal for its employees, Mulroney argued. It was a strong performance that managed to bring onside the Quebec government officials conducting the hearing, the press attending it and even, to a large extent, the union.

Up in Labrador City, people were less impressed.

Labrador City was another remote northern town that owed its existence to the Iron Ore Company. It was built in the late fifties in the bleak Labrador interior, where trees were few and temperatures hovered around minus forty degrees Celsius from late fall to early spring. By Hallowe'en, it was already too cold to walk more than a short distance without long underwear. The town's sole purpose was to provide labour for the nearby mines. The town was largely built by the company, and virtually everything in it — including the houses — was owned by the company. There was no road into the town, only a railway, owned and operated by the company.

For all its disadvantages, Labrador City had attracted a hardy set of workers who were drawn by the high wages. By the early eighties, average pay in the town had already reached the handsome rate of $32,000 a year. For those who had been accustomed to the poverty and uncertainty of life in mainland Newfoundland, Labrador City offered an escape, a chance to make good through hard work and willingness to put up with isolation and a bitter climate. Newcomers generally spent their first few years living in the town's grim trailer park; trailers were relatively cheap to buy since the company brought them in on its railway at no charge. Workers who managed to save enough moved up to a house after five or six years, many with intentions of spending a lifetime there.

The same world economic downturn that had brought things to a halt in Schefferville had afflicted Labrador City too. But the company decided to keep Labrador City — and Sept-Iles — operating, although at greatly reduced capacity. Whereas Schefferville's 526 workers found their jobs terminated, some 1,900 workers in Labrador City and Sept-Iles merely found themselves laid off. The difference was crucial. "Terminated" workers qualified for the generous severance and relocation allowances, and anyone who wanted to remain in Schefferville could buy his or her company-owned house for $1. But laid-off workers got no such deal. They were deemed to be on three-year recall, which meant they had the right to be recalled to work, in order of seniority, if the company decided to increase its work-force. But even company officials admitted the chance of recall was very low, except perhaps for those with the most seniority. For most, it meant sitting and waiting, with little real hope of returning to work. And, at the end of three years, they would simply be let go, without any severance or relocation benefits.

Most of the Labrador City workers quickly saw they were in a no-win situation and decided to leave. But leaving wasn't that easy either. Suddenly, now that the town no longer had a future, their homes were virtually worthless. Workers who had bought homes for $50,000 several years earlier found there were no buyers. They simply walked away from them, handing the keys over to the bank before they left town.

But this depressing option wasn't even available to some seventy families, whose mortgages were privately insured by the Mortgage Insurance Co. of Canada. The insurance company informed the families that, if they abandoned their homes, they would still have to pay the balance on the mortgage. Forty-six-year-old Mary Birmingham discovered just what this meant. Laid off after sixteen years with Iron Ore, she found herself unable to sell her $48,000 house, and eventually had to turn it over to the bank. When the mortgage insurance company sued her for the balance owing on it, she declared personal bankrupty, and ended up losing her 1977 Oldsmobile as well. A devastated Birmingham returned to Petty Harbour, Newfoundland, to live with her parents. But Iron Ore tracked her down there, sending her a letter demanding payment for $9.26 she owed her former employer for the electrical bill on her house! The curt letter from Iron Ore threatened to take her to court. Said Birmingham: "I think that was kind of low."

The situation in the trailer park was equally bleak. It was home to the younger workers with the least seniority and the least chance of recall. But, if the option of leaving seemed the only sensible one, again it proved difficult. Many of the young families had sunk as much as $25,000 into their trailers, which were virtually their only possessions. Although the company had brought the trailers in on the railway for free, it was offering no such free passage out — even though it owned and operated the railway. Rayfield Sutton, one of the laid-off workers, found that Iron Ore planned to charge him $10,000 to move his $28,000 trailer to St. John's — $10,000 that he certainly didn't have.

Ironically, hundreds of those laid off in Labrador City had originally worked for Iron Ore in Schefferville, but the company had transferred them to Labrador City in the months before the shut-down. That way, they no longer qualified for the benefits when Schefferville was closed, and they also found themselves at the bottom end of the seniority list in Labrador City.

Furthermore, the company was highly selective in its treatment of laid-off workers. Among the 1,200 people laid off in Labrador City in 1982, some 300 were supervisory staff. These supervisors received full severance pay and relocation allowances. No such generosity was extended to the unionized workers, many of whom even found themselves faced with exorbitant bills when they tried to take their luggage and belongings out on the company train.

The tragedy of the situation was more poignant because of the hope that had accompanied the workers when they came to Labrador City. They had uprooted themselves from more agree-able surroundings in their home towns and sought out a better life for themselves in true pioneer spirit. "These were the success stories. These were the ones who had the initiative to move up here," said Ernest Cordon, a teacher at the local high school. Indeed, in many ways, these were the types of workers celebrated in the mythology of free trade: they rejected the safety and security of their past and went to wherever they could find a job, even if that meant living in a less hospitable terrain. And yet, after years, many left with nothing to show for it, not even able to pay their own way out. Clive Hamilton, a twenty-five-year-old worker who lived with his wife and three children in the Labrador City trailer park, was laid off in January 1982 after five years working for Iron Ore. Six months later he declared personal bankruptcy, losing his trailer and his van and the $22,300 he had spent on them.

While Mulroney basked in the glow of good publicity for his "civilized" shut-down in Schefferville, the workers in Labrador City were hurting badly — far from the glare of TV cameras. Since the lay-offs there lacked the drama of the Schefferville shut-down, they never received the same media attention. It was months before the union realized how bad the situation was in Labrador City — a situation as much Brian Mulroney's making as the "generous" Schefferville settlement for which he received ample credit. But by this point, it was too late. Mulroney had left Iron Ore. His new office declined an interview request on the subject on the grounds that Mulroney was no longer with the company. Clearly, an opposition leader had no time to answer questions about the plight of his former employees who were left stranded in a virtual ghost town.

Mulroney's tenure at Iron Ore turned out to be a stepping stone to his political career. The world-wide collapse of iron ore prices left him surprisingly unscathed. He escaped with far more than a relocation allowance or the right to ship a trailer on the company train. Indeed, his years at Iron Ore contributed greatly to his financial prosperity. His personal friend and biographer, the journalist L. Ian MacDonald, who had Mulroney's co-operation for the preparation of a 1985 biography, *Mulroney: The Making of a Prime Minister*, notes that the deal Mulroney negotiated for himself with Iron Ore back in 1976 was so generous it would "assure Mulroney of lifetime financial security."

MacDonald also notes how Mulroney later looked back on his appearance in the Schefferville auditorium with considerable satisfaction. Mulroney himself described it to MacDonald as "quite a performance." MacDonald goes on to describe how, after his impressive performance, Mulroney left the remote northern town with his worries behind him, focussed on the real business of organizing his campaign, content that he had done his best to minimize the "negative fallout" from Schefferville.

The negative fallout that concerned Mulroney was clearly any possible bad publicity from the Schefferville shut-down that might have damaged his leadership bid. But it never happened. Mulroney went on to win the Tory leadership in June, without the Iron Ore lay-offs — and the shabby treatment of hundreds of his employees — ever becoming an issue. As for Ray Sutton, Clive Hamilton, Mary Birmingham and others who were left behind in the snowbanks as their former boss began his rise to power, L. Ian MacDonald doesn't mention if Mulroney ever worried about what happened to them.

BRIAN MULRONEY GOT his first big break at the age of seven. A man showed up at the Mulroney family home in Baie Comeau one afternoon and asked if Brian would come out and sing. Brian, who sang in the small local choir, was being invited to sing for the Colonel. Like everyone in Baie Comeau, Brian knew who the Colonel was.

The Colonel was Colonel McCormick, a powerful U.S. news-paper baron whose empire included the New York *Daily News* and the Chicago *Tribune*. The Colonel had more or less created Baie Comeau in the thirties from a wilderness site, in the interests of milling local timber for his newspaper empire. It was very much a company town, and the Colonel was the legendary super-boss. The finest building in town was the magnificent guest house that the company built to accommodate the Colonel and his entourage whenever they visited the area.

It was to this guest house that young Brian was driven that first day he met the Colonel. He was placed on top of the piano and sang "Dearie," at the Colonel's request. A few other songs followed and the Colonel, apparently satisfied, pulled a $50 (U.S.) bill out of his wallet and gave it to the wide-eyed boy. After that, whenever the Colonel was in town, young Brian was summoned to sing.

What is remarkable about this incident is not so much that it happened, but that Mulroney relishes the story. It's recalled fondly in some detail in MacDonald's book, quoted directly from Mulroney. And Frank Common, Mulroney's former law partner, says that he has heard Mulroney recount the tale "about a thousand times." Why is Mulroney so delighted with this story? Clearly, in some way it captures how Mulroney sees himself and his life.

Mulroney's pleasure with the story would make more sense if, for instance, he had gone on to become a great singer, with his performance for the Colonel being the big break that opened doors to later stardom. But of course we know that Mulroney made his mark in politics, not singing. Does the episode hold the key to his success in politics? This is an intriguing possibility. What apparently excites Mulroney about the story is not the fact that his singing skills were appreciated, but that he received recognition and reward from a very powerful man — a man who, perhaps, loomed even more powerful in young Brian's eyes because he was from a big city far away.

For young Brian, the Colonel represented the glamour of life beyond Baie Comeau, even life beyond Canada. Was it possible that there was someone out there this rich and this generous? Was this what Americans were like? Unlike Bill Loewen, who grew up in Elkhorn thinking Americans talked too loud and too fast, young Brian had a different view of these foreigners. Baie Comeau owed its very existence to them and their money; there was little anti-Americanism in this town.

Americans seemed so prosperous. You sang a few little ditties and the Colonel reached into his pocket and pulled out $50 *U.S.* The mundane Canadian world of pulp and paper and belching smoke stacks and schoolwork and everything else Brian saw around him in Baie Comeau utterly lacked this kind of excitement; Baie Comeau was dreary and grinding and boring. But the big, wide, wonderful world of power and money lay beyond, and you could gain access to it. All you had to do was please the Colonel . . . sing him a little song. . . . It was fun, it was easy and you wound up with $50 in your pocket.

Young Brian learned how to please the Colonel: "Any time he came to Baie Comeau, he asked for me, and I'd go sing. I'd perform any song that he'd want. He'd just name them and I knew them," Mulroney later told his biographer. There was clearly something pleasing in the demeanour of this earnest young man that kept the Colonel asking for more.

For Mulroney, singing for the Colonel appears to have been a pivotal experience, as his interest in reliving the event in later years attests. For many, such a story would be recalled years later with a tinge of embarrassment. Of course, no one can blame a seven-year-old for being excited by a $50 bill and a leathery smile from the legendary godfather from America. But Mulroney's gig for the Colonel had such overtones of Sambo performing for the big white boss that many — particularly anyone who went on to lead a country — might happily abandon the memory of it, along with the other silly little things that happen in childhood. But not Mulroney. He sees no problem with his performance. Wasn't he just doing the logical thing — satisfying the whims of those with power?

In many ways, Mulroney is still very much that young boy who took the $50 bill and probably wondered why someone would give him so much just for singing a song. He may have marvelled too, years later, at how the Iron Ore Company gave him lifetime financial security for simply lowering the axe on several thousand of his compatriots. And he probably also marvelled at how easy it was to raise millions of dollars in financial backing from the business community — the Conservative Party collected more than $52 million from business between 1984 and 1989 under Brian Mulroney — simply for promoting the business agenda. What Mulroney learned from performing for the Colonel was that it was possible to become rich and important, and that it felt good too. All you had to do was please the powerful. It was a lesson that would take Mulroney a long way.

YOU HAD TO expect highs and lows in politics, but this was beyond low. This was downright humiliating.

It was August 1983, only two months since the Conservative convention had swept Mulroney to within striking distance of his lifelong dream; for the first time the prime ministership hovered just above the horizon. The glare of cameras, the crush of bodies, the intensity of the negotiations, the fear of defeat, the high of winning, the surge of the crowd to be near him; it was all still alive in his mind. But after the months of heady excitement, now it came down to this: he couldn't even draw a crowd at a nursing home when he was the only attraction.

The reception area of the Glen Haven nursing home in Trenton, Nova Scotia, where he was scheduled to speak to the residents, was empty. But then he was a little early. That had to be the explanation. It was inconceivable that the bed-ridden residents had something better to do than meet the future Prime Minister of Canada. Mulroney, fresh from his leadership victory, was running in the federal by-election in the riding of Central Nova on August 29, in a bid to win a seat in the House of Commons — something he had never bothered to try for before.

Central Nova was a safe Tory seat, and its long-time MP, Elmer McKay, had assured himself a choice portfolio in an eventual Mulroney cabinet by stepping aside to let the new leader run there. Still, safe or not, Mulroney wasn't taking any chances at this point. He was doing the full campaign routine. He had even coaxed Joe Clark into joining him for an afternoon campaign rally there, leaving himself open to the humiliation of watching as more children pressed for autographs from Clark, who, as a former Prime Minister, had more stature than someone who had never even been elected to a school board. These kinds of humiliations were inevitable. Still, he wasn't prepared for a putdown from the nursing home set.

Mulroney headed back to his car, after his aides suggested to the Glen Haven staff that they round up some live bodies for his return. The small Mulroney entourage then drove off, briefly canvassed some nearby homes, and drove around the block a few times. (A photographer and I, the only media representatives there, followed in a car directly behind.) Finally the Mulroney car pulled up in front of the nursing home again, and the Conservative leader bounded out, apparently confident that the situation was under control. But his hopes faded as he walked back into the spacious reception area and found only five elderly people waiting to meet him.

To say these people were not Mulroney's crowd is perhaps a bit of an understatement. Their lives were as limited and confining as his was expansive and full of promise. There were no deals to be cut here, no power to be brokered. There were only five votes in the whole room, and it was dubious whether any of them would even bother to vote. "Don't make any dates for August 29th," he joked to three elderly women. "I don't want you going out on heavy dates."

The conversation soon petered out, leaving an awkward calm hanging over the half-empty room. Mulroney, dressed casually in slacks and an open-necked shirt, could think of virtually nothing to say to these people — these people whose needs were so great, but who had so little to offer him.

Three minutes into the event and it was starting to lag. Worse, there was someone from the press sitting in the far corner of the room; what if she mentioned this embarrassing little episode in *Maclean's* and it made his campaign look ineffective?

"Well, it's nice and quiet, eh?" said the future Prime Minister of Canada.

Within ten minutes, Mulroney was gone, on to the next appearance, with the nursing home visit written off as a campaign blunder. Chalk it up to the need for better advance men.

A year and a half later, Mulroney made one of the biggest political mistakes of his political career when he removed the full indexation protection from the old age pension. It was a particularly bumbling move that anyone with a feel for the country could have warned him would cost him dearly in terms of public trust.

The people at the Glen Haven nursing home could have alerted him, if he'd taken the time to ask them about their lives.

IN THE SUMMER of 1984 — after Pierre Trudeau's resignation and before Brian Mulroney's victory as Prime Minister — the Department of Finance in Ottawa was busily preparing a new agenda for Canada. Although the changes being mapped out were quite dramatic and promised to alter Canada in some very fundamental ways, the voters hadn't yet been consulted. That wouldn't happen until September 4, the day of the federal election. But business had already communicated what it wanted. It wanted a new agenda for Canada.

If ever there was a golden opportunity for the business community, this was it. After a decade and a half of Canadian politics dominated by Trudeau, the master survivor was finally, truly gone. Business had never liked Trudeau. He was too erratic and uncommitted to the needs of business. One minute he could be singing its tune, the next he could be musing about the end of capitalism. It often seemed that, for Trudeau, the economy was little more than a diversion from the real business of government: constitutional and cultural matters.

Furthermore, the final four years of Trudeau had been the worst as far as business was concerned. The Trudeau crowd had bounded back into office in 1980 full of reformist enthusiasm, after their brief appearance on the opposition benches during Joe Clark's prime ministership. Clark's few forays into policy, such as his plan to sell PetroCanada and move the Canadian embassy in Israel to Jerusalem, had seemed out of sync with the sentiments of most of the Canadian public. And Trudeau had swept back into office promising a nationalistic approach that would give Ottawa a much more interventionist role in the oil industry and would put some backbone in the government's Foreign Investment Review Agency.

If business moguls had consoled themselves that this was all just campaign rhetoric, the freshly elected Trudeau regime gave them pause when it proceeded with its National Energy Program and undertook to make good on its FIRA commitments. If that wasn't bad enough, there was the problem of Herb Gray, the dour, serious-minded nationalist of the Liberal party who had been pushing for tough controls on foreign investment since the early seventies. Gray had been elevated to the post of Industry Minister in the new activist Trudeau regime, and was even travelling the country advocating the ultimate bogeyman of international business — a national industrial strategy. It all reeked of government intervention and control.

But perhaps the final straw was the tax reform in the Liberal budget of November 1981. In an attempt to close loopholes that had become gaping caverns, Finance Minister Allan Mac-Eachen had brought down a budget that unabashedly went after the rich. The reforms would have cut off many avenues for tax avoidance enjoyed by corporations and high-income professionals, and it produced some of the wildest hoots of derision ever to emanate from Canadian business and the business press. The relentless business attack mounted on the MacEachen budget lasted for months and eventually drove the government to retreat. Few of the controversial MacEachen measures were ever enacted: business scored an incredible victory.

In the aftermath of the budget retreat, business was swelled with its own sense of power. It had tasted blood. By howling and screaming, it had managed to topple one of the most powerful ministers in the Trudeau cabinet. MacEachen and his deputy, Ian Stewart, were soon removed to other locations outside the Department of Finance. Furthermore, business was being treated with a new respect, which was reflected in the increasingly flattering portrayal of its leaders in the press. Ironically, the fight against the MacEachen budget had helped raise the profile of business with the public, which had no real inkling that the budget was fundamentally an assault on the rich and that business was simply defending its own interests. In the press, it had looked as if business was fighting a budget that would gouge all Canadians. MacEachen was cast as the evil knight: but for the grace of business, we would all have been impaled on the end of his spear.

If business was enjoying a new respect, it was partly due to some clever repackaging of the business message — largely the work of the Business Council on National Issues. Set up in 1976, the BCNI was an unabashed replica of the U.S. Business

Roundtable. The central formula of both organizations was to greatly increase the clout of the largest and most powerful corporations by banding together in an exclusive, by-invitation-only club. The club was made up of a single representative of each of these super-companies — and each representative had to be the chief executive officer. No substitutions allowed. Without a lot of puny vice-presidents cluttering up the club, it would speak with more authority.

By the early eighties, the BCNI had honed itself into a slick operation, under the deft direction of Tom d'Aquino. With a background in international law, the glib d'Aquino cut new ground in business lobbying with a whole new image for his organization: no longer just the greedy barons of business mythology, BCNI members were presented as wise and caring men who would guide the country to a better future. What had changed was style not substance: d'Aquino stressed the importance of business and labour working together, while still advocating policies that would raise unemployment. But in d'Aquino's agile hands, the business message seemed much smoother, more forward-looking. Tom d'Aquino was to old-style business lobbying what Globalization was to world trade.

In no time, d'Aquino had won the confidence of the country's top CEOs, who conferred on him the honour of being made a CEO himself — of the BCNI. This was no small gesture; he wasn't just the spokesman or executive director of the big business group. He was the *CEO*. Indeed, he was the CEO of the council of CEOs. It was hard to get much more important than that.

As the BCNI took stock of the situation in the aftermath of the MacEachen budget, it saw an opportunity. In its victory against the budget it had felt the power of its own muscle. It was on a roll. Now there were bigger battles out there to win. The MacEachen budget was really just a symptom of a whole approach that irked business, an approach that said big business and the rich were getting away with too much.

This idea seemed to be gaining currency in the tough economic times of the 1982 recession. The Canadian Conference of Catholic Bishops — a group that most business leaders felt should confine itself to prayers and confessionals — had intruded on the scene with a report advocating less emphasis on business profits and more on the downtrodden worker. In tones reminscent of the hated MacEachen budget, the bishops were calling for new taxes on investment. It was disturbing that even a conservative group like the Catholic bishops was thinking along such lines. These kinds of ideas, left unchecked, could catch on. Now was the time to regroup and launch a new assault — an assault much broader and more all-encompassing than the assault on the MacEachen budget.

What business had in mind was a fundamental reorientation — an end to the dominance of government and a shift of power to the private sector. This process had already been successfully launched in the U.S., where Ronald Reagan was entrenching corporate power even further and tying the hands of government. But Canada wasn't the United States. Canadians had long accepted a strong role for government, with crown corporations, government agencies and control boards playing a major role in the economy. And Canadians had long believed that government was responsible for social welfare, for providing a wide range of basic services, for making sure the country's resources were divided up fairly and for guaranteeing that the disadvantaged were protected. These attitudes were part of the Canadian psyche, as much as carrying guns and running the world were part of the American psyche.

To change these basic Canadian notions would be a tall order. For the BCNI, it would involve a "program of reconstruction," as d'Aquino told the staid crowd of Toronto's Empire Club in January 1983 in an address billed as a "business response" to the bishops' proclamation on the economy. While praising the bishops for their good intentions, d'Aquino suggested that their solutions would further harm the economy and, therefore, the poor. Rather, he said, members of the BCNI had been working on a reconstruction program. "And by reconstruction we mean fundamental change in some of the attitudes, some of the structures and some of the laws that shape our lives." What d'Aquino was talking about — as later events would show — was a fundamental alteration of the political landscape. He was talking about changing Canada and the way Canadians thought about Canada.

Over the next eighteen months, the BCNI honed its ideas into a coherent program, which it presented in a detailed discussion paper in August 1984 — one month before the federal election. The paper included many familiar notions long advanced by business, such as the perennial plea for more tax breaks (for business). There was also a new emphasis on reducing the role of government in the economy — by getting rid of airline regulation and stripping government of its power to set oil prices, for example.

But the most crucial thrust of the new BCNI approach was its attack on something that was central to the concept of Canada in the eyes of most Canadians — the social welfare system. Interestingly, the BCNI was well aware of the importance Canadians attached to it. In its discussion paper, the business group acknowledged that there was a "broad consensus" in Canada in favour of large public sector spending, which amounted to some 40 percent of the Gross National Product (GNP) — compared with 35 percent in the U.S. Canadians supported this greater spending, said the BCNI, "reflecting the greater priority that Canadians put on social welfare."

The BCNI also noted the fact that social spending in Canada, while higher than in the U.S., was dramatically lower than in many European states, such as Sweden and the Netherlands, which devoted more than 60 percent of their GNP to the government sector and which were — although the BCNI didn't mention this — prosperous, well-developed countries. What concerned the BCNI was not the large gap between the European and North American countries, but rather the small gap between Canada and the United States. "The divergent trend in the government share of GNP in Canada and the United States is most telling. The United States is Canada's most important trading partner," said the business group. And then, in a line that foretold the shape of the BCNI's battle plan for the next decade, it continued, "The Canadian economy will have more difficulty competing with the United States if the private sector has to support a government sector which has been allowed to get too far out of line." Clearly, any plans to draw Canada closer into a trading relationship with the U.S. was only going to exacerbate this problem of higher Canadian government spending, in the eyes of Canada's most powerful business leaders.

For the BCNI, then, the government sector had been allowed to get "too far out of line," growing bigger than the U.S. government sector. Never mind that this higher public sector spending in Canada was, as the BCNI itself noted, supported by a "broad consensus" of Canadians "reflecting the greater priority that Canadians put on social welfare." For the BCNI, this would have to change. Canadians would have to change. They would have to abandon their priorities. With a month still to go before the September 1984 federal election, the most powerful business group in the country had already decided that, no matter what Canadians decided at the polls, the country had to change.

And the BCNI wasn't leaving anything to chance. In the same paper, it outlined in detail exactly what the new government was to do. It even provided the argument for the changes it envisioned — changes that would amount to an undoing of the Canadian consensus. The argument was simple — we could no longer afford the social programs we evidently valued so much. The deficit had changed all that.

In its simplest form, the deficit boiled down to a shortfall in government revenue. The government was spending more than it was taking in. At least part of the problem lay in the fact that, as government spending had increased over the previous two decades, Ottawa had at the same time introduced a wide array of tax breaks — particularly for business — that left the federal treasury with less and less money to pay for the programs. Corporate taxes, for instance, had declined from roughly 50 percent of total revenues to little more than 30 percent. Personal income taxes had not grown enough to make up the difference, partly because the tax system had been indexed to inflation in the early seventies, so that taxpayers didn't pay more tax simply because inflation had bumped them into a higher tax bracket.

Despite this central problem — insufficient revenue to cover the cost of Ottawa's programs — the system more or less hobbled along, as long as the economy kept growing. The crunch came with the recession of the early eighties. With a badly shrinking economy, tax revenues plummeted still further and the deficit became even more bloated. When the economy began to recover in 1983 and 1984, the deficit still grew, largely because the government's high-interest rate policy was forcing Ottawa to pay out billions in interest payments on money it borrowed to cover the carrying costs of the federal debt.

But while the deficit problem was real, the solution advocated by business — cut popular Canadian spending programs and raise taxes on ordinary Canadians — was by no means the only solution. Business had defined the solution in a way that suited its own interests. It was happy to part with social programs, to make Canadians tighten their belts. It was less keen about tightening its own belt.

At the risk of being glib, let's, for a minute, compare Canada to an anthill with thousands of ants scurrying around. If there's a sudden shortage of food, how should the ant community respond to the crisis? Would it make sense to cut back the portions of the thousands of scurrying little ants, many of whom have very little to eat anyway, or to look instead to the large, oversized ants who are hoarding large supplies of food? The large ants, predictably, suggest the solution is for the little ants to work harder and to learn to do with less. Certainly the large ants see little merit in the idea that they should share more from their own stockpiles. Indeed, even the mention of such an idea makes them threaten to pack up and leave, and take their stockpiles with them.

Now Canada is, of course, more than an anthill. But some of the same problems apply. The BCNI posed the question: With such a serious deficit situation, can we any longer afford social programs? But we might just as well pose another question: With such a serious deficit situation, can we any longer afford such tremendous inequality in our society? Perhaps dramatic inequality was a luxury that belonged, if at all, to more bountiful times, when there was lots to go around. In the face of hardship, perhaps inequality is one of those luxuries we just have to give up — in the name of reducing the deficit.

If the spotlight were turned around in this way and focussed on the rich, a very different picture would emerge. Every indulgence — an extravagant home, an exotic car, a fur coat, a yacht, a costly piece of jewelry — would look vulgar and unpatriotic, evidence of the unwillingness of the rich to make sacrifices clearly needed to restore fiscal responsibility. Instead of always blaming the middle and lower classes for their unwillingness to make sacrifices, we'd focus instead on those with money. Why won't they open up their stockpiles? The country needs them.

Indeed, there is something striking in the tendency of business and the rich to urge restraint for others while continuing on an indulgent fling themselves. The *Financial Post*, for instance, has been among those leading the charge against government social spending, yet it sees no irony in its magazine running articles promoting an expensive life-style for executives. As the recession took hold of the country in 1990, the *Post* magazine ran features on costly wines and spirits, cellular phones as "executive toys," private airplanes for CEOs and lavish entertaining "as a corporate art form." Haven't these people heard we have a deficit crisis? Don't they read their own editorials? Are they completely unaware, for instance, that more than a billion dollars are added to the deficit each year from businesses writing off expenses under the corporate entertainment tax deduction — an unnecessary indulgence if ever there was one.

While the BCNI insisted that its deficit-reduction agenda would hurt everyone, including business, this was simply not the case. The BCNI axe fell largely on spending that business disliked anyway. The council called, for instance, for cuts in government support for agriculture, which would hit farmers. It also wanted significant cuts in government spending on rail transportation, which would hit passengers, particularly those who lived outside large cities. And it called for cuts in regional development programs, which provided government grants for firms that located in depressed parts of the country, largely to the benefit of employees who were thus able to remain in their native provinces despite poor economic conditions. The BCNI noted that business would be happy to exchange these grants for a reduced corporate tax burden; that way, business could enjoy government largesse without having to locate its plants in remote or depressed parts of the country.

In the area of energy, the BCNI was even happier to see spending cuts — along the lines it advocated. The council, whose membership included such oil giants as Texaco, Shell and

Imperial Oil, took up the cry of the oil companies to get the government out of the oil patch and leave it to the industry. Specifically, the BCNI called for the end to Ottawa's Petroleum Incentives Program (PIP), under which grants for exploration and development were linked to Canadian ownership and to activity in remote areas where reserves were costly to develop. These were variations on the "performance requirements" that U.S. business so disliked. The BCNI joined the foreign-owned oil companies in its ranks in asking the government to let the PIP program expire and be replaced by a new system of tax breaks that would provide benefits equally to foreign interests and to companies that preferred to pump oil from cheaper, already developed locations.

But the most dramatic changes business wanted were in the touchy area of social programs. This was the fat that business was really keen to trim, and it foresaw annual savings of billions of dollars. The BCNI started from the premise that Canada could no longer afford its existing level of social programs: "[I]t is important to recognize that the extremely favourable macroeconomic circumstances that existed when many of Canada's present social programs were put into place no longer exist." Basically, the BCNI wanted to reduce the overall amount the federal government spent on its broad social programs, such as the old age pensions and family allowance. Those at the very bottom of the scale would be protected, even possibly receive larger benefits, but the vast majority of Canadians would see their benefits diminish over time. The BCNI also proposed cutbacks in payments to the provinces — payments that covered a large part of the cost of Canada's free medicare program as well as subsidizing low-cost education for Canadians at universities and colleges throughout the country.

Still, business had to tread carefully. Using a battering ram against something that enjoyed a "broad consensus" of support was poor politics, and was likely to rally the country to its defence. So a frontal assault against social spending was out. What was needed was something that attacked from an unprotected flank, something that would lead to cuts in social spending without coming right out and saying so, something like . . . well . . . the deficit.

Unlike social programs, the deficit was a neutral concept that stirred no patriotic feelings in Canadian breasts, that claimed no hold over the Canadian pscyhe. Indeed, most Canadians didn't even know what it was back in 1984. An all-out assault on the deficit had a nice, clean ring to it. It was so clinical — a set of huge, incomprehensible numbers that could be said to threaten our future, even our social programs. While politicians wouldn't last long railing against Canadian social programs, they could freely travel the country denouncing the deficit. And once the public had been prepared for a war on the deficit, the government could then start chopping social programs — in the name of fighting the deficit. Canadians might sense something was wrong at this point, but the Trojan horse would be well inside the gates. Thus the deficit became a crucial weapon in the business arsenal, a powerful concept that could be trotted out to back up the business claim that government spending was out of control.

The BCNI was calling for changes that would have a profound effect on the country, and it released its proposals in the heat of the summer election campaign. But the paper was not really addressed to the public so much as to the new government. Indeed, it was really aimed specifically at the new Prime Minister. As it stated in the introduction, "what is required is a clear political commitment *at the Prime Ministerial level* to begin the painful process of reducing the federal government's spending and program commitments as a *key priority in the autumn of 1984*" (italics added). The members of the BCNI didn't want to waste time dealing with mere deputy ministers or even cabinet ministers. After all, they were the top CEOs in the country, and they intended to deal with the top politician in the country. And they wanted their deficit concerns at the top of his agenda from the moment he took office.

In fact, they had already managed to get their deficit concerns at the top of the agenda of at least one of the contenders: John Turner. In the summer of '84, Turner was enjoying his brief stint as Prime Minister following the resignation of Pierre Trudeau. After a decade spent lining up political support on Bay Street, Turner had learned to listen carefully to the thoughts of senior business leaders. He had certainly listened carefully to their recent thoughts on the deficit, and, as the September '84 election approached, he had taken to referring to the need for deficit reduction in his campaign speeches — much to the horror of his political handlers. Sensing that deficit reduction had all the popular appeal of higher taxes or compulsory military service, Turner's staff tried to steer him clear of the subject, preparing speeches for him that never mentioned the subject. But often just before a speech, Turner would reach into his breast pocket and pull out his own set of notes. The aides would cringe as he launched into an attack on the deficit. "Those speeches went over like a lead balloon," recalled one former Turner staffer.

Meanwhile, in the Department of Finance, Deputy Minister Mickey Cohen had picked up on the theme of the new Prime Minister, setting some of his senior officials to work preparing a paper that would define deficit reduction as the centrepiece of a new Turner government. "I gather Turner was prepared to make [Cohen's deficit-reduction paper] the basis for the Speech from the Throne," said one former senior Finance official. While the actual writing was done largely by Assistant Deputy Minister Fred Gorbet, Cohen kept a close eye on the deficit paper, the political line of which fit well with his own leanings.

Although his successful career had included long stints in government, Cohen had also spent time in the private sector and was really a "private sector person," as one former Finance official described him. Indeed, Cohen had been brought in to run the Finance department in the fall of '82, largely to win back the support of business after the fiasco over the MacEachen budget. And he had proved himself up to the task, loosening the tax laws in ways that won business support.

Cohen quickly established himself as a major force and, if anything, he acquired even more clout after the Conservatives came to power in '84. "Mickey just towered over the bureaucracy," recalls Charley McMillan, Mulroney's chief policy advisor. Cohen's strong pro-business orientation allowed him to fit in well with the new Cabinet, and he became a trusted advisor of both the Prime Minister and the Minister of Finance.

If it seemed that Cohen's true inclinations lay in the private sector, he soon followed them there. He left Finance in the summer of 1985 to take on the job of running the Reichmann family's massive business empire. From there he moved on to become CEO of Molson's, and a full-fledged member of the BCNI.

Although the deficit paper was an internal document, prepared with Turner in mind, Cohen was well aware that the paper's theme would also go down well with the Conservatives, who had raised $11 million from the business community to finance the party's '84 campaign. Indeed, the Conservatives were made aware of the thrust of the paper during the election campaign. "Finance made known to both parties what it was up to. Both agreed," said a former Finance official. "The department recognized that, regardless of which party won, there would be a new government. The Trudeau guys had left. [The new Prime Minister] would be starting fresh."

So before the public even went to the polls on election day, the new agenda for reshaping the country had already been largely worked out inside the Department of Finance, with an eye to satisfying business. Government, business, the Liberals and the Conservatives all supported the thrust of the changes proposed. The only people who had had no input or knowledge of what was being planned were the members of the Canadian public. If we want to find any evidence of how the public felt about deficit reduction during the election, one place to look might be the campaign results of John Turner — the one candidate who dared to mention the subject, only to go down to humiliating defeat.

But, despite Turner's sporadic forays into the subject, it's probably fair to say that Canadians generally were not really aware of the deficit as an issue in the September 1984 election. Although the government had mapped out an agenda to put the deficit front and centre the day after the election, no one had told the public this. So Canadians happily spent the campaign trying to figure out how to vote, in the naive belief that they were going to determine their country's future. What they didn't realize was that the key decisions about the direction of the new government had already been made.

Within six weeks of the new Conservative government taking office, it came out with its first major pronouncement, an

"Economic Statement" that slashed $4 billion from the deficit. (Although this was a dramatic cut, some within the new inner circle had wanted to go much further; McMillan, for instance, had pushed for a cut of $7 billion.) Accompanying the new government's statement was a brushed-up version of Mickey Cohen's paper that had been mostly prepared before the election. Now titled "A New Direction for Canada: An Agenda for Economic Renewal," the paper bore the name of the new Finance Minister, Michael Wilson, and laid out almost everything the Conservative government planned to do to remake the country. "That was the economic agenda for the government," says Bill Fox, former press secretary to Mulroney. "It was deliberately done separate from the budget process so it would be seen as an economic blueprint paper. Each of the budgets would be measured against it." Recalls another highly placed official, "It became the Bible."

Interestingly, the "Bible" bore an uncanny resemblance to the BCNI's August 1984 proposals. The central focus of the government's paper was also the need to reduce the deficit, and the recommended areas to cut were familiar too. Like the BCNI paper, the Finance paper singled out nationalistic energy programs, rail subsidies, agriculture and regional development programs. It also followed the BCNI's lead in the area of social policy, arguing for greater selectivity and possibly reducing indexation of old age and family benefits. Like the BCNI, it also wanted to save money by cutting back on Canada's foreign aid spending. Furthermore, the one area that both the BCNI and the Department of Finance found worthy of increased spending, despite the deficit, was the military. When it came to the need to beef up Canada's military might, concerns about the deficit suddenly subsided.

Ironically, the revised post-election version of Cohen's paper implied that this "new direction for Canada" was somehow the result of the election. "On September 4, Canadians voted for change. . . . The mandate of September 4 reflects as well a sombre judgment about Canada's poor economic performance in the recent past. Canadians looked back on a decade of soaring government deficits and rising unemployment; of expansive, intrusive government. . . . They saw that their government and their economy had gone dangerously off course and off balance." The wording of the paper had been cleverly crafted to suggest that the new government was acting on a mandate from the Canadian public to bring in this new agenda — an agenda that Canadians had hardly heard about before the election.

As for Mulroney, who had shrewdly kept quiet on the subject of deficit reduction during his campaign, he quickly became a crusader after the election. The BCNI had called for a commitment on deficit reduction at the prime ministerial level, and Mulroney delivered. In speech after speech, he began hammering away on the subject, describing deficit reduction as the number one priority of his government. The script for this harangue had been largely written before the election — in the offices of the Finance department and the boardroom of the BCNI. All that was needed was a new actor in the lead role. And Mulroney took to the task with all the gusto of learning a new song for the Colonel.

IN THE DIMLY lit splendour of the upscale Italian restaurant, a former top Mulroney aide is explaining the government's agenda when he is confronted with a delicately presented veal piccata.

To call Stanley Hartt merely a former top Mulroney aide perhaps underbills him. Before leaving the government to return to his law practice in the summer of 1990, Hartt, a friend from Mulroney's days as a Montreal labour lawyer, had served in two of the most sensitive spots in the Mulroney administration. During the Tories' first term, he had replaced Mickey Cohen as deputy finance minister, overseeing tax reform and the development of the GST, and had played an important role in the evolution of the free trade agreement. And in the second term, Mulroney had brought Hartt even further into the inner circle, appointing him to the top job of chief of staff in the Prime Minister's Office — the person with the closest access to the Prime Minister, the person who controls whom the Prime Minister sees and, to a large extent, what the Prime Minister does.

"He [Mulroney] knew that he had to clean up the lethargy and the laxity," says Hartt.

Hartt is explaining the Mulroney agenda. And make no mistake about it, Hartt sees it as an agenda — a coherent and cohesive plan to change the country.

"Canadians seem to think you don't have to do anything to remain a rich, high-standard-of-living country. We need someone to wake us up," he says.

The waiter approaches our table with a large cylindrical object that turns out to be a pepper grinder. But this is no ordinary pepper grinder. As the waiter grinds it, a light on the bottom flashes on, illuminating the food below and preventing over-peppering of food. A world-class pepper grinder. With technology like this, it's hard to believe we're slipping behind in the race for global competitiveness.

The root of the problem, according to Hartt, is what he calls the "Canadian paradigm." By this, Hartt says, he means the attitude on the part of Canadians that, "I'm entitled to a living; the government owes it to me."

"If there's a drought, the government has to fix it for me. They [the people who run the government] convince me they care about me by the amount of money they spend on me. And if someone says, 'Who's going to pay for all this?' the answer is 'Nobody.' It just gets added to the deficit. And if for some reason it can't go on the deficit, then the answer is, 'Let the rich pay.'"

Hartt argues that, in order to remain competitive in the world, these attitudes that he attributes to Canadians have to change. Canadians must learn that "there's no free lunch."

This richly decorated restaurant in the heart of Montreal certainly exudes a sense of high living. Around the restaurant, diners tucked into cosy corners look like they're enjoying a very high standard of living indeed. At the next table, an immaculately dressed couple in their late thirties appear indifferent to the opulence and finery, and to each other. The look of boredom on their faces suggests this is one of many exotic restaurants they frequent.

Hartt continues to explain the problem with Canada. "We are a spoiled and lazy country," he says.

A recent column in the *Financial Post* expressed the same idea more bluntly. Anthony Hampson, a former CEO of Canada Development Corp., who now describes himself as a venture capitalist and "social commentator," painted a highly negative view of the Canadian psyche: "Many historians and sociologists agree Canada is a nation of losers, with all the bad attitudes losers usually develop — a sense of entitlement, a tendency to freeload, a reluctance to change, and an inability to face both reality and their own weaknesses."

A nation of *losers?* A tendency to *freeload?* A *spoiled* and *lazy* country?

Now I'm perplexed. Hartt and Hampson are portraying Canadians as a bunch of no-good lay-abouts. But this just doesn't fit with the country I know. Canada has always seemed like an industrious little nation, full of prosperous, well-meaning people — a kind of Switzerland of North America.

It occurs to me that what Hartt and Hampson are really saying is not that Canadians, as individuals, are lazy people, but that the Canadian system fills Canadians with a sense of comfort and security, a sense of well-being. Unlike the everyman-for-himself world of the United States, Canada has always enjoyed more of a feeling of community. This has traditionally been reflected in our political and social system, which has aimed to provide a decent standard of living for everyone.

We subscribe, for instance, to the notion that everyone has the right to proper medical care; indeed, that no one has the right to superior care simply because he or she has more money. Yet in the U.S., where Cadillac care is available to the rich, some 20 million Americans have no access to medical care, and would be turned away at many hospitals even if they arrived by ambulance. In Canada, we also subscribe to the view that education — even at the university level — is something everyone with basic ability should have an opportunity to take advantage of. In the U.S., however, higher education is almost exclusively the preserve of the privileged, and middle-class parents spend their whole working lives saving up to give their children a university education. Furthermore, Canadians believe that those who can't or simply don't earn an adequate living on their own should receive subsidies to help them get by. As a result, our poor people have generally been cushioned from devastating poverty, while much of the American underclass has been relegated to a life of abject poverty in violent, teeming ghettoes largely cordoned off from middle-class society.

Maybe being a nation of losers isn't so bad.

But Hartt — and the Mulroney government in which he played such a pivotal role — are determined to change that. They want to bring Canada, kicking and screaming, into what they say is the real world — a rough and tumble, cut-throat sort of place, far removed from the comfort and security of the Canada we know. In this new world, Canada will be leaner and more competitive, and Canadians will cease to be freeloaders.

But wait. Freeloaders? Freeloaders on whom? Freeloaders, presumably, on government. But how can we be freeloaders on government if we're paying for government, which we certainly are with our tax dollars? Aren't we, then, just freeloading on ourselves? Or to put it another way — aren't we simply pooling our resources, combining them to create a more efficient and equitable society, a better functioning community?

Indeed, if freeloaders do exist, they are probably people like us — Stanley Hartt and me. Our dinner at this exotic restaurant is being subsidized by the Canadian taxpayer. Let me explain. I invited Hartt to dinner to interview him for this book, so I'm legally entitled, under our absurd tax laws, to deduct most of the cost of the dinner as "business entertainment" when I fill out my income tax form. I suspect most of the people in this restaurant are doing the same. Just ask any restaurant owner how many clients are on business expense accounts, and he or she will likely answer that most are.

Whether or not the restaurant patrons are actually discussing business is, of course, another matter. Since it's virtually impossible to police that sort of thing, the government doesn't even try. That bored couple at the next table is likely deducting the cost of their dinner, even though they appear to be mostly squabbling about domestic matters. But every time they — or I — deduct the cost of meals like this, we're saving ourselves taxes, and the federal treasury is losing money. Revenue Canada estimates that the business entertainment deduction costs more than one billion dollars a year — a billion dollars that could go to pay off the deficit.

Surely, if we are trying to find ways to reduce the deficit, this would be an excellent place to start. It's clearly not essential that this interview be conducted in such splendour. If the tax deduction didn't exist, Stanley Hartt and I would probably be discussing Canadian laziness over coffee and a doughnut. Somehow we'd get by. And maybe we'd both get a better understanding of the government's austerity measures if we were sitting amongst the kinds of people we'd see in a doughnut shop. But business executives, despite their "acute concern over the deficit," as the BCNI has described it, have shown no willingness to abandon this government subsidy for their high living. How can we take these people seriously?

All this talk of freeloading has made me hungry, but a lovely, suitably peppered lasagna lies invitingly before me. As I indulge myself, it occurs to me that many of my compatriots — the lazy and spoiled lot of them — have never known the luxury of a meal like this. As we sit here talking, sipping fine Alsatian wine, nibbling haute Italian cuisine, with a pepper grinder that makes food glow in the dark, it's easy to idly entertain notions about making Canada more competitive. But what does it mean? Does it mean fewer indulgent meals for people like us? Will the bored couple at the next table have to start worrying about where their next extravagant dinner is coming from? I suspect not.

Rather, I suspect, the Canadians who will grow leaner are the ones closer to the bottom. It is they who will see their wages driven down in the name of making Canada more competitive with the low-wage countries of the world.

Hartt admits that the rich may be the first to benefit from a more competitive Canada: "That's the nature of capitalism. The benefits go initially to those who are successful competitors. They certainly don't go to the foreman or the machinist on the plant floor."

But Hartt insists that the benefits trickle down to workers too, by increasing their job and income prospects. This, of course, is what Ronald Reagan always promised. But Reagan is now gone, and with him went the bagmen and scallywags who reaped hundreds of millions of dollars from the lax, help-the-rich regime he put in place in the U.S. The poor are still waiting for the trickle to start.

The Mulroney team has always insisted that the most disadvantaged members of society will continue to be protected in the new competitive Canada it is creating, but the record suggests otherwise. For the first time since the Depression of the thirties, food banks and soup lines have sprung up around the country, and the streets of Montreal and Toronto are getting crowded at night with the homeless. Rather than responding to these emergencies with extra aid, the government has brought in changes that exacerbate the situation. It has made unemployment insurance harder to get, even as its high interest rate policy has driven up the number of unemployed. And it is imposing a cap on payments that cover welfare cost increases in Ontario, Alberta and British Columbia — the "rich" provinces, as if welfare recipients in these provinces are somehow rich too. This puts the lie to any Mulroney government claim of protecting the disadvantaged. By cutting welfare subsidies, the government is potentially leaving vulnerable some of the neediest members of society — single mothers, young children, the disabled.

Hartt acknowledges that there's a lot of resistance among Canadians to the changes. "They say, 'You're changing the venerable ground of Canada. We like the old guys, we like the old ways.'" What does the government do in the face of such opposition? Stop? Listen? Slow down? Reassess its course? No; it perseveres, insisting that it is right.

Hartt says that Mulroney knows his agenda is unpopular with Canadians. "But he knows what Canada needs, what is good for Canada."

It never seems to occur to Mulroney that Canadians are neither lazy, nor spoiled nor a nation of losers. They just have a different vision of how to run a country.

INDEED, "VISION" MAY not be the best way to describe Brian Mulroney's notion of how to run a country. Mulroney is more a gambler than a man of vision. He finds his soul mates not among the true believers who strut occasionally across the public stage, but among the fast-living speculators who came to dominate the business scene in the eighties, turning it into a kind of casino for those willing to roll the dice — for either a corporate empire or a country.

5 • CASINO CAPITALISTS: SOUL MATES ON A ROLL

It seemed like one of those touching humble-boy-makes-good stories. In the magnificent splendour of the Governor General's official residence in Ottawa, a man from modest Winnipeg roots stepped forward to receive Canada's highest honour, the Order of Canada. In the moving ceremony — Ottawa's equivalent of the Olympic moment of glory when the medal is placed around the neck of the triumphant athlete — Ross Johnson bowed as the red and white cloth garland was lowered over his head by the Queen's representative in Canada.

It had been a long road for Johnson from Depression-era Winnipeg to the velvet chairs of the Governor General's palatial official residence. As a child, Johnson had rented out his comic book collection in a show of entrepreneurial zeal that would eventually take him to the top of the corporate world and now to a spot on Canada's honour roll. While few Canadians had heard of Johnson when this honour was bestowed on him in April 1987, he would become better known the following year when, like a tiny number of Canadians before him, he would make it onto the cover of *TIME* magazine; the real *TIME* magazine, not just the Canadian edition.

A cover story in December 1988 showed Johnson under the less-than-flattering headline "A Game of Greed," and noted that he stood to pocket personally anywhere from $100 million to $1 billion in a corporate manoeuvre known as a leveraged buy-out (LBO). The cover headline asked if things had, perhaps, gone too far. Even in capitalist America, Johnson was perceived to have pushed things beyond the limit, to have risked blackening the very name of a system that thrives on the ambitious greed of the entrepreneur.

This would suggest that Ross Johnson was a Dr Jekyll and Mr Hyde sort of character — a corporate hero to Canadians by day who turned into a greedy manipulator south of the border at night. But it would be misleading to see him this way. Ross Johnson the hero and Ross Johnson the villain were one and the same: a free-wheeling, life-in-the-fast-lane gambler and deal maker, a casino capitalist. It was these very qualities that led Johnson to gamble everything in his brash bid for ownership of RJR Nabisco, the U.S. corporate giant, over which he already presided as CEO. And it was these same qualities that had made him a close personal friend and soul mate of Brian Mulroney.

For Johnson, the *TIME* magazine rebuke was as harsh and unexpected as the dramatic tumble in the polls of 1990 and 1991 — down to the mid teens — would be to his friend Mulroney. Both men had operated in the only way they knew how: rolling the dice, going for broke, playing a game of high-risk poker that had always worked for them in the past. But eventually their worlds came crashing down around them when they came up against guys who were simply better with a deck of cards.

For both men, the stakes were high and the fall was devastating. Mulroney, who had won the largest back-to-back majorities in Canadian history, lost his dream of being remembered as one of the country's most popular prime ministers. And Ross Johnson, who had risen from nothing to control one of the largest corporations in the U.S., lost his LBO bid, and with it the dream of joining the ranks of the world's billionaires. Yet, in both cases, the real risks these men took were not with their own lives, but with the lives of others.

SINCE LEAVING CANADA in 1974 after a modest career in marketing, Ross Johnson had lived a charmed life as a rocket-propelled up-and-comer in the corporate world. Perhaps it was the whiff of entrepreneurialism in the New York air, but Johnson was quickly transformed from a smooth-talking light-bulb salesman — his forte in Canada — into one of the top moguls of U.S. business. His spectacular climb to the top was all achieved through clever manoeuvring and corporate politicking. Twice he threatened to quit unless he took over the boss's job and both times he ended up being the boss. By 1986, he was CEO of RJR Nabisco, the tobacco and grocery giant that claimed annual revenues of $16 billion and a spot among the top twenty corporations in the U.S.

He even started to act the part. Gone was any trace of the lanky salesman in horn-rimmed glasses smiling in front of the light-bulb display stand. Johnson had become more American than the Americans themselves, with his loose-talking, shoot-from-the-hip bravado. He was brash, genial and cocky, and thrived on a kind of corporate chaos, discarding staff like tissue paper and creating for himself and his close coterie of top managers one of the most lavish life-styles in America — all on the company tab.

His spending was legendary — endless dinners, parties, limousines, celebrity sports events, golf-club memberships, and travel in RJR Nabisco's fleet of ten corporate jets, the main function of which seemed to be to transport Johnson, his friends and members of the company's board to a constant stream of social events. He kept a stable of sports celebrities — including Jack Nicklaus and Don Meredith — on lavish company retainers and trotted them out at special functions, ostensibly for company promotion, but also to satisfy Johnson's love of rubbing shoulders with stars. Johnson had no respect for budgetary restraint. Certainly, when it came to spending company money on himself and his cronies, he was nothing but indulgent. He considered restraint at the senior executive level a sign of nit-picking small-mindedness. And by coddling and indulging the company's directors as well, Johnson managed to convince them that all this personal extravagance had something to do with corporate creativity and helping RJR Nabisco sell cookies and cigarettes.

With a salary of $1.7 million a year, Johnson was the envy of the corporate world. But he set his sights higher still. From his early days at the helm of RJR Nabisco, Johnson began entertaining ideas of a leveraged buy-out — the popular eighties business scheme whereby a small group, often from within management, buys control of a large public company.

Typically, they do this by offering to buy up a majority of the company's shares with vast sums of borrowed money, which they raise using the company's assets as collateral. If their bid succeeds and they gain control of the company, they pay off this mountain of debt by stripping the company's cupboard bare — shutting down less profitable divisions, selling off parts of the corporate empire and firing large numbers of employees. In the process, these individuals become the owners of a major corporation that generates hundreds of millions of dollars a year in profits, delivering themselves personal fortunes that would turn heads at a garden party of oil sheikhs.

The LBO typified everything that had gone wrong with business in the eighties. The LBO bidders used the company's corporate treasury to pay for their acquisition. In the U.S., $1.3 trillion dollars — money that could have been spent on research and development or upgrading plants and equipment to make companies more productive — was diverted instead to the cause of paying for buy-outs or mergers, which served no purpose but the further enrichment of the already rich. U.S. economist Robert Pollin and journalist Alexander Cockburn have noted that this sum amounted to about one-third of the amount spent on new productive plant and equipment in the eighties, and that a shocking $13 billion was spent on the fees of the lawyers and bankers who did nothing more socially useful than arrange these deals. Meanwhile, employees of the target companies were unceremoniously dumped. And the whole scheme was subsidized by taxpayers: since the interest costs on corporate debt are tax deductible, corporations legally avoided paying billions of dollars in taxes through these LBO schemes.

Ross Johnson's attempted LBO — which failed when someone else outbid him — represented greed on the grandest scale. Johnson himself confessed that he eventually stood to make $100 million; outside analysts said that his personal stake could have been more in the $1 billion range. The hundreds of lawyers and investment bankers involved stood to take tens of millions out of the RJR Nabisco corporate trough as well. The lost revenue for the federal treasury was estimated to be somewhere in the $2 to $5 billion range.

If Johnson's LBO bid was the ultimate deal, it was simply the culmination of a long career that focussed on clever bargaining and skillful deal making. Johnson was never one to be concerned about substance or tradition. In this sense, he was the quintessential eighties manager. As journalist Larry Black expressed it in the *Globe and Mail*'s *Report on Business* magazine, "All the Yankee know-how that once went into perfecting automobiles, airplanes, refrigerators, chewing gum and nylon stockings [was] in the 1980s poured into power plays, deal making and creative accounting. At this new game of business, Ross Johnson is a grand master." Indeed, Johnson took little interest in the actual grocery products he was peddling, focussing instead on which firms the company could take over or how the company could drive up the value of its stock to please shareholders.

Johnson's indifference to substance was evident throughout his career: when he took over New York-based Standard Brands in the mid seventies, he quickly abandoned the company's basic approaches for product development. Gone was the time-honoured company practice of consumer taste-testing, for instance. In its place, Johnson assembled a team of number crunchers and technological wizards to assess a new product's potential. When the new team developed a "gravy stick" that was guaranteed not to turn lumpy when melted, it looked on paper like a winner. Johnson decided to launch the new product with costly fanfare. But, although Smooth 'N' Easy, as it was called, had been carefully studied for its marketability and technological perfection, the experts had failed to detect one problem: it tasted awful.

The ambitious, extravagant Johnson found plenty in common with Brian Mulroney. The two had met and become friends back when Johnson was working in marketing for Canadian General Electric in Montreal. Even back then, in his light-bulb-selling days, Johnson had had a penchant for high-flying, expense-account living and he moved in the same circles as the up-and-coming Mulroney. Both men had been befriended by prominent Montreal businessman Paul Desmarais and both hung around the ritzy Mount Royal Club, where women were encouraged to enter by the side door.

Mulroney and Johnson had become fast friends by the time they were both at the pinnacle of their careers, with Johnson running RJR Nabisco and Mulroney running Canada. When a White House dinner was held for Mulroney during his visit to Washington in September '84, Ross Johnson was among the honoured guests. Mulroney and Johnson, who both had married women more than a dozen years their junior, socialized privately as well, with the Mulroneys spending time at the Johnsons' lavish Florida retreat near Palm Beach. And, with Johnson at the helm of RJR Nabisco, the company's Canadian subsidiary made a generous contribution to the Conservative Party's election coffers in 1988 — a donation of $102,000. (The following year, after Johnson had left the company, the Canadian subsidiary gave nothing.)

The friendship between Mulroney and Johnson was not difficult to fathom. Both men rose from modest circumstances in the Canadian provinces, and aspired to the glamour and bright lights of the big world far beyond their home towns. Johnson left the country to achieve his success while Mulroney achieved his in Canada, yet they were both, in a sense, expatriates — fortune-seekers drawn to the high-stakes, wheeling-and-dealing world of power and big business that finds its centre south of the border.

Mulroney was, after all, a branch plant manager for a large U.S. company before making it to the top of Canadian politics. And chances are, had he failed in his second bid for the Tory leadership, he might well have ended up joining his friend Ross Johnson in the world of U.S. business, maybe even tried his hand at a leveraged buy-out. Certainly Mulroney maintained his connections with the U.S. business world long after leaving the board of Cleveland-based Hanna Mining. Former Mulroney aide Bill Fox says that Mulroney kept up contacts with a wide range of senior business figures in the U.S. as well as in Canada. While Mulroney was not above playing the little Canadian boy from Baie Comeau when he thought it would strike a sympathetic political chord with the electorate, his nostalgia for his roots seemed to be limited to these public manifestations. "He found his fortune in Montreal," says a long-time Mulroney friend. "There is no boy from Baie Comeau left in him."

Above all, Mulroney and Johnson were gamblers, with Mulroney playing the odds on free trade — and later on the Meech Lake constitutional accord — just as Johnson went for broke on the LBO. Free trade was just the sort of risky venture that appealed to Mulroney. It involved breaking with tradition, taking what amounted to nothing more than a "leap of faith" into the unknown. Of course it helped that the real risks would be borne by others — Canadians who could end up losing their jobs if businesses began streamlining their operations by closing their Canadian plants. Mulroney conceded there would be some "dislocation" during the "transition period."

Johnson conceded the same about his LBO, even using the same language. Asked by *TIME* magazine if an LBO wouldn't be hard on his employees, Johnson replied, "While you are going through a *transition period* it is. If you take 120,000 RJR Nabisco people, yes, there will be some *dislocation*" (italics added). Like Mulroney with his free trade gamble, Johnson was unlikely to face any personal hardship should his roll of the dice turn up snake eyes. Although he found himself out of a job when his LBO bid failed, he did not leave RJR Nabisco empty-handed. He had carefully arranged a golden parachute for himself, worth some $30 million. He now lives behind electronically operated gates on a verdant estate just outside Atlanta, with rolling gardens and a Georgian-style home.

It is not surprising, given Johnson's taste for risky deals, that he felt at home promoting free trade for his friend Mulroney. In January '86, when there was still some wavering over free trade in the Canadian business community, Johnson flew up to

Toronto to make a speech wholeheartedly endorsing free trade to a Canadian business audience at a meeting of the Board of Trade. As a Canadian heading up a major U.S. corporation, Johnson represented the kind of easy cross-border links that made closer business ties between the two countries look like a boon to Canadians. In his speech, Johnson stressed the numerous potential benefits for Canada, but could apparently only come up with a few minor benefits free trade could offer the U.S. Oddly, he utterly failed to mention the key benefit the U.S. hoped to achieve — getting an international agreement on the three areas of services, intellectual property and investment — even though, as a member of the American Express Board of Directors, Johnson was well versed in these objectives.

Johnson also played a pivotal role in providing Mulroney entry to the top echelons of U.S. business. As chairman of the most prestigious U.S. dinner club, the Economic Club of New York, Johnson arranged for Mulroney to make a major speech there in December '84 at a black tie dinner attended by 1,700 corporate titans. Declaring Canada "open for business," Mulroney used the speech to signal clearly to American business leaders that he planned to turn Canada into a haven for foreign investors. For the corporate executives gathered that night, Mulroney's words were electric. From then on, they felt he was someone they could count on.

The New York speech also brought Mulroney right onto the home turf of a third casino capitalist — a man who was to play a major role in the crucial career gambles of both Mulroney and Johnson: American Express chairman Jim Robinson. Like Mulroney and Johnson, Robinson was a deal maker who lived in the fast lane, and both of their deals were his kind of venture. On the free trade front, Robinson, more than any other U.S. businessman, was pivotal in pushing for a deal from his strategic posts as co-chairman of the Business Roundtable and head of the U.S. President's top private sector trade advisory panel. And the lobbying effort that Robinson set up supporting free trade with Canada was, according to a number of Washington insiders, unmatched in terms of sheer thoroughness, in a city where sophisticated lobbying efforts were as common as homeless people.

Jim Robinson was also a central character in Johnson's LBO attempt. He was not only a close friend and confidant of Johnson's, he was also head of the company that owned Shearson Lehman, the Wall Street brokerage house that Johnson teamed up with to raise the capital for the LBO bid. Furthermore, Linda Robinson was retained by Johnson to handle his public relations for the deal. She was thus saddled with the Olympian task of trying to dispel the image of Johnson as greedy — a task that would prove insurmountable even for the most powerful woman on Wall Street.

For Ross Johnson, as well as for his good friends Brian Mulroney and Jim Robinson, free trade was really just another project, another deal — like taking over a company, marketing a new product, laying off a work force or launching a leveraged buy-out. It was something to be pulled off through power brokering, dishing out favours, calling in favours and doing whatever wheeling and dealing was necessary to put the transaction in place. The aim was to increase your own power and wealth, or the power and wealth of those whose interests you represented. Whether or not free trade would be good for the majority of Canadians was evidently one of those questions — like whether the gravy tasted good — that Johnson, Mulroney and Robinson didn't consider very important.

IF FREE TRADE had quickly worked its way to the top of the Mulroney government's agenda, that was largely because it was the sexiest of the initiatives Mulroney found on his desk when he took office. Although free trade had not been part of his '84 campaign — indeed, when asked, he had rejected it as the path for Canada — it seemed, in some ways, to be the least objectionable of the many grim initiatives that business had put on the new Prime Minister's platter. Unlike most of the items on the business agenda — such as deficit reduction and social spending cuts — free trade was something that could be presented to the public as positive, something potentially flashy and splashy and dramatic enough to capture the imagination.

But it hadn't begun that way. While the U.S. had from the early eighties been focussing on putting in place a wide-ranging new world trade agenda, Canada's interest in a trade agreement had more modest origins. Certainly, the first Canadian moves towards free trade had not grown out of a desire for dramatic change, but rather out of the traditional fears of losing access to the U.S. market. In the Trudeau years, much of this initiative had come from Ed Lumley, the rough-hewn Minister of International Trade.

Unlike most of the seasoned political veterans of the Trudeau cabinet, Ed Lumley saw himself first and foremost as a businessman — a small-time, small-town businessman who understood the world in simple terms and thought almost anything could be achieved through straight talk. Lumley had worked as a truck washer in Windsor and owned a Coke bottling plant in Cornwall, Ontario, and years later would still talk about himself in the third person as: "Ed Lumley, Coke bottler" or "Ed Lumley, truck washer." He had become one of the few real friends of business in the Trudeau cabinet, and was constantly jetting off to far-away places on government trade missions with a gaggle of businessmen in tow. "The business community was crying for help," he recalls. "My motto became, 'Have bag, will travel.' I said to business, 'If you've got a problem, let's go.' "

Lumley had little patience with his own government's nationalistic policies, particularly the Foreign Investment Review Agency, which he spent considerable time fighting from inside the cabinet. He had been mayor of Cornwall, which hugs the U.S. border, and he had a simple, folksy solution to U.S.-Canadian problems: just get everybody together and talk. After all, Canadians and Americans were so alike that there was no need for a lot of silly squabbles. He was fond of pointing out to U.S. audiences that his mother lived in Florida, his father in Detroit and his mother-in-law in Idaho.

All this was bound to make Lumley an easy-going buddy for William Brock, Reagan's appointee to the key job of U.S. Trade Representative. Brock had a southern charm that made it hard not to like him. A Tennessee millionaire, he had a graciousness and sophistication that allowed him to fit in easily with the finely-bred business and political figures he dealt with around the world. But Brock also understood the Tennessee outback, and could adjust himself to whatever level on the social scale the situation demanded. "Brock can play the Tennessee boy or the millionaire. He can go up or down; he has the social skills to deal with labourers or kings," said one Ottawa insider who has seen him in action. Such social dexterity made it easy for Brock to relate to Ed Lumley, Coke bottler and truck washer.

When the jovial Lumley presented himself at Brock's door shortly after Brock had been installed as U.S. Trade Representative in 1981, Lumley's let's-be-friends, we're-all-the-same attitudes came rambling out in a genial flow. Lumley explained to Brock that he had come for an unofficial goodwill visit before bureaucrats got involved and complicated their relationship. Lumley was direct and unabashedly upbeat; he recalls saying to Brock, "How can we get together and take on the world?"

Brock was delighted by this tall, easy-going, easy-talking Canadian who was spouting thoughts that would go down easy in the State Department. In Brock's short time as U.S. Trade Representative, he had already come to see that the Trudeau government's nationalist policies, which U.S. business found highly irritating, promised to be a problem for him. Now here was a member of that odious Trudeau cabinet talking a language the Americans understood; here was a potential ally for them on the inside.

But Lumley went even further during that first meeting: he floated, in vague terms, the idea of free trade between Canada and the U.S. This was a pet idea of Lumley's; the Trudeau cabinet had by no means endorsed it. But it was music to Brock's ears. If there was one thing that almost everyone in U.S. business and political circles had been raised on from birth, it was free trade. And Brock, as the U.S. Trade Representative, was even keener about it than most. Lumley and Brock became fast friends. They even socialized together. When Brock came up with prime tickets for the Super Bowl (at the fifty-yard line, just behind then Vice-President George Bush), Lumley provided the transportation, jetting them both to Detroit in a Canadian government plane.

Although Brock could charm just about anyone from labourers to kings, one person his soft touch utterly failed to reach was Herb Gray, Lumley's cabinet colleague who occupied the more senior post of Minister of Industry, Trade and Commerce. More than anyone, Gray was the embodiment of the kind of nationalism so abhorred by the Americans. The steady, plodding Gray — whom even his enemies credit with sincerity — had long been a strong and committed champion of greater Canadian ownership of the economy and a national industrial strategy. In 1972, he had overseen a comprehensive government report, known as the Gray Report, which called for a screening agency to monitor the performance of foreign investment in Canada, with an eye to forcing foreign firms to provide greater economic benefits to the country. It was the Gray Report that prompted the Liberals to set up FIRA in 1973. FIRA fell considerably short of the sweeping review agency envisioned by Gray but still managed to provoke widespread disgruntlement among U.S. business leaders.

Gray notes that the U.S. seemed far less willing to tolerate any form of economic nationalism in Canada than in other countries, including France, Britain and Japan. "They accepted things from France without a peep, as far as I can see, and yet our rather mild, limited up-front, visible review process was an ongoing source of irritation," says Gray. "Overall, American business as a whole was not willing to look upon Canada quite the same way as it looked upon France or other sovereign countries."

Apart from Gray's politics, there was the problem of his personality, as far as Brock was concerned. While Lumley was an easy-going, knee-slapping, roll-with-the-punches kind of guy, Gray was more withdrawn and careful, uncompromising when he thought principles of Canadian sovereignty were involved. "Herb's style is not consistent with the good-old-boy system," explained one former Canadian government official. "He's a fervent believer. It must not have been very enjoyable for Brock. The last thing he needed was to go and face an earnest true believer." One U.S. trade official said that Brock found dealing with Gray "like talking to a brick wall."

With Gray heading the Department of Industry, which oversaw FIRA, Brock and his colleagues in the Reagan administration, together with the U.S. business community, grew more and more impatient with Canada. "Consideration was given to retaliatory measures," recalls Bill Merkin, who at that point was serving in the Canada Office of the U.S. Trade Representative, under Brock. Among the retaliatory measures seriously considered by the Reagan administration, according to Merkin, were restrictions on trade or access to U.S. capital markets. Although the measures never made it beyond the drawing board, the U.S. made its protests to Ottawa vocal and frequent. Merkin says that the dissatisfaction with Trudeau's regime reached to "very high levels in the U.S. government" and included "senior people in the State Department and Treasury Department . . . which are normally sympathetic to Canada." Relations between Canada and the U.S. began to ease a little only in the fall of '82, after Gray was removed from the sensitive Industry portfolio and replaced by the more congenial Lumley.

In a sense, Gray met the same fate as Allan MacEachen, who was shifted out of the Finance Department after business complained bitterly about his soak-the-rich budget. Both men had been senior government figures with important posts in the reformist Trudeau regime that came to power in 1980. Both were pushed aside gently, and allowed to keep their dignity intact: they were shifted to prestigious cabinet posts — MacEachen to External Affairs and Gray to Treasury Board. But, in both cases, their new portfolios put them in less sensitive positions, where they could no longer pursue the policies that had so infuriated business.

But the image of Canada as aggressively nationalistic stuck south of the border. Ironically, the Reagan administration was highly nationalistic itself, but had little patience with nationalism in other countries, particularly countries like Canada that it had always regarded as more or less part of the U.S. A hostile anti-Canada mood took hold in U.S. business and political circles. At the same time, protectionist sentiment was on the rise in the U.S. Congress, largely because U.S. industry was finding itself unable to compete effectively in its own markets with cheaper Japanese products. As Congress contemplated action to protect its own industry, Canada became lumped in with Japan as a country in need of a little trade discipline from the U.S.

In Canadian business circles there were growing fears that Canada was going to be locked out of its biggest market. Much of this fear turned to anger towards the Liberal government for so antagonizing the U.S. with FIRA and the NEP. Alfred Powis, chairman of mining giant Noranda and one of the founders of the BCNI, blames the Liberal government for the "soured relations" with the U.S. "Here was the government of Canada beavering away to make itself as unpopular as possible with the U.S., at a time when the U.S. was becoming increasingly protectionist. If suddenly, in that context, the Americans had retreated to Fortress America, we'd have been ruined up here," says Powis. "If the U.S. was going to put up walls, we'd better get in behind them."

The BCNI responded by appointing a small internal task force in 1982 to look at how to get behind those walls. The task force, which included Alcan Aluminium CEO David Culver and Canadian General Electric CEO Alton Cartwright, was chaired by Powis. Although the focus of the task force was broad, it quickly centred on the issue of trade problems with the U.S., recalls Powis.

Inside the Ottawa bureaucracy similar ideas were taking root, as the Canadian government toyed with the idea of trying to establish new trade agreements with Washington in a few key sectors, such as informatics — an idea being pushed by Rowland Frazee from the Royal Bank — as well as steel and petrochemicals. The idea sprang from a trade policy review conducted in External Affairs in 1982 under Deputy Minister of Trade Robert Johnstone, and largely prepared by senior department official Derek Burney.

Burney would later go on to play a key role in developing free trade initiatives for Mulroney's Conservative government, but under the Liberals he confined himself to advocating sectoral trade agreements. Even this was startling enough in the early eighties within the Ottawa bureaucracy, where the orthodoxy had long been that trade problems should be resolved through multi-country GATT negotiations, not through closer relations with the United States. Burney's paper, which was released in August 1983 by International Trade Minister Gerald Regan, endorsed the idea of sectoral trade talks with the U.S. while specifically rejecting more comprehensive free trade. The idea was to duplicate the success of the Canada-U.S. auto pact, under which Canada had built up an auto industry that employed tens of thousands of Canadians and had become the backbone of Ontario's industrial heartland.

But if that idea had a strong appeal in Canada, it had virtually none south of the border. The auto pact was perceived in the U.S. as unduly favourable to Canada. Even though ownership of the industry remained firmly in the hands of the three big U.S. auto companies, the pact specified that a certain amount of production take place in Canada: essentially, for every car sold in Canada, one had to be built here. This was a variation on the "performance requirements" so disliked by the Business Roundtable. By the early eighties, trade agreements like the auto pact were no longer of interest to Washington.

The BCNI task force chaired by Powis found this out abruptly when it requested a private meeting with Brock in January '83. Brock met with the BCNI committee over breakfast at 7:30 a.m. on a cold winter morning in Toronto. Powis says that his committee raised the idea of sectoral trade agreements with Brock, but Brock was immediately cool to it. "He said, 'You can try, but we're not interested,'" recalls Powis.

But Brock had another idea: comprehensive free trade between the two countries — a relationship with their overpowering neighbour that Canadians had traditionally been wary of. Under a comprehensive free trade agreement, there would be no production guarantees along the lines of the auto pact. Companies would have access to markets on both sides of the border — and would be free to locate their production facilities wherever they wanted.

Furthermore, a comprehensive free trade agreement could be broad enough to address the three new trade issues that had become so crucial to the U.S. — issues that cut across specific sectors and would, therefore, be virtually impossible to address in a series of sectoral agreements. Brock had spent much of 1981 and 1982 touring the world, arguing everywhere he went for a new round of multilateral talks to address these new issues — services, investment and intellectual property. But Brock had encountered tremendous resistance from Third World countries. Tim Bennett, a U.S. trade attaché who had worked under Brock, says that this Third World resistance had the effect of making Brock and the U.S. trade establishment interested in trying a bilateral approach — that is, a two-country deal, rather than a multi-country agreement through the GATT. "There was the belief that, gee, we've got a lot of leverage bilaterally," Bennett recalled in a recent interview in Washington, where he is now a trade consultant. "There was a feeling of powerlessness multilaterally."

If Brock had been toying with the idea of finding a partner for bilateral negotiations, he seemed to have stumbled into the right place at this early morning breakfast. Certainly these Canadian business leaders seemed more agreeable than the people he had been meeting on his world-wide travels. Indeed, the Canadians seemed downright keen. This meeting was their idea. And even if they had started out talking about sectoral trade — something that the U.S. had no real interest in — they appeared amenable to comprehensive free trade too. This could be just the kind of situation — offering just the kind of leverage — that Brock had been waiting for.

Powis says that he asked Brock at that meeting why the U.S. was keen for free trade. Brock responded by telling him about a lush type of grass that grows in the American south, in his home state of Tennessee. "He said, 'You know, you plant a little clump of it here, a little clump of it there, and pretty soon it covers the whole damn lawn. You get an agreement here and an agreement there, and pretty soon you're going to free up the whole world.'" Since Brock's job as U.S. Trade Representative was to do just that — free up the whole world for U.S. trade and investment — his enthusiasm for free trade with Canada was perhaps not surprising.

But Brock had already thought through the political delicacy of the situation, and told the Canadian business leaders on the BCNI task force that the initiative could not be seen to be coming from the U.S. "What Brock was saying to us was that . . . politically the impetus had to come from Canada," says Powis. "He was very strongly in favour of it, but if the United States started talking about free trade, it would be torpedoed just like that. But if Canada screwed itself up to ask for it, he would certainly go along with it." Brock was essentially counselling the BCNI members how to sell free trade to Canadians: make it look like it was a Canadian idea, even though, in reality,

Brock had suggested it. For the BCNI committee, the message was unmistakable. "It became obvious at that meeting," says Powis, "that if we asked for it [free trade], they would start negotiating."

After that, the members of the BCNI task force abandoned any thoughts of pushing for sectoral trade agreements and switched its focus to the possibility of a comprehensive free trade deal. "We threw out sectoral pretty fast. The Americans weren't interested," says Powis. "We'd have been beating our heads against the wall with that. It just wasn't a starter."

For the BCNI task force, there was formidable work ahead, beginning with the task of bringing the rest of the BCNI onside. Tom d'Aquino recalls that, at the early stages, there was considerable hesitation over free trade among the CEOs on the council, including Rowland Frazee, the Royal Bank chairman who had been pushing for sectoral trade in informatics. But the task force set out on a marathon trek to win support for the idea of a comprehensive free trade deal, within their own organization, within business and government circles and, eventually, within the Canadian public.

While little progress was made during the Trudeau administration, the pace picked up dramatically with the arrival of Mulroney's Conservatives in September 1984. Powis recalls his task force getting a positive response to its free trade idea from the new Conservative Trade Minister, James Kelleher, shortly after he took office. "That is my first recollection of a serious discussion on the subject with the government," says Powis.

In March 1985, Brian Mulroney and Ronald Reagan emerged from their first summit, known as the Shamrock Summit, in Quebec City, and announced a plan to explore the possibility of a comprehensive free trade agreement between the two countries. They emphasized that the initiative had come from Canada.

ONE OF THE first places to feel the impact of the free trade plan announced at the Shamrock Summit was a small corner of the Department of Consumer and Corporate Affairs in Ottawa. For years, the department had been under considerable pressure from multinational pharmaceutical companies. These large brand-name drug companies — which were all foreign-owned — were determined to get Canada to abandon its policy of compulsory licensing, or allowing the sale of cheap, generic copies of brand-name drugs.

A small Canadian industry had grown up manufacturing and marketing the generic drugs and Canadian consumers had become accustomed to the dramatically lower prices of the no-name copies. Despite this competition, the brand-name companies were still reaping large profits in the range of 18 percent a year, exceeding profit levels for all manufacturing industries. Even so, they felt cheated, insisting that the Canadian generic companies were taking profits that were rightfully theirs. The grievance was an old one and the brand-name companies had kept up an almost constant stream of pressure — a pressure that had intensified after 1981 when the Reagan administration took up their cause.

Although the lobbying on the issue had been intense in the early eighties, the Liberal government had been in no hurry to do anything. The generic policy seemed to work in Canada, keeping prices down by forcing the brand-name companies to compete with the low-cost generics. The Canadian government's policy of allowing generics actually dated back to 1923, and had been extended in 1969 after three government-initiated investigations had concluded that drug prices and brand-name profits were still too high in Canada. But by the eighties, the brand-name drug industry was fighting back. It retained former Liberal cabinet minister Martin O'Connell, who had become an Ottawa consultant, to lobby for changes and it increasingly managed to enlist the support of Liberal MPs from Quebec, where about half of the Canadian subsidiaries of the brand-name companies were located.

The Liberal government responded cautiously, listening to the grievances of the brand-name companies and making tentative steps in the direction of change. It set up an interdepartmental task force to study the issue, and in an attempt to appease the brand-name firms appointed O'Connell as an advisor. But none of this produced any government action.

Besieged by executives from the Canadian subsidiaries of the multinational firms, Consumer and Corporate Affairs Minister Judy Erola appointed a royal commission in April 1984 to examine the issues more carefully.

Headed by University of Toronto economist Harry Eastman, the Commission took a year to conclude, like the three previous investigations into the issue, that the compulsory licensing policy had basically worked well and served Canadian interests. In his detailed 474-page report, handed in after the Conservatives had taken power and just weeks before the Shamrock Summit of March 1985, Eastman recommended a few changes favourable to the multinational drug industry, such as higher royalty rates to be paid by the generic firms to the brand-name companies holding the drug patents.

But the brand-name companies were deeply dissatisfied with this solution. They were not interested in receiving piddling royalties that were just a small percentage of a very low-priced product. Rather, they wanted the right to keep generics out of the market completely, allowing them to enjoy a monopoly that let them set the price as high as they wanted. This way, the consumer would have no choice but to pay the brand-name company's price or do without the drug. In the U.S., for instance, where the brand-name companies enjoyed a seventeen-year market monopoly on a new drug, the price of small amount of Valium was $345.93. The same amount of its generic equivalent, Diazepam, sold in Canada for a mere $2.31! It was examples like this that had led Eastman to hesitate about abandoning Canada's generic drug laws.

But if Eastman's findings were not at all what the industry had in mind, it had no intention of abandoning the struggle — certainly not now that Canada had indicated an interest in negotiating a free trade agreement with the U.S. In the aftermath of the Shamrock Summit, the pressure on the Department of Consumer and Corporate Affairs suddenly escalated. "It got much more intense," recalls Tom Brogan, who was the department's chief advisor on the issue.

Part of the problem was that the issue had become immensely important in the U.S. Indeed, by the early eighties it had become one of the top items on the U.S. trade agenda. This was a remarkable development in itself, since the issue had been a relatively minor one only a few years earlier. The transformation was, to a considerable extent, due to the diligent efforts of Edward Pratt, chairman of Pfizer, one of the largest U.S.-based drug companies. Pratt, a no-nonsense ex-marine who played a leading role in the Business Roundtable, was appointed by Reagan in 1981 to chair the government's top private sector trade advisory panel — the position later occupied by Jim Robinson. The panel carried considerable clout with trade negotiators, Congress and the President. Pratt used this entrée to the highest levels of power to get the issue of patent protection for brand-name drugs — under the guise of the protection of intellectual property — onto the U.S. trade agenda.

His results were phenomenal. Joe Gavin, a Washington-based official of the U.S. Council for International Business, says that the issue in trade circles went from relative obscurity to being virtually at the top of the trade agenda in only a few years. Pratt pulled together a small but powerful coalition of U.S. businesses interested in the subject — drug companies as well as those with similar copyright concerns, such as computer, electronics and film companies. The coalition identified the growing number of countries that were doing nothing to protect the rights of patented and copyrighted products, and showed how this resulted in the U.S. losing its edge in some of the few areas where it still enjoyed supremacy in world markets. Pratt and his coalition managed to line up support from key businesses in Japan and parts of Europe, putting together a formidable international business coalition in only a couple of years — a lightning pace for an issue that only a few years earlier had been known in trade circles as "intellectual *what*?"

One of Pratt's key objectives was to get the intellectual property issue onto the agenda for the upcoming round of GATT talks that were being planned for Uruguay in 1986. A delegation from Pfizer went down to Puenta del Este, the Urugayan capital where the agenda for the GATT talks was being negotiated, to back up efforts by U.S. trade negotiators to keep the issue in the forefront.

But the U.S. negotiators encountered strong resistance, particularly from the Third World. For many countries, producing cheap generic copies of everything from drugs to computer programs was a legitimate way for them to try to make up ground with advantaged countries. "There was a very strong current of belief among a lot of countries that, 'You rich boys may have developed this, but Christ, the only way we can catch up is by leapfrogging. Your stuff is fair game for stealing; pirating is a legitimate way of catching up,'" says Tim Bennett, the former U.S. trade attaché.

In the area of drug patents — the one that most concerned Pratt — the problem had become particularly acute by the mid eighties. And it was by no means confined to Third World countries. France, Italy, Belgium and even, increasingly, Britain and West Germany were adopting policies that the brand-name drug industry considered highly punitive. These European countries not only permitted the sale of generic drugs, but also placed limits on the prices of the brand-name products, and even in some cases restricted the profits that could be earned by the brand-name companies. Although the Canadian laws were actually less punitive to the brand-name firms than the laws of many European countries, Canada was in a special situation, since it had come forward and asked for a free trade agreement with the U.S. For Pratt, this represented the perfect opportunity to force the issue onto the agenda of an international trade negotiation. A red flag had been waved in front of a frothing bull.

With Pratt in the key role of the President's top private sector trade advisor, it was inevitable that his pet issue of "intellectual property" was going to be front and centre in any free trade negotiation with Canada. Indeed, in June 1984 Mulroney, before he was even Prime Minister, had been given a taste of how strongly the U.S. felt about the issue. He was then leader of the Conservative opposition and had been invited to meet President Reagan in the White House as part of an effort by Washington to bolster the Canadian Conservatives in the hopes of damaging the electoral chances of Trudeau's Liberals. Bill Fox, a Mulroney aide who did much of the preparatory work for that June '84 trip, recalls that intellectual property was one of the items raised by Reagan in his meeting with the would-be Canadian Prime Minister.

The subject was also raised as a key U.S. trade concern by Brock just days before the Shamrock Summit, when he addressed a group from the BCNI at a closed-door session in Washington. The meeting, which had been arranged for the BCNI by *TIME* magazine, included briefings from senior members of the administration and was typical of the kind of closer U.S.-Canada business ties that were evolving under the Mulroney government. Brock's flagging of intellectual property, only days before the joint Reagan-Mulroney announcement of the free trade talks, highlights the importance the U.S. attached to the issue as it prepared to embark on the free trade venture.

Within the U.S. administration, the issue was already well established. Certainly U.S. negotiators, who met regularly with the business advisory panel chaired by Pratt, knew the importance of satisfying the panel's members. Bill Merkin, who became the U.S. deputy chief negotiator in the talks with Canada, notes that, "It's important to keep that committee happy" because its members have so much influence that they can potentially scuttle the passage of any deal that goes before Congress for approval. "It's unavoidable," says Merkin. "If American Express cares about a particular aspect of the negotiations — or Ed Pratt or somebody else on that committee. . . . We're not naive. We know that, if we can solve a lot of their problems, they will be more active on our behalf."

Merkin says that the importance of pleasing powerful business interests was one of the first things he learned in his fifteen years as a U.S. trade negotiator. "You've got to have a feel for what politics are at play. When you bring an agreement to Congress, Congress listens to what the business community has to say. . . . You would prefer to have that top blue-ribbon committee with you rather than against you."

And Pratt was not shy about pushing the intellectual property issue to the forefront of the Canada-U.S. talks. Pratt's intense interest in the issue was not lost on the U.S. negotiating team. "Certainly we felt that the issue had to be resolved to the industry's satisfaction before [a free trade] agreement went up to Congress for approval," says Merkin. "You've got to remember that our top private sector advisory group at the time was chaired by Pratt. He was in a position to be helpful —

and was helpful — in getting support for the agreement in Congress. If he had been unhappy, we couldn't have counted on his help."

All this presented enormous problems for Mulroney. Like the Liberals who had tackled the issue before him, he could see that it had little upside in Canada. Four major Canadian investigations, including the exhaustive Eastman Commission, had more or less declared the matter an open-and-shut case. Canada was on the right track, they had said. Although the multinationals could rightly argue that they spent tens of millions of dollars researching a new drug, the studies showed that the companies were already recouping their costs handsomely, and that Canada was contributing generously to their profits even with generic copies on the market. In any case, it generally took eight to ten years before a generic made it to market, during which time the brand-name company enjoyed a total monopoly on the sale of its patented drug. (It was true, though, that generics were beginning to appear more quickly.) Altogether, the multinational drug industry enjoyed higher profits in Canada than in European countries. Furthermore, as Eastman discovered, the industry's profits in Canada had risen "sharply higher for the last four years."

Apart from the embarrassing economics, the issue was fraught with political pitfalls. There was the difficult fact that all the multinationals were foreign-owned, mostly American, firms. Pitted against them was the generic drug industry, which was largely Canadian-owned, as well as Canadian consumers, whose interests the Canadian government was supposed to champion. A study done for the Eastman Commission found that generics allowed Canadians to save $211 million a year in drug costs. And the product in question wasn't some trinket that people could easily do without. In many cases, these were life-saving drugs. To allow companies to set outrageously high prices — and there were many examples where this had happened in Canada before a generic equivalent was on the market — seemed like condoning highway robbery of the most vulnerable people.

Since the U.S. was demanding changes that would be extremely unpopular with most Canadians, the Mulroney government feared the issue would make the public suspicious of any free trade agreement from the start — if giving in to the Americans on the drug issue was perceived as part of the price of free trade. Free trade was a departure from traditional Canadian politics, so it had to be presented as a positive, beneficial change, not one that threatened to strip Canadians of the traditional protection they had enjoyed in, for instance, drug prices. Free trade would have to be sold as something that would bring prices down, not drive them up. Above all, Canadian negotiators could not be seen to be bartering away a proven system that Canadian governments had stood firm on for decades simply to appease the enormously rich U.S. pharmaceutical industry.

The Mulroney government's solution was, in fact, to barter away much of the Canadian system to appease the U.S. pharmaceutical companies, but at the same time to deny vehemently that it was doing so. Whatever heat the government would have to take over the issue — and it would be considerable — would be kept from tarnishing the image of the free trade talks.

And so it was decided at the outset that the issue would be dealt with immediately, but outside the free trade negotiation process. As Merkin explains, "Ottawa didn't want it [intellectual property] to be in the free trade negotiations. They didn't want to *appear* to be negotiating that away as part of the free trade agreement. Whatever changes they were going to make, they wanted them to be *viewed* as, quote, 'in Canada's interest.' " To this end, the Mulroney government repeatedly denied that there was any connection whatsoever between the free trade negotiations and its decision to overhaul the country's generic drug laws. The U.S. negotiators played along with this charade because they understood, as Merkin explains, Ottawa's need to keep up a false appearance on the subject.

Still, if the U.S. was happy to help Mulroney keep Canadians in the dark, it did not lose sight of the fact that, in reality, the generic drug issue was very much a part of the free trade negotiations, even if it was being handled separately. "It was a high priority issue for us," says Merkin. "We were not above flagging the importance of resolving the issue [to the Canadian negotiators] for the success of the overall negotiations."

With the Mulroney government determined to keep the two issues separate, at least as far as the Canadian public was concerned, there was suddenly an enormous push to get the generic drug question settled as quickly as possible. After years of the Liberals dragging their feet, the Conservatives wanted the issue dealt with rapidly, to get it settled before the free trade talks were fully underway.

Michel Coté, the new Minister of Consumer and Corporate Affairs who was considered a rising star in the Conservative caucus, waded right into the swamp by trying to get the generics and the multinationals to negotiate some kind of compromise. But the talks had little success; neither side was very interested in compromise. The multinationals, who were represented by an association made up of their Canadian subsidiaries, wanted a guaranteed ten-year monopoly period for each new drug before the generics were allowed to compete with it. The generics, who sensed the public was on their side, felt little inclination to give up ground at all to what they could easily portray as a bunch of foreign bullies.

With the failure of the industry to resolve the issue, the Department of Consumer and Corporate Affairs was pressed to start drafting legislation. The pressure was coming directly from the minister's office, and when proposals were sent up from the department staff recommending monopoly periods shorter than ten years, they were sent back with the comment that the monopoly period wasn't long enough. For those working on the new legislation, it was clear that the pressure was connected to the free trade talks. "The more free trade grew, the more [the draft legislation] was forced," said one department official who worked on it.

Still, the issue was dragging on at a snail's pace as far as the government was concerned. Part of the problem, it seemed, was Coté. Although he was from Quebec, where the multinationals enjoyed some popular support as well as the official support of the Quebec government, he had never really warmed to the issue. His lack of enthusiasm was only reinforced in early June 1985 when he watched his colleague, Health Minister Jake Epp, take a thorough beating from the opposition, the press and the public over the government's decision to remove full indexation protection from old age pensions — a decision that would take millions of dollars in pension benefits from struggling senior citizens all over the country. It was the government's first major crisis, and it sent shock waves through the Tory cabinet. Coté was in the West meeting provincial health ministers about the generic drug issue when the pension crisis struck, but he saw enough of Epp's discomfort on TV to get a chilling taste of what public disdain might be in store for a minister who forced Canadians to pay hundreds of dollars more per year in drug prices.

Indeed, the issue was already earning the minister considerable bad publicity. Coté did eventually produce new draft legislation, but, due to poor planning, his bill never made it onto the order paper and died when the parliamentary session ended in the summer of 1986. The free trade negotiations had formally begun a couple of months earlier, so there was growing pressure to get the drug issue resolved before it became any more difficult to keep up the charade that the two matters were not connected. Furthermore, the public was growing increasingly hostile to the proposed changes, as the generic firms trotted out more and more horrific examples of overpriced brand-name drugs.

Determined to see the changes through quickly, Mulroney replaced Coté with Harvie Andre, an MP from Calgary who had championed the multinational cause inside the cabinet for months. Andre, an engineer by profession, was as much a true believer in intellectual property as Herb Gray was in economic nationalism. Andre had attended virtually every cabinet committee meeting that dealt with the subject, even before he was minister. He had little patience for the generic firms, which he saw as technological pirates, and argued that the only way to entice the brand-name companies to increase their Canadian research budgets was to give them the monopoly protection they were demanding. His appointment to the Consumer post was Mulroney's way of ensuring the legislation was given the high priority the Americans were demanding.

The legislation tabled by Andre in the fall of '86 was a significant departure from the existing law. The brand-name companies were given the ten-year monopoly they requested in cases where the chemical ingredients in the generic were imported into Canada. If the ingredients were actually manufactured in Canada, generic competitors were to be allowed on the market after seven years of brand-name monopoly. Either way, it was a far cry from Eastman's recommendation that the monopoly period be no longer than four years. The brand-name companies had basically got their way. Inside the Department of Consumer and Corporate Affairs, where the changes had been unpopular, a joke went around reflecting the consensus that the government had given far too much to the multinationals: "We didn't give them one nickel more than they asked for."

Still, the multinationals were not entirely satisfied. The new law had some strings attached. An agency would be set up to monitor prices and, although critics charged it lacked the power to control the kind of price gouging that could take place in monopoly situations, it was nonetheless a step towards closer surveillance of the industry — something the industry resented. Worse still, as the public debate over the changes had heated up, the industry had been obliged to make promises about increasing its research and development spending in Canada. The new agency was going to keep tabs on this as well, and at least report deficiencies to Parliament. Although there was no guarantee Parliament would take any action, the whole notion came dangerously close to the idea of "performance requirements" so disdained by U.S. business.

Despite the lack of gratitude on the part of the multinationals, the Mulroney government had gone through amazing contortions to deliver as much as it had. The issue had been generally portrayed in the press as a clash of interests between U.S. multinationals and the Canadian public — a portrayal that was difficult to avoid. No matter how good a face the Mulroney government tried to put on the situation, it was unavoidably true that the pressure for change had originated south of the border, and the Canadian public remained heavily opposed to the changes.

The situation only looked worse when the consumer cause was championed in the Senate by Lorne Bonnell. Bonnell was a grandfatherly country doctor from Prince Edward Island who could recall patients going without medication in the thirties and forties because they couldn't afford the drugs he prescribed them. Bonnell had gone on to become the province's Health

Minister and was eventually appointed to the Senate by Trudeau. But years in politics had not softened his distrust of the multinational drug industry. As chairman of a special Senate committee that travelled the country hearing citizens' groups complain about the changes, Bonnell cut a strikingly sympathetic figure who made the Mulroney government's bombast on the subject seem all the more hollow.

So, right up to the final passage of the legislation in December 1987, the Mulroney government maintained the fiction that the concessions to the brand-name companies were wholly unconnected to free trade. Eventually the American side — apparently inadvertently — exposed this as the distortion that it was.

In a hastily-prepared summary of the final free trade agreement, the Office of the U.S. Trade Representative released a statement on October 4, 1987 that included a section on "Intellectual Property." The six-page summary of the key features of the trade deal stated that: "The two sides agreed to resolve long standing trade irritants in broadcasting (Canada will protect satellite re-transmissions) *and to make progress towards establishing adequate and effective protection of pharmaceuticals in Canada by liberalizing compulsory licensing provisions.*" [italics added.]

The sentence was a blatant contradiction of the Mulroney government's position that there was no connection between free trade and the drug issue, and it was corrected in a revised version of the summary that was issued four days later by the U.S. Trade Representative's office. The revised summary, which was virtually identical in every other aspect, simply removed the portion of the sentence italicized above. This airbrushed version was then released to the press by the U.S. Embassy in Ottawa, in an attempt to help Ottawa keep up its fiction.

In fact, the U.S. was not long appeased by the concessions Canada had made. As plans for a free trade deal with Mexico heated up in the winter of 1990–91, U.S. trade negotiators once again spotted an opportunity to gain new ground on the issue — both in Mexico and Canada. Although Mexico offered no patent protection for brand-name drugs in the past, it bowed to U.S. pressure in the run-up to free trade negotiations and drafted a law that would guarantee full protection in the future.

With Mexico suddenly co-operative, the U.S. pharmaceutical industry sensed it now had new leverage over Canada and it launched another fierce lobbying campaign with Ottawa. It even publicly suggested that the favourable developments in Mexico might lead it to unilaterally abandon the commitments it made to Canada in 1987 about increasing research spending here. As Harvey Bale, spokesman for the Pharmaceutical Manufacturers Association, told Linda Diebel of the *Toronto Star:* "Can [the commitments we made to Canada] be sustained when you have a Mexico that has gone from zero to 100 miles an hour on a patent law in the matter of the past year." With surprising bluntness, the U.S. industry was signalling to Canada that it had no qualms about using its breakthrough with Mexico as leverage for getting a better deal from Canada — and that it felt in no way bound by previous commitments it had made to Canada.

Indeed, this time, the industry wasn't going to take "no" for an answer. It wanted nothing short of an end to compulsory licensing — the system that had allowed Canadian generic manufacturers to flourish and Canadians to enjoy lower drug prices. Barry Sherman, president of the Canadian generic manufacturer Apotex, said that he got a clear sense that the federal government was considering dismantling compulsory licensing altogether when he received a visit in the spring of 1991 from Dr Elizabeth Dickson, the director of the federal division that oversees health care products in the Department of Industry, Science and Technology. Sherman says that Dickson asked him what steps the government could take to soften the blow for Canadian generics if compulsory licensing were eliminated. "She talked about it as if it were a fait accompli," he said. For her part, Dickson says that she met with Sherman as part of an attempt to prepare the generic industry for the "significant likelihood" that Canada will move further in the direction of strengthening patent protection in the next ten years.

The Mulroney government's handling of the drug issue provides a revealing glimpse of the way it approached free trade. In the interests of securing a deal, it readily abandoned a system that had served Canadians well for decades, with apparently little concern about the negative consequences of such a change.

But what was most revealing perhaps was the government's willingness to resort to secrecy — even deception — in vociferously denying there was a connection between the changes and what was going on in the free trade talks. Why was it necessary to keep up this elaborate charade? Surely Canadians are capable of understanding that any deal involves trade-offs on both sides. Why couldn't Brian Mulroney come forward to the Canadian public and simply tell the truth: that the Americans seemed to be unwilling to do a free trade deal unless they got some satisfaction on the generic drug issue; and that, in the opinion of the government, this was an acceptable concession to make in order to achieve the goal of free trade. Had Mulroney levelled with the Canadian people, they could have judged for themselves whether this was a reasonable trade-off.

Mulroney's secrecy and dishonesty in the matter raises the question of what he was trying to hide from us. Could it be that he didn't level with us because he feared that, if we knew the whole story, we'd decide the trade-off he was proposing was not a reasonable one, that the gravy tasted lousy? Could it be that even he sensed it was an awfully large concession, both in terms of dollars and in terms of sovereignty, that it amounted to an admission that we were willing to overhaul our laws for no other reason than to suit U.S. business? Could it be that he suspected not all Canadians were willing to follow his lifelong pattern of doing whatever was necessary to please the powerful?

IN INTERVIEWS WITH those involved in the free trade negotiations, it is striking how often people on both sides of the border go out of their way to make the point that the initiative for the talks came from Canada. Since this is not a matter that can be easily verified — nobody suggests that a document exists proving the case — it is interesting that so many people assert it with such certainty. It seems to be one of those notions — like the lack of connection between the pharmaceutical legislation and the free trade deal — that is deemed to be very important.

The reason appears to be that those who advocated free trade want us to believe that Canada entered into the process willingly, even eagerly, that the decision to open up our market in a way that leaves our industries highly vulnerable to foreign competition and to relocation south of the border was a decision we made of our own volition, not under pressure from Washington. Yet, in any meaningful sense, is this true?

The root cause of the concern that led Canadians to contemplate free trade was the fear of being shut out of the American market as the U.S. Congress became highly protectionist. But the initial response to this problem both within the Canadian government and within the Canadian business community was to think along traditional Canadian lines: to protect ourselves by negotiating new sectoral trade agreements, similar to the auto pact. That had long served as an example of how Canada could prosper industrially. It wasn't the pure nationalist's ideal — a Canadian-owned industry along the lines of Sweden's Volvo would have been — but it was, nonetheless, a suitable Canadian-style compromise. The auto industry remained foreign-owned, but we benefitted greatly from it. Both sides seemed to prosper. We traded access to our market for an ample return to Canada in terms of jobs and tax revenues.

It's not surprising, then, that when Canadians grew twitchy about their relations with the U.S. they thought in terms of more auto pacts. The federal government's August 1983 trade paper argued that sectoral trade possibilities should be explored. Furthermore, as Alf Powis notes, the BCNI was considering the idea of sectoral trade agreements when U.S. Trade Representative Bill Brock made it clear the U.S. just wasn't interested. Sectoral agreements smacked of auto pact-style performance requirements. Worse still, they offered no opportunity for the U.S. to get the crucial three new items on the U.S. trade agenda into the deal. But Brock, a smooth and dexterous diplomat if ever there was one, spotted the Canadian keenness.

No, he told Powis and his committee, sectoral trade agreements weren't possible; but wait, my friends, before you go, how about comprehensive free trade? The charming Brock was like the salesman who smoothly deflects the customer from what he's come in to buy and directs him to what the salesman wants to sell. No, says the salesman, you don't need a new set of windshield wipers, you need a whole new car! Let me show you our brand new Corvette Stingray XKE. Now there's a car! It takes a real man to drive that car.

The committee of Canadian businessmen quickly abandoned all thoughts of a new pair of windshield wipers and began looking over the Corvette with real interest. The committee later went up to Ottawa and began pushing the idea with the freshly elected Mulroney government, which was searching for a way to make a big splash — preferably with an initiative that would please its friends, such as the members of this committee. A flashy new Corvette seemed like just the thing.

It was this new idea that quickly became the focus. The clever Brock cautioned the Canadian business leaders not to let their fellow Canadians think that the new idea had come from outside the country, lest they be suspicious.

And Powis's recollection of Brock's position on this subject is backed up by others. Rowland Frazee, former Royal Bank chairman, also recalls Brock's enthusiasm for free trade and Brock's insistence that the initiative would have to come from Canada. Frazee recalled Brock making this point at the *TIME* magazine-sponsored meeting in Washington. "He [Brock] really believed in open trade," says Frazee. "But he felt the initiative had to come from Canada. If it came from the States first, Canadians would immediately become suspicious."

Of course, Brock was right. Canadians turned out to be highly wary of free trade, and undoubtedly would have been more so had they thought that the initiative had come from the U.S. But this, along with the connection between the pharmaceutical changes and the free trade talks, was one of the things it was deemed better for Canadians not to know. They would like free trade more if they didn't know the whole story.

Yet by taking the initiative on free trade — at Washington's suggestion — Canada was not only misleading the Canadian people, but sacrificing a lot of leverage in the talks that followed. Since we had asked for it, we were the ones who looked keen for it. Like a fifteen-year-old desperate for a date, we weren't in a position to be too picky. We showed our weak bargaining stance right off the top with our willingness to knuckle under on the drug issue. The more the Canadian government hyped up free trade, the more pressure it put on itself to come up with a deal. The Americans, however, maintained their low-key approach — partly through Carrot Top's indifference — and did little to play up the issue with the American public. If they didn't get what they wanted at the table, they could simply walk away, and no more than a few trade negotiators — and Jim Robinson — would even notice the difference.

The problem sprang from Mulroney's hunger to do a deal, to deliver at any cost. It would be a side of Mulroney Canadians would see again — as he faced the provincial premiers around the constitutional table in the aftermath of drawing up the Meech Lake accord. After the headstrong federalism of Pierre Trudeau, the premiers found in Mulroney what amounted to a virtual indifference to the fundamental constitutional shape of the country. What mattered to Mulroney was getting a deal. And as he told the *Globe and Mail* in June 1990, he was prepared to roll the dice to get his deal.

It was the same with free trade. Once Mulroney had fixed on free trade, it simply became a question of how — not whether — to push it through. The gravy might taste terrible in the long run, but as long as most Canadians didn't know that, in the short run it would go down Smooth 'N' Easy.

6 • FREE TRADE: DON'T LEAVE HOME WITHOUT IT

Brian Mulroney wasn't the only player in the free trade process who enjoyed the cover of secrecy. Perhaps even more interesting is the shyness of Jim Robinson, because if there was one thing that Robinson had never been accused of, it was shyness.

While many CEOs of Robinson's stature attracted relatively little press, he had always generated a lot of media attention and even seemed to revel in it. Unlike many powerful businessmen, he co-operated with interview requests, even ones that seemed to border on the invasion of privacy. In 1989, he allowed a *Fortune* magazine reporter to tag along with him for days of meetings, luncheons, a trip to Chicago and an afternoon at his Connecticut farm. Robinson also went along with a photographer's request to demonstrate his muscles by hoisting his wife into the air. Indeed, he seemed to enjoy and promote his image as something of a muscle-man. When rumours surfaced that the U.S. best seller *Barbarians at the Gate* was to be made into a movie, Robinson reportedly told a friend that he wanted his role in the movie version of the RJR Nabisco takeover battle to be played by Arnold Schwarzenegger.

Robinson made a point of finding time in his busy schedule for all this because he liked publicity and saw its value. And the press lapped it up. Thrilled by the unusual degree of access to such a powerful CEO, *Fortune*, for instance, ran a flattering cover story on Robinson in November 1989 titled, "American Express: Service that Sells," glossing over a slew of trouble spots at Amex as well as Robinson's role in the RJR Nabisco fiasco. Graced with photos showing an intent Robinson hard at work on his corporate jet and taking charge of a meeting of commodity traders in Chicago, the *Fortune* piece was a virtual advertisement for Robinson; Linda Robinson's firm would have had trouble designing a more desirable bit of coverage. And the *Fortune* article followed on the heels of a *Business Week* cover story earlier that year that gave Robinson credit for transforming American Express into "the unrivalled colossus of financial services." U.S. journalist Connie Bruck commented that, while Robinson's press had nearly always been good, it had "by the late eighties become breathless."

Yet Robinson was oddly shy about the central role played by himself and his company in the Canada-U.S. free trade deal — at least as far as a Canadian audience was concerned. Through his spokesman, Frank Vaccaro, Robinson declined repeated requests for an interview for this book about his role in the free trade process and about the coalition of U.S. businesses that he assembled to support the deal. Calls to others at American Express who were involved in free trade were referred to Vaccaro's office. After months of delays, Vaccaro finally responded with a final "no" to all interview requests for this book.

Perhaps it was not surprising that Robinson did not have the time to give an interview to a Canadian reporter writing a book for a Canadian audience. But what was surprising was that Robinson also barred everyone else at American Express from giving an interview. Vaccaro explained that "Mr Robinson felt that it was not appropriate to spotlight the role he played when so many others were involved. He did not want to be seen as grabbing the spotlight." And yet Robinson didn't seem shy about grabbing the spotlight when it came to putting himself front and centre for *Fortune* or *Business Week,* or, for that matter, having Schwarzenegger do so in a blockbuster movie.

Furthermore, by all accounts, Robinson was far more than simply one of many involved. Virtually everyone acknowledges his central role as the instigator and navigator of the whole process in the U.S., the general overseeing strategy and marshalling troops from his command centre in the American Express tower. Indeed, Robinson is invariably identified as the central U.S. character in the free trade deal by everyone involved, including several who worked for the lobbying firms hired by American Express to organize the free trade coalition and conduct an elaborate pro-free trade campaign.

"American Express provided the greatest organizational resources," said Gail Harrison, vice-president of the firm Wexler, Reynolds, in an interview in her lovely high-ceilinged office, complete with fireplace, in a charming old Washington building not far from the White House. "Robinson was the most active business leader on the issue." Paul Fekete, an analyst with Government Research Corporation, another firm retained by American Express for the free trade campaign, says that "American Express served as the catalyst . . . it served as the spark to get other companies thinking in this fashion."

Canadians involved also pinpoint Robinson's central role in the free trade process. Tom d'Aquino from the BCNI agrees that Robinson was the driving force behind free trade in the U.S. "No question about that, absolutely no question. He stood out head and shoulders above everyone else, and had the highest profile in terms of marshalling the forces." Certainly, Canadian business leaders knew to seek out Jim Robinson if they wanted to talk to U.S. business about free trade. "I can remember two or three sessions we had with him [Robinson] — there was one in Washington and one in his office in New York," says Powis. D'Aquino, too, recalls meeting with Robinson on a number of occasions — perhaps four or five times a year — to discuss the free trade negotiations. He says that the meetings took place in New York and Toronto, and usually included BCNI member David Culver. D'Aquino also recalls Jim Robinson being very much a hands-on leader in the whole process, with Harry Freeman, Amex's executive vice-president, taking a back seat to Robinson on the issue. "Harry advised Jim; Jim had the lead role," says d'Aquino. "It wasn't

as if Jim delegated to Harry and then Harry did all the work.
. . . Jim came to meetings, Jim represented the views, Jim
explained the positions and so on."

Robinson also met with Brian Mulroney on at least one
occasion. Freeman, who, as a former American Express
employee, was not bound by the company's ban on giving
interviews for this book, says he was present for one meeting
that took place during the negotiations, and believes there may
have been another meeting between Robinson and the Canadian Prime Minister. "I remember them meeting in a [hotel]
suite late one night in Washington," said Freeman, who
described the encounter as informal. Mulroney seemed very
interested in knowing what U.S. business thought about the free
trade talks, Freeman recalls.

Robinson was careful to ensure that, publicly, his free trade
efforts didn't look like a one-man show. Fekete says that
Robinson "wanted a coalition of some sort, because there would
be more credibility than American Express on its own." American Express also played the lead role in another U.S. business
coalition championing free trade, the Coalition of Service
Industries. The Coalition's newsletter instructs the interested
reader to contact either its executive director in Washington or
Beth Bogie at American Express in New York.

Robinson also felt it was important to get a broad range of
American businesses involved in promoting the Canada-U.S.
deal in order to head off any possible problems in Congress.
Robinson's fear was that a vocal minority of regional interests,
concerned about increased competition with Canada in certain
specialized sectors, could scuttle an agreement, while the vast
majority of U.S. businesses simply sat on the sidelines barely
paying attention. Congressmen and senators were highly sus-
ceptible to the grievances of their constituents, particularly
when those constituents were important regional industries that
employed a lot of voters. These grievances had led to a surprising degree of opposition within the special Senate committee
that was charged with giving authorization to the President's
free trade initiative with Canada. The final vote had been
nerve-rackingly close, with only a one-vote margin giving the
go-ahead for the formal talks. Robinson wanted to avoid a

replay of that when the final deal was presented to Congress for ratification.

So, in late 1986, Robinson began putting together a truly impressive lobbying effort. He decided no one company could handle the scale of the lobbying effort he had in mind. Instead, four top Washington firms were retained — each with different connections and specialties — to handle the campaign. No expense was spared as the massive lobbying effort swung into action, conducting a detailed person-by-person approach to every member of the House and Senate. "It was probably the most gold-plated lobby — the most organized, the most resources, the most systematic and first-class effort — that I've seen," says Joe Gavin, the associate Washington representative of the U.S. Council of International Business, who has spent a decade watching the lobbying scene in the capital.

Although the firms retained for the lobbying effort had good connections to the Reagan administration and the Republican party, the White House was already onside on the free trade issue. So the main emphasis was on enlisting firms with strong ties to the Democrats in the House and the Senate who would ultimately determine the fate of the free trade deal in the U.S.

Press relations, particularly handling presentations to newspaper editorial boards, were to be handled by Ogilvy, Mather, whose principals included Jody Powell, former press secretary to Democratic President Jimmy Carter and an important link to Democratic Washington. Wexler, Reynolds — the Reynolds was Nancy Reynolds, a close personal friend of Nancy Reagan — was retained to organize a coalition of businesses supporting free trade and keep them informed and active on the issue. Government Research Corporation, a public policy consulting firm with links to Ottawa, was retained to do the substantive analysis of the negotiations.

The final and most important leg of the four-part team was the prestigious law firm Akin, Gump, Strauss, Hauer & Feld, which counted Robert Strauss among its senior partners. Strauss was a formidable figure in Washington, the kind of dominating character who has entrée with both political parties. A Texas-born lawyer, Strauss was part of a clique of heavy-hitting Texans whose ranks included Jim Baker, Lloyd Bentsten and George Bush. Strauss, a one-time FBI agent, had risen to the top of the Democratic Party, serving as chairman of the Democratic National Committee. During the Carter era, he had been the President's personal representative for Middle East peace negotiations and also the President's trade representative, earning the lifelong rank of "Ambassador." It was as trade representative that he had made his mark in Washington, gaining credit for orchestrating the successful results of the Tokyo Round of the GATT negotiations in the late seventies. With superb political connections and enormous prestige as a negotiator, Strauss was a highly influential figure on Capitol Hill. "You probably couldn't get a more effective voice on trade than Ambassador Strauss," says Gavin.

The lobbying effort was personally overseen at American Express by Freeman and his assistant David Ruth, who flew constantly to Washington to meet with the high-powered team that had been assembled. Although the core of the effort was conducted by the team, a coalition of businesses was also formed in early 1987 to give the lobbying effort credibility. Known as ACTE/CAN (American Coalition for Trade Expansion with Canada), the coalition consisted of major business organizations as well as a host of key multinationals, including General Electric, IBM, Dow Chemical, Ford Motor Co., RJR Nabisco, Metropolitan Life, Honeywell and, of course, American Express. Some smaller businesses were also recruited.

It turned out to be surprisingly easy to line up support for the free trade deal among U.S. multinationals, who could see the potential for consolidating their positions in an expanded North American market and for winning new ground in services, investment and intellectual property. "We easily got over 1,000 companies," says Freeman. Indeed, as the lobbying team mapped out a strategy, one of the biggest problems turned out to be how to keep in check the tremendous excitement U.S. business felt about the prospect of a Canada-U.S. free trade deal. Of course, the fact that U.S. business was excited about a deal would only help assure its passage in Congress. But, as Strauss and the other skillful strategists noted, there was another audience that also had to be played to: the Canadian public, which, in the end, turned out to be more problematic than Congress. Too much enthusiasm on the part of a coalition of powerful U.S. business interests was bound to make the already suspicious Canadian public even more suspicious.

Ron Pump, Washington lobbyist for the U.S. telecommunications giant AT & T, which was a member of the coalition, recalls Strauss playing a key role in toning down the public expressions of enthusiasm on the part of U.S. business. Pump recalls that it was Strauss "who gave us the very, very sage advice: you can't appear as if this is the greatest thing in the world for Americans. Then it's going to have a negative reaction in Canada." Pump says that this was not always easy advice to follow. "How do you try not to be as enthusiastic as we were about this? Up until the end, we were sitting on pins and needles. . . . Ironically, that was one of the hardest things — trying to contain some of the enthusiasm we had here."

The American strategists realized that too much enthusiasm from U.S. business could harm not only the chances of the deal gaining support in Canada, but also Mulroney personally, since he had put so much of his personal prestige into the initiative. Mulroney had already proved to be a godsend for American business. His declaration at the Economic Club in New York that Canada was "open for business" had gone a long way towards wiping out the negative memory of Pierre Trudeau in American business circles. And Mulroney had followed up with concrete actions that had greatly pleased U.S. businessmen, dismantling Trudeau's National Energy Program and replacing FIRA with the more welcoming Investment Canada. Gavin, from the U.S. Council for International Business, says that U.S. business had been highly pleased to see Mulroney undo the nationalistic programs brought in by Trudeau. Asked if this had earned Mulroney greater respect than his predecessor in U.S. business circles, Gavin was careful to make a distinction. "*Respect* isn't the word. We were just pleased and relieved, and happy where we could be supportive of Mulroney."

Certainly the last thing American business wanted was to throw Mulroney to the wolves up in Canada, where anti-free trade sentiment was building. Strauss and the other strategists for the ACTE/CAN coalition were well aware of the delicacy of the situation in Canada and wanted to do their best to shield

Mulroney from negative political fallout. "We all saw it as a precarious thing to begin with. Mulroney was up there out on a limb," says Gavin. The White House was also sensitive to Mulroney's difficult situation at home, and was anxious to do what it could to protect a prime minister who had already proved so accommodating to U.S. interests.

Indeed, the Reagan administration was so protective of Mulroney that U.S. negotiators feared the White House would pressure them to compromise more on the final free trade package than they felt was necessary. According to R.K. Morris, director of international trade for the U.S. National Association of Manufacturers, this was particularly a fear for Peter Murphy, the tough, uncompromising U.S. top negotiator who was accustomed to getting his way at the negotiating table with the textile-producing countries that he'd dealt with in the past.

Morris, who sat in on briefing sessions given by Murphy, said that Murphy was worried that the White House would tie his hands and prevent him from driving a really tough deal with the Canadians — in order to protect Mulroney politically. "He [Murphy] was afraid he would lose control," said Morris, "and that a deal that was less advantageous than the one he could get would be forced upon him by a nervous White House that didn't want to lose all or *have an embarrassment for Mulroney.*" Mulroney had become so useful to the U.S. government that it was trying to protect the Canadian Prime Minister from his own voters.

The U.S. business strategists working for the ACTE/CAN coalition figured the key thing was for the coalition to keep a low profile in Canada, and have the deal championed north of the border by Canadian business. Pump, from AT & T, recalls that some U.S. businessmen wanted to charge up to Canada and start promoting the free trade deal themselves, but cooler heads prevailed, and cautioned them to leave it to their Canadian counterparts. Still, Pump remembers there was frustration among the U.S. business leaders because Canadian business was initially sluggish in promoting the deal. "It's not that we pointed the finger," says Pump, recalling the mood inside the ACTE/CAN coalition, "But, geez, it would be nice if the Canadian business community would get out in front on this issue."

The concern of U.S. business was not surprising. Just as U.S. trade strategists had correctly figured out that free trade would have a better chance of success in Canada if the initiative at least *appeared* to be coming from within Canada, so too were the American business planners now seeing the importance of having Canadians "out in front on this issue." As Pump notes, "We were very, very conscious of our efforts not to make it appear that this thing was being directed from here [Washington]."

This perhaps explains why Jim Robinson was so reluctant to give an interview for a Canadian audience — or to allow anyone from his company to be interviewed. His claims of modesty and reluctance to steal the spotlight conceal another motive: his desire to prevent Canadians from seeing his company's central role in orchestrating the free trade deal. Robinson knew well that an accurate description of his company's role would only intensify Canadian suspicions that free trade was really part of an American — not a Canadian — dream. Better to say nothing, and let Canadian business be "out in front" on the issue.

And yet, interestingly, if we look at the Canadian business leader who was perhaps most "out in front" on the issue, we once again find a strong American Express connection. David Culver, who was at the very centre of the free trade issue in Canada from the early eighties, was a director on the American Express board in New York, where he came into monthly contact with Robinson.

Culver, who was chairman of Alcan until 1989, was probably as deeply involved with free trade as anyone in Canada. He was a member of the BCNI task force that met with Brock back in January '83 and served as a catalyst for pushing comprehensive free trade at an early stage. He also served as chairman of the BCNI from '86 to '89, when the BCNI was leading the free trade drive in Canada. And, as d'Aquino notes, Culver was usually present at meetings with Jim Robinson in New York and Toronto to discuss the free trade issue. Culver was also instrumental, he acknowledges, in setting up the Canadian business coalition supporting free trade — the Canadian equivalent of Robinson's coalition. Indeed, the Canadian coalition, called the Canadian Alliance for Trade and Job Opportunities, operated out of Alcan's Montreal headquarters with the help of a full-time Alcan employee. Culver, who ran the Alliance as chairman of its executive committee, says that he devoted about one-tenth of his time to the cause. Under his direction, Alcan donated $250,000 to the Alliance, the company has disclosed.

Exactly where the idea for setting up a Canadian alliance came from is not clear. But it's likely that Culver picked up the notion at one of his regular encounters with Jim Robinson in New York. Since 1980, Culver has served on the American Express board, bringing him into constant contact with Robinson as well as Freeman. (Another familiar face on the American Express board in this small interconnecting world was Ross Johnson, Brian Mulroney's friend and fellow free trade advocate.) Culver notes that free trade and open competition were constant themes at American Express board meetings, and he acknowledges that the subject of the Canada-U.S. deal did come up in conversation, sometimes with Robinson, sometimes with Freeman.

While Culver insists that the business coalitions on both sides of the border started independently, he acknowledges that his personal relationship with Jim Robinson helped co-ordinate the efforts of U.S. and Canadian business. Says Culver: "Because we happened to be people who knew one another, it was easy for us to occasionally check our readings." Culver said that he couldn't remember who first raised the idea of setting up coalitions — himself or Robinson. "Jim was heading for it anyway," says Culver. "I think he was about to form something. I can't say whether he already was doing it when I mentioned it."

It appears, however, that Robinson had already made plans to launch his coalition when the BCNI began to initiate one in Canada. Fekete recalls that American Express was seeking proposals to put together a coalition at the end of '86, and says that he clearly recalls that the U.S. coalition was already in place by the time the Canadian one was launched in March '87. So it seems likely that the subject of a Canadian coalition came up between Robinson and Culver before the idea surfaced among a small gathering of BCNI members, including Culver, at the York Club in Toronto in February '87.

Culver recalls that the small group had dined together following a BCNI committee meeting and was relaxing after dinner when the conversation turned to the need for Canadian business to promote free trade more vigorously. The members agreed, and the business group soon established the alliance, which was mostly a regrouping of BCNI members, largely organized and run by BCNI stalwarts Culver and d'Aquino. Alf Powis says that the original intention was to create a coalition much broader than the BCNI, but that plan never materialized. "I think if you look at how it [the Alliance] was financed, it was financed by BCNI members."*

Once the Canadian alliance was in place, it co-ordinated its efforts with Robinson's coalition. Although Culver plays down the connection between the two groups, Powis recalls extensive co-ordination. "We worked very closely with them," he says. "Culver was — and still is — a director of American Express. Jimmy Robinson of American Express was heading it [the U.S. coalition] up. We used to go to the [American Express office] and talk to them and co-ordinate efforts." Freeman also recalls frequent co-ordination between the two sides, and adds that the private sectors in the two countries got together more than once and put the free trade negotiations back on track after things had run into an impasse at the negotiating table.

This is not to suggest that some sort of conspiracy was hatched in the boardroom of American Express. What does seem likely, however, is that much of the impetus for free trade came from south of the border, particularly from American Express, and that there was a careful effort on the part of the sophisticated lobbyists assembled by the company to disguise this fact from Canadians. An important part of this strategy was to suppress evidence of the overwhelming enthusiasm for free trade felt by certain powerful American corporations and to get Canadian business "out in front" on the issue. Accordingly, a small group of BCNI members, including American Express director David

---

* The Alliance produced a financial accounting in August 1989 showing that it had raised $5.2 million from more than 250 corporate and individual donors. It did not, however, provide a breakdown of the amounts contributed by the donors.

Culver, proposed setting up a coalition of Canadian business leaders, similar to the one that had just been set up in the U.S. Culver ran the Canadian coalition, which worked closely with the American coalition organized by his fellow American Express director.

None of this amounts to a conspiracy. But it is a different version of events from the one presented to Canadians — and questions about it render a usually confident, gregarious Jim Robinson surprisingly shy.

JIM ROBINSON WAS his confident, gregarious self at a breakfast meeting he arranged in Washington in July '87. With only three months to go before the deadline set by Congress for the signing of the Canada-U.S. free trade deal, Robinson had invited a team of Canadian businessmen from David Culver's coalition to meet with a group of influential U.S. senators. But no sooner had the Canadians taken a bite of their eggs than they were confronted with some jarring news: the U.S. senators were telling them that under no circumstances was Canada going to win an exemption from protectionist U.S. trade laws.

This was disturbing indeed. From the outset, Canada's first and foremost goal in entering into free trade talks — indeed, really its only clear goal — had been to win secure access to the U.S. market. This essentially required a common set of rules to govern trade between the two countries, so that Canada was shielded from the potentially punitive U.S. trade laws. But the Canadian businessmen were now being told that the senators wouldn't allow such a measure. And the senators had the power to accept or reject the final agreement. Without their ratification, the agreement could never become law in the U.S. Culver remembers the senators being adamant at the breakfast meeting: "They said, 'If you people think you're going to get a special deal out of this country, you're barking up the wrong tree.' "

For the Canadian businessmen, the breakfast was as sobering as the strong coffee that was served. And the bad news came hot on the heels of a disturbing confidential study, prepared the

month before by the Bank of Nova Scotia's economics department, and quietly circulated among key segments of the Canadian business community. That study showed in dramatic terms
how free trade could end up being an economic disaster for
Canada. It pulled no punches, since it was prepared exclusively
for internal bank purposes to allow the bank's credit managers to
assess the risks involved for businesses trying to borrow money. It
concluded that, with the exception of natural resources, the free
trade deal would hurt every sector of the Canadian economy:
"Beyond resources, all other sectors are net losers."

And the biggest loser, the report said, would be the services
sector — the sector that Jim Robinson was targetting with his
new set of rules. Those new rules would allow U.S. firms selling
services full access to the Canadian market, on the same terms
as Canadian firms. Such competition could prove disastrous for
the Canadian service industry, which accounted for 70 percent
of Canada's employment. "In general, the Canadian service
sector is smaller, weaker and less competitive compared to the
service sector in the United States," the bank study said.

The study certainly cooled the enthusiasm for free trade at
the very highest level of the Bank of Nova Scotia. "Everyone
associates free trade with the physical movement of goods," said
bank chairman Cedric Ritchie in a recent interview. "But it's a
question of the service side — data processing, banking, insurance, advertising, engineering — that was what the U.S. was
after." Ritchie suspects that the Canadian team was not properly prepared to deal with this new area. "When you ask who
was on that group who had skills in terms of services, it was
weak," said Ritchie. "When you get into the question of cross-
border financial services — American Express was the classic
illustration — I don't think we knew what we were talking
about."

As Ritchie's concerns grew, he began to voice them among his
colleagues at the top of Canada's business establishment. But he
found them surprisingly uninterested in such concerns as they
closed ranks in support of the deal. "Nobody would sit back and
challenge some of the statements. It was just sort of euphoria to
get it done, and solutions would fall in afterward," he said. "You
were either aboard 100 percent, or if you started to ask some of

these questions, you were against it and trying to scupper the agreement."

The Bank of Nova Scotia study, grim as its findings were, was based on the upbeat assumption that Canada would achieve its objective of gaining secure access to the U.S. market. But the businessmen at the Washington breakfast were now finding out that Canada was not going to achieve this objective. Yet business had already fully committed itself to free trade, launching its alliance months earlier and embarking on a nation-wide promotion campaign that included speeches and media appearances almost every day. Retreat at this point would, at the very least, involve a massive loss of face. The problem was exacerbated by the fact that the Mulroney government had dangled the possibility of guaranteed access to the U.S. market so temptingly in front of Canadians. Indeed, Ottawa had made it clear that this was the central goal of free trade, and without it, there would be no deal.

Ottawa had also made this position abundantly clear to the Americans, right from the beginning. In the months before formal negotiations between the two countries were launched, there was an informal series of pre-negotiations in which both sides had communicated their priorities to each other. These pre-negotiations had culminated in a crucial, if relaxing, meeting aboard a sailboat in Chesapeake Bay just off Washington on the last day of July 1985.

The sailboat belonged to Mike Smith, the deputy U.S. Trade Representative. He had invited a small group of Canadian and U.S. officials to have this final discussion in the privacy of his comfortable boat, in the hope of clarifying for both sides whether there were sufficient grounds to proceed with formal talks. Smith's wife came along and served sandwiches and coffee for the group, which included Bill Merkin, who headed up the Canada desk at the U.S. Trade Representative's office, and Canadian officials Derek Burney and Michael Hart.

As the sun beat down and the boat drifted past the scenic Washington shoreline, both sides spoke frankly. Smith made it clear that, for the U.S., the top priorities for a free trade agreement were new rules to cover investment, services and intellectual property. The Canadians, who were getting burned in the hot sun as the afternoon wore on, stressed that their top priority was security of access to the U.S. market. This would include a common set of trade rules to shield Canada from U.S. trade laws and a dispute settlement mechanism to enforce the common rules. Both sides left the boat that afternoon feeling that a deal was possible.

From the outset, then, the U.S. was well aware that securing access to its market was Canada's top agenda item. And Merkin, who became the deputy chief negotiator for the American side in the formal talks that followed, recalls that "the Canadians tried absolutely everything they could" to achieve their goal. But the U.S. negotiators, led by Peter "Carrot Top" Murphy, simply never budged — partly because they knew Congress would never approve something that amounted to an exemption from U.S. trade law. Congress protected its lucrative home market like a nervous mother bear watching over her cubs, and was unwilling to grant exemptions to any country. "That was not in the cards, ever," says Claude Barfield, a trade specialist with the Washington-based American Enterprise Institute. "Congress would never have allowed it."

But, even though the U.S. negotiators knew all along that they could not offer Canada what amounted to an exemption, they never made this clear — not on the sailboat in Chesapeake Bay, nor through the long months of negotiations. Indeed, they did just the opposite, stringing the Canadian negotiators along. "I guess we led them on on that issue," says Merkin. "We knew we were never going to be able to deliver. . . . Peter was very coy on the issue." The U.S. agreed to the establishment of a working group to study the issue of subsidies, with the idea that if they could come up with a common definition of subsidies then they could perhaps work out a common set of rules to govern them. (The issue of subsidies was crucial, because U.S. trade laws often penalized foreign goods on the grounds that foreign governments were subsidizing them, giving them an unfair advantage over domestically produced goods in the U.S. market.)

But the working group on subsidies never made any real progress, so the negotiations never got to the key issue of whether the two countries could come up with a common set of rules. "We really didn't have to mislead explicitly," says Merkin. "We implicitly, I guess, misled by acting like there were prospects of something coming out of that working group." Merkin believes the Canadian negotiators were drawn in by the U.S. ruse. "The Canadians made it clear that [secure access] was essential to the agreement, so they assumed we wouldn't continue the dialogue if we didn't expect to do something in that area."

Reisman bristles at the suggestion that the Canadian team might have been fooled. Asked about Merkin's assertion that Murphy's stonewalling was a deliberate strategy, Reisman explodes with anger. The charming, highly personable side of Reisman — something I'd seen quite a bit of in nine hours of interviews with him for this book — was instantly gone, submerged in his sudden transformation into the legendary 800-pound gorilla. "Look, I'm not going to spend my time answering Merkin!" he bellowed. The question had obviously touched a raw nerve, wounded his pride. It became clear that part of his anger sprang from the insult of being asked to respond to the statements of someone who had held a lower rank in the negotiations. "Merkin was a member of their damn team. . . . He was number two. If you want to know about Merkin . . . go to [Gordon] Ritchie. Ritchie was number two [on the Canadian team]." The little outburst provided a flashing insight into just how chaotic the negotiations must have been.

Whether or not Murphy's obstinance was a deliberate strategy or merely a personality flaw — as some on the Canadian side argue — it allowed the American team to keep the Canadians on tenterhooks while conceding no ground. And the approach seemed to be endorsed by those at the very top of the U.S. administration. Reisman himself notes that, at his urging, Mulroney raised the subject with Reagan at two summit meetings, but still no orders seemed to trickle down to Murphy, who continued with his intransigence.

For months, the negotiations remained in a stalemate. Finally in late August '87, with less than two months to go before the Congressional deadline for a deal, the two teams retired for a week to Cornwall, in the hope that a more relaxed setting might produce better results. There, a charming Simon Reisman spent long hours trying to establish some kind of personal rapport with Murphy over a game of horseshoes, out fishing in a boat and on long walks. Sometimes the chief negotiators were joined by Merkin and Ritchie; sometimes they went alone. Recalls Reisman, "I sat with Murphy for hours. At no point did I get a 'no,' at no point did I get a 'yes.' " At the end of the week, the whole exercise had produced nothing.

An exasperated Reisman reported to Mulroney that he thought the Canadian team should formally walk out of the negotiations, as a last-ditch attempt to get the attention of higher-ups in Washington. If the walk-out failed to produce real concessions, that would be the end of the talks. With Mulroney's agreement, Reisman called Murphy's bluff. After the long months of negotiations, Murphy finally produced a proposed solution. But the solution offered nothing of substance. Murphy was proposing a common set of rules that, in essence, would be much harder on Canada than on the U.S. The rules would impose tough restrictions on the subsidy of exports, while imposing virtually no controls on domestic subsidies. Such a system would punish Canada, which was primarily an exporter, while doing nothing to prevent the U.S. from continuing its massive domestic subsidies. It was the same pro-American solution that the U.S. had managed to impose for years on GATT, making it very difficult for export-oriented countries throughout the Third World to get into the American market. Reisman stormed out of the negotiations as planned.

Ottawa now had to wait to see if its gamble would pay off. Within twenty-four hours a call came from the White House. It was a Reagan aide telling an official in the PMO that the President wanted to speak to the Prime Minister. But officials in the PMO quickly determined that the call was just a goodwill gesture, with no concessions. A high-level decision was made that Canada should politely decline the call. "The call never took place," said Reisman. Over the days that followed, there was a flurry of calls between senior officials in both capitals, and a trip to Washington by Derek Burney and Michael Wilson, all to no avail.

Finally, Treasury Secretary James Baker phoned Burney and said he thought he'd worked out a basis for a deal, after consulting with members of Congress. Under Baker's solution, there would be no common set of rules, but there would be provisions for dispute settlement panels — composed of representatives from both countries — which would ensure that the separate laws of the two countries were correctly applied. In other words, the Americans would continue to use their trade laws, and the Canadians would continue to use theirs. The dispute settlement panels would simply replace the court systems of the two countries in deciding whether each country was applying its own laws correctly.

It was hardly a great victory. Although it gave Canada something no other U.S. trading partner had, it was far from the solution that Canada had said all along was its bottom line goal. It certainly was not guaranteed or secure access to the U.S. market. Without a common set of rules, Canada was still subject to the full range of U.S. trade law. The only difference would be that the disputes panels could, presumably, ensure U.S. trade laws were not applied capriciously. But many critics argue that the laws themselves are a problem, whether applied capriciously or not.

In many ways, Baker's offer seemed like slim pickings. Reisman admits that, had he known at the outset that the U.S. would never agree to a common set of rules, he would have backed out as the chief negotiator long before, told the Prime Minister to "get yourself another boy." If the talks had broken down at the beginning, Mulroney might have felt freer to walk away from them. Now, after he had relentlessly hyped the issue for more than two years, the stakes seemed much higher. Merkin comments that the U.S. was "able to play it out so that the process was so far along" that anything appeared better to the Mulroney government than failure.

The Americans had analysed the situation correctly. Mulroney decided Baker's half-offer was more appealing than admitting defeat. Putting the best face on the situation, the government tried to generate a sense of expectation and excitement as it sent a Canadian delegation back to Washington for a final round. Heavy-hitters like Michael Wilson, Derek Burney and International Trade Minister Pat Carney were now involved, and were negotiating directly with one of the most powerful men in the U.S. government — Jim Baker. The press was full of insider stories about negotiating teams camped out in the halls during late-night sessions and motorcycle engines revving outside as official couriers waited to take the final package to the White House for Reagan's signature. It was all part of the drama. Could we or could we not pull off a deal? The question of whether or not we *should* pull it off somehow got lost in the media drama, in the roar of the motorcycle engines.

Like a Hollywood script, the drama continued right to the end. With three hours to go before the midnight deadline, the Canadian team was still in a serious quandary about whether to accept or reject the whole deal. The remaining obstacle was critical: Baker's deal didn't rule out the possibility that the U.S. could change its trade laws in the future, making them still more punitive. In the ante-room off Baker's office where the Canadian delegation was gathered, Reisman argued vociferously that this was a serious flaw that made the deal unacceptable. He recalls Alan Gotlieb, Canadian ambassador to Washington, urging acceptance of the deal even without a clause preventing the Americans from changing their trade laws, but Gotlieb vigorously denies this. "I disagree 100 percent with any notion that I thought we should proceed without that clause," says Gotlieb. "I was convinced it was absolutely essential. Without that clause, you could drive a coach and four through [the agreement]."

The delegation phoned Mulroney in Ottawa and after private conversations with Reisman, Burney, Wilson and Gotlieb, he sent Burney back into Baker's office at 9:15 p.m., insisting that the agreement must hold both countries to their existing laws. This risked throwing the whole deal, since Baker might well come back and say he simply couldn't bind the hands of Congress like that. But, by 11:20, Baker came up with a solution that appeared to accommodate the Canadian concern: a section was written into the deal saying that any new laws must conform with the principles spelled out in the agreement. The deal was done; the couriers dispatched to the White House.

It is easy to see how the negotiating team would itself get caught up in the excitement and drama of trying to get a deal, as the clock ticked towards the artificial deadline set by Congress. The setting was seductive — with the motorcycle engines roaring, the President supposedly waiting up to put his signature on the deal before the midnight deadline, the Canadian team stuck in an ante-room off the office of the powerful U.S. Treasury Secretary. It all increased the desire for a deal, making it appear to be an opportunity that must be seized now, while it was still offered, before the deadline expired or Reagan fell asleep. Reisman notes that the Americans deliberately structure these kinds of negotiations so that the other side "is always working towards their deadlines." Yet, interestingly, when the Americans tried the same thing with the Europeans in the dying moments of the Uruguay Round of the GATT negotiations in December 1990, the Europeans refused to be played with like that. Notes Reisman, "The Europeans said 'Go to hell,' " letting the deadline expire without a deal.

Such irreverence towards the U.S. giant is perhaps easier when there is a bunch of countries involved, just as it's always easier to defy the schoolyard bully when you're part of a gang. This is, of course, the reason why one-on-one negotiations between puny Canada and massive United States posed problems from the beginning. As Tim Bennett, the former U.S. trade attaché, noted, one of the major reasons that the U.S. began flirting with the idea of bilateral negotiations in the early eighties was that Washington realized one-on-one negotiations would give the U.S. more "leverage."

The Canadian side knew that the final free trade package fell far short of its expectations. Asked if he's happy with the agreement, Reisman says, "Well, I'm not happy, but I'm not unhappy." Hardly a ringing endorsement. Alfred Powis recalls considerable uncertainty over whether the BCNI would even be able to support the final deal. He recalls being briefed by Tom d'Aquino on Sunday, after the final late-night climax on Saturday night. Powis asked d'Aquino if he felt the final package was good enough to win the BCNI's support. "I think so," Powis recalls d'Aquino saying. Powis flew to Ottawa on the Monday after the Saturday deadline for a briefing with Reisman. "We were not at all sure the deal was good enough," says Powis. "We certainly didn't get everything we wanted. It was not a perfect deal, but on balance we finally reached the judgement that it was better than the status quo."

This lukewarm enthusiasm didn't prevent the business community from selling the deal to Canadians with gusto. Indeed, the business alliance concealed its lack of enthusiasm and moved into full gear with its promotional campaign — a campaign in which the alliance alone would eventually spend more than $5 million selling the idea of free trade to a skeptical Canadian public. In part, the reason for the BCNI's willingness to go along with the final package, despite misgivings, was that the business agenda had changed somewhat in the years since the trade initiative was launched. While winning secure access to the American market had been the prime concern in the early eighties, a whole new motive had emerged by the mid eighties. Free trade had become a potential tool for a dramatic overhaul of a country that business had come increasingly to dislike.

A LITTLE BROOK in the corner of the garden produced a gentle gurgling sound, giving the pretty back yard, complete with swimming pool, patio and flowers, the feeling of an English country garden. It was a beautiful summer morning and the yard was full of birds and water sounds. It all fit perfectly with the tranquil atmosphere of Toronto's Rosedale, with its lovely tall trees and stately old homes. In a shaded spot at the corner of the garden, David Braide was serving coffee and talking about free trade.

Braide clearly belonged in his garden. He was finely mannered and soft-spoken and, even after fifty years in Canada, maintained his British accent, just as Rosedale somehow maintained an old-world refinement in the midst of Toronto's bustle. A successful businessman, Braide had risen to be vice-chairman of CIL, the British-owned paint and chemical giant, but had also found time to be active over the years in a number of business associations, serving on a series of business committees and as president of the Canadian Chamber of Commerce.

Perhaps because of his international background — he was born in Britain and raised partly in India, where his father served in the British army — Braide had always taken an interest in international trade. When the business community became concerned about its trade relations with the U.S. in the early eighties, Braide seemed like a natural to organize a committee of businessmen to contemplate the problem. At the urging of several colleagues, he set up an ad hoc committee of about forty senior business figures from across the country and held a series of meetings at CIL executive offices in Toronto in 1984 and 1985. Although some of the businessmen initially had doubts, Braide says that all forty eventually endorsed the concept of free trade with the U.S. The Mulroney government later set up a similar committee, with mostly the same members Braide had assembled, to advise the government formally on the issue.

Like others, Braide recalls that interest in free trade in the business community arose initially over Canadian fears of being locked out of the U.S. market. "I think the thing that really got it going was the threat of American protectionism, and the desire of a lot of people to avoid getting caught up in that net," says Braide, sipping his coffee and nibbling on a shortbread cookie. "That got the debate going, but it broadened out to more important questions."

More important questions? Wasn't access to the U.S. market *the* important question, the raison d'être for the whole exercise? The more important questions Braide had in mind, it turned out, revolved around the need to make Canada more competitive, to gear it up for the tougher competition of the world marketplace — for Globalization. "Canadian business, in my view, has had a relatively easy time of it, protected by significant tariffs or huge captive markets and resource industries. It has developed a mind-set based on an inward-looking concept of competition," said Braide.

For Braide, and others in the business community, ripping down these tariff barriers was the first step towards making Canada more competitive. Braide was convinced that Canadians could compete with their larger American neighbours but, even if it turned out that they couldn't, free trade would still have its advantages. "To the extent that we can't compete, the pressure to become more efficient resulting from the elimination of duties would be healthy," he said. "Competition began to be regarded as a refreshing, invigorating kind of experience, rather than a threatening one. In my view, that's the most important aspect of the free trade arrangement."

According to Braide, then, free trade was above all a method of disciplining Canadians out of their old protective "mind-set," of forcing them to adopt a leaner, more efficient approach. This view is echoed by David Culver, who says that the BCNI came to see free trade as a way of gearing Canada up for world competition. "We were thinking that the only way we were going to be competitive on a world scale was to get to be competitive on a North American scale," said Culver. "The competition that Canadian industry has to face as a result of the free trade agreement is the very competition that's going to make Canadian industry world-class competitors." Culver volunteered that there would be "some pain involved" as Canadians adjusted themselves to a more competitive scene, and added, "If you can't stand the heat in the North American kitchen, you won't stand it outside."

A key benefit of free trade to these businessmen, then, was what we could call the "cattle prod theory." Free trade would be like the electric shock in the metal prod that drives the cattle on to where the rancher wants them to go. Canadians would feel the shock of increased competition, experience the fear of job loss, and respond, as the business-ranchers wanted, by lowering their expectations and their wage demands. Canadians finding themselves in head-to-head competition with U.S. firms that pay their non-unionized workers much lower wages would respond by accepting lower wages themselves. And when Canadians next found themselves in competition with Mexican workers who earned even less, their wage expectations would fall still further.

An Economic Council of Canada study, prepared in 1988, provides an insight into how this all works. The study showed that the free trade deal would cost Canadians both jobs and output — unless Canadian productivity was boosted well above historical trends. In other words, free trade would end up *hurting* Canadians unless they changed significantly, unless they increased their productivity by, for instance, working for lower wages. And yet, despite the fairly depressing scenario revealed by the numbers in the study, the Economic Council endorsed free trade! This is not the contradiction that it seems to be at first glance. The economists at the Council, like the business leaders in the BCNI, clearly saw an advantage to a free trade deal that would act like a cattle prod in making Canadians change their behaviour.

In this view, free trade was not so much seen as a boon to Canadians but rather a way to whip them into shape, strip them of their old expectations — expectations of a high standard of living based on Canada's ample natural resources and prosperous home market. This market was now to be opened fully to outsiders, and Canadians would have to scramble to keep a foothold in it. In the new, ultra-competitive world to be created right on Canadian soil, Canadians would have to learn to expect less. There would be no guarantee of employment and less in the way of a social security system. Just why all this was suddenly necessary was never adequately explained. It was vaguely blamed on factors beyond our control — the international market, the demands of foreign investors — things ordinary people were supposed to trust the experts to figure out.

As Braide described how to make Canadians more competitive, it became clear that the pain involved in all this revamping of the Canadian pscyhe was not likely to be evenly shared. One of the key needs in making Canada more competitive, according to Braide, was to reduce the tax burden on Canadian corporations so they could compete more effectively with corporations from countries with lower corporate taxes. But lower corporate tax rates meant higher taxes for someone else, and that someone else inevitably turned out to be the vast majority of Canadians. Indeed, as it turned out, free trade and tax reform came to be seen by business as two sides of the same coin — the coin that was supposedly going to make Canada more competitive in the world. It's not surprising then that in 1986, when free trade was still in the negotiation stage, the BCNI came out with a tax reform paper urging substantial tax *cuts* for corporations and the rich, with the missing revenue to be made up by a comprehensive new sales tax. Although almost no one paid attention at the time, the BCNI's tax reform paper heralded the birth of what later became the hated GST.

But as I sat in David Braide's lovely English garden, sipping coffee in the fresh morning air with the blue sky reflected in the swimming pool and the little brook gurgling gently in my ear, I was struck by a sense of déjà vu, a memory of dining with Stanley Hartt at the fancy Italian restaurant in Montreal. Just like Hartt, Braide was talking about the need to change Canada, to discipline Canadians into a more competitive mind-set. And once again, it seemed clear that the punishing effects of all this discipline were going to fall on less affluent Canadians, the ones who had never enjoyed the luxury of swimming in their own back-yard pool or relaxing in a delightful garden in the heart of Rosedale.

It was this vast majority of Canadians — the spoiled and lazy, the nation of losers — who would be forced to tighten their belts and learn to do without. It was these ordinary people who were somehow found wanting, who had to be remoulded to fit the new Canada business wanted to create. This disdain for Canadians as they were was reflected in a column Diane Francis wrote in the *Financial Post* in November 1990. Francis proposed Ottawa give Canadian passports to "every single one of Hong Kong's 5.81 million residents" who was willing to settle in Canada's "lacklustre" Maritime provinces. "These talented people would bring to the sleepy Maritimes a work ethic, business smarts and factories. . . ."

Francis, who was born and educated in Chicago, went on to argue that the newcomers would not be allowed to make claims on Canadian social programs for two years and would also be exempt from paying Canadian tax for two years. The idea, presumably, would be to create a mini-Hong Kong right in the midst of the Maritimes, to establish a kind of free-fire economic zone outside the Canadian mainstream, complete with all the ingredients that have contributed to the Hong Kong economic miracle: sweat shops, brutal working conditions, a vastly different standard of living for rich and poor. Newcomers from Hong Kong who failed to make it in the new world would presumably end up without any social assistance, destitute, hungry and cold. A new culture of unbridled capitalism — a purer strain of the ideology than even that found in Francis's native U.S.A. — would be transplanted onto Canadian soil, to shake Canadians from their lethargy and show them how to live by transporting them back to the mean realities of life as it was here a century ago. What was evident in all this was a scorn for the Canadian way of life, a desire to transform the civilized world of Canadian communities into a ruthless economic jungle.

AS FOR THE Americans, it was not hard to see what they liked in the free trade deal. There had been considerable progress on the three new items on their agenda — services, investment and intellectual property — as well as a dramatic breakthrough in the key area of energy. With U.S. business and the Reagan administration strongly backing the deal, it sailed through Congress and, with the signatures of Mulroney and Reagan, became law in January 1988. It would be beyond the scope of this book to attempt a detailed analysis of the agreement, which has been summarized and analysed in detail elsewhere. But, just as we looked at how Canada fared in achieving its original objective, it is worth noting how well the U.S. did in winning its primary goals.

In intellectual property, the U.S. had managed to force Canada to greatly expand the monopoly rights of brand-name drug companies, despite overwhelming sentiment against such changes among Canadians. Although the free trade deal made no mention of this Canadian retreat, Canada's willingness to change its laws was clearly linked to its desire to appease the Americans in the free trade negotiations, as we've seen.

The U.S. also achieved much of what it was seeking in Jim Robinson's target area of services, where $11 billion in trade was at stake. Significantly, Canada agreed to allow U.S. firms in the service field the same rights as Canadian firms, whether they established themselves in Canada or merely sold their services in the Canadian market from across the border. By winning this right, the U.S. had not only opened up new markets for its strongest sector, but had set a timely precedent for the GATT negotiations where the U.S. was still encountering strong resistance. As the influential publication *Inside U.S. Trade* pointed out on October 9, 1987, "The free trade agreement between the U.S. and Canada is an international breakthrough because it is the first pact that sets binding rules for services trade between any two countries."

Canada also gave considerable ground in the key area of financial services, where barriers to entry had traditionally been strongest. Under the Canada-U.S. agreement, for instance, American banks, securities firms and insurance companies would be entitled to virtually the same privileges as their Canadian equivalents in the Canadian market. Since the Mulroney government was embarking on a wide-ranging liberalization of rules governing its financial markets, this opened up tremendous opportunities for American firms. Under the new rules, for instance, Canadian banks were entitled to own securities firms, so American banks would now receive this privilege as well.

But no such new privileges were won by Canadian banks in the U.S. market: a U.S. law called the Glass-Steagall Act prevented banks — American or foreign — from owning securities firms, And, as Peter Nicholson, vice-president of the Bank of Nova Scotia, points out, even if the U.S. relaxed these restrictions on its own banks, the new privileges would not necessarily be extended to Canadian banks. The free trade agreement only required that *amendments* to the Glass-Steagall Act be extended to Canadian banks. Instead of amending the act, the U.S. is now granting American banks the right to own securities firms on a case-by-case basis — a scenario not covered in the free trade deal. According to Douglas Peters, senior vice-president and chief economist of the Toronto Dominion Bank, "There is no particular breakthrough in the free trade agreement to allow Canadian banks any greater access to U.S. markets than they already have."

The U.S. negotiators were so pleased with their free trade bonanza that they wrote in a confidential briefing paper, later leaked to *Inside U.S. Trade*, that "essentially, in the text we got everything that we wanted." Indeed, they even got something they hadn't originally expected to get — a breakthrough in the crucial field of energy. Before the free trade initiative was even launched, the U.S. had already succeeded in pushing the Mulroney government to retract the National Energy Program. But in the free trade agreement, it was able to go much further, winning a deal that would bar any future Canadian government from imposing a similar nationalistic energy policy.

The agreement also gave the U.S. equal access to Canada's energy resources. This meant that, even in times of scarcity, Canada was prohibited under the free trade agreement from withholding supplies to the U.S. market, and had to provide "proportional access to the diminishing supply." Furthermore, Canada could not set a special preferential energy price for Canadians. Essentially, the U.S. achieved what it had long wanted but had been unable to twist Canada's arm into accepting: a continental energy policy.

In exchange, Canada was given a guarantee that Canadian energy would not be excluded from the U.S. market. While Canadian producers in the past had run into problems selling energy to the U.S. in times of surplus, this concession on the part of the U.S. was nowhere near as important in an energy-hungry world as the one Canada made. Indeed, Canada's willingness to give so much ground on the energy front took many in the U.S. by surprise. It hadn't really occurred to the U.S. National Association of Manufacturers that a free trade deal could include access to Canada's energy, but the association was delighted when it did. "When we got such a great deal on energy, we were crusaders for the deal," says the association's R. K. Morris.

And, although the Americans were clearly thrilled with the energy deal, it was obtained almost without effort. According to U.S. negotiator Merkin, the Canadian side put up little resistance to the U.S. demands on energy. "Believe it or not, while it was very controversial [in Canada] once the agreement was announced, it was not controversial in the negotiations," Merkin recalls. Reisman agrees that the energy provisions weren't controversial, and he dismisses the Canadian environmentalists who expressed concerns about them as "tree huggers."

But perhaps the most stunning U.S. victory was in the area of investments. In the past, the U.S. had bristled when Canada had established nationalistic programs that favoured Canadian business, consumers or workers. Such programs limited the rights of American investors in the Canadian market, placing restrictions on their ownership or requirements on their performance. But under the free trade agreement, Canada agreed to abandon these types of policies, making itself a safe haven for U.S. investment.

For the U.S. National Association of Manufacturers this was perhaps the most important achievement of the free trade deal. "For us, it linked Canadian trade policy to Canadian investment policy. You could no longer adopt an extremely interventionist investment policy without jeopardizing the gains . . . of the trade agreement," says R. K. Morris. In other words, from now on, access to the U.S. market would be linked to Canada's willingness to put in place investment policies the U.S. found acceptable. For the U.S., this was a guarantee that any future Canadian government would remain committed to a market-oriented approach or would face being shut out of the U.S. market — Canada's ultimate fear. "Even if you have a new Liberal government, there won't be a dramatic swing back to [interventionist] economic policies, *because the cost for you would be very high*," said Morris. "It would be hard to overstate the importance of that."

Ottawa, in effect, handed the U.S. a powerful lever over Canadian economic policy and limited Canada's ability in the future to chart an independent course. Morris sums up the situation well: "Canada is still a sovereign country, and can do whatever she pleases, *but not without incurring a risk of damaging trade benefits*, because she has by agreement with us made a link between the two. . . . The two issues have for too long been kept separate around the world." Under the free trade deal, then, Canada retained its sovereignty — as long as it didn't step out of line. This is the freedom of a dog on a leash; as long as he trots obediently at his master's side, he feels free. But if he strains to get away, the leash holds him in check.

By surrendering sovereignty in this way, Canada was not really handing power over to the U.S. government, but rather to the private sector. The U.S. government was simply the enforcer, the police officer who would impose trade penalties on Canada if it deviated from its pro-market commitments. The real recipients of power in the deal were the powerful private interests — on both sides of the border — who had longed to see the hands of government tied. Michael Hart, one of the Canadian negotiators, explained that the Canadian team had little trouble agreeing to U.S. demands on energy because, like the U.S., the Mulroney government took the position that energy allocation should be determined by the marketplace, not by government. Ottawa was willingly abdicating much of its power to control the economy, handing it over to private hands.

"This way, they're finally achieving what a certain segment of the business world wanted — to put a strait-jacket on government," comments Lloyd Axworthy, Liberal MP and outspoken free trade opponent. Axworthy says that he made this point over dinner one night at the Swedish ambassador's Ottawa residence with several prominent pro-free trade advocates. The unanimous response, Axworthy recalls, was agreement: that was exactly what the Canadian negotiators were attempting to do.

The desire to put a strait-jacket on a freely elected government, when it comes right down to it, springs from the desire to place limits on democracy. For all its flaws, government is, after all, the closest thing to the expression of the popular will. To some extent, in a democracy the government is accountable to the people, imperfect as that method of accounting often is. The desire of segments of the business community to place limits on the power of government was really a move to wrest power from the public and place it in the hands of private interests, which were not obliged to go to the polls every few years. The public couldn't vote out the Conrad Blacks or David Culvers if it didn't like the way they operated.

And the Canadian business community showed that it had no particular loyalty to Canada. Indeed, the fact that much of the private sector in Canada was controlled by Americans was not seen as a problem. Key sectors of the Canadian business community became convinced that their interests were more closely aligned with U.S. business than with the Canadian public, which after all might do something rash like elect a government that favoured dangerous reforms — such as redistributing income, insisting on protections for Canadian jobs, or raising corporate taxes. American business was far more reliable.

What business on both sides of the border had in common was a desire to reassert its rights, to ensure for itself a large and growing share of a shrinking national pie in the economic crunch of the eighties and nineties. By putting a strait-jacket on government, business had transferred to itself an enormous amount of power over the economy and the allocation of resources. Business wanted Canadians to learn to expect less, to adjust to the possibility of a lower standard of living and to accept a more passive role in an economy where decisions would increasingly be made, not by the Canadian public, but by private interests. All this could be justified in the name of Globalization and the compelling need to become internationally competitive.

David Culver notes that the concept of Globalization — now a central theme of the business community — had not really crystallized in the minds of Canadian business leaders until the mid 1980s. "I don't think Globalization really came into our vision clearly until '83, '84, '85," he said. Certainly the ideas behind Globalization were really just warmed-over dregs from the past, just the same old survival-of-the-fittest concept dressed up as a new-wave philosophy for the nineties. But its convenient arrival as a repackaged, saleable, even sexy notion in the mid eighties was timely. Just as it became clear that free trade was not going to offer Canada its cherished dream of guaranteed access to the U.S. market, Canadian business became fixed on what free trade really did offer — the perfect prod for getting Canadians to accept a meaner, leaner way of life.

IN JANUARY 1989, well after Mulroney had won his second national election and free trade had become law, a small item in the government's official bulletin, the *Canada Gazette*, set off a small political storm. In its usual dull language, the *Gazette* revealed that the Mulroney government had, some two months earlier, given preliminary approval for a foreign bank licence to American Express.

Almost immediately, it was charged that Mulroney granted Amex the licence as a pay-off to Jim Robinson for his help promoting the free trade deal in the U.S. Certainly there is ample circumstantial evidence to support such a claim.

American Express wanted the license badly, because it would allow the company to gain access to the highly sophisticated network of automatic teller machines that had been developed by the five big Canadian banks. Harry Freeman, the Amex executive vice-president, had spelled out the importance of such access in a February '87 speech to Washington's Brookings Institution: "In consumer finance, linkages with automatic teller machine networks and point of sales networks are crucial for financial services companies." The Canadian banks had invested hundreds of millions of dollars developing the automatic teller system, but a bank licence would permit American Express to plug into the network for a relatively small fee. It would allow Amex to offer its 1.5 Canadian cardholders virtually full banking services, while costing the company almost nothing.

Amex's decision to apply for a foreign banking licence in Canada in 1986 was in keeping with the company's aggressive marketing policies. The only problem was that Amex didn't meet several of the Canadian government's specifications for receiving a licence, as outlined in a series of guidelines prepared by Ottawa in the early eighties. The most serious problem lay in Amex's failure to meet the requirement that a company receiving a foreign bank licence be regulated as a bank in its own home jurisdiction. The purpose of this requirement was to ensure that the parent company was solvent and properly regulated, and thus to prevent bank failure. Because of Amex's extensive involvements in other commercial fields, it had never qualified as a bank in the U.S. Under Canada's guidelines, this would disqualify it for a foreign bank licence.

But Amex was persistent in making its claim, meeting repeatedly with high-ranking government officials, including junior Finance Minister Tom Hockin and deputy Finance Minister Stanley Hartt. A flurry of meetings over a two-year period were recorded in government documents obtained by the press under Freedom of Information requests. They suggest that there was resistance within the bureaucracy to the Amex request — hardly surprising since Amex failed in an important way to meet government guidelines.

Still, on November 21, 1988, the Mulroney cabinet decided to ignore Canada's own guidelines and approve the licence anyway. This alone would have been enough to set tongues wagging. But what made the situation particularly interesting was the fact that this was no ordinary day. It happened to be the day of the highly contentious federal election — the one fought over free trade. It seemed like an odd day for cabinet ministers to be sitting around idly tidying up housekeeping matters; after all, they could have been out of a job the next day. The timing suggested that there was something unusual and important about this approval.

When the approval came to public attention almost two months later, there was immediate speculation that the government had delayed approving the licence until its very last day in power for fear that news of it might leak out and provide fodder for the opposition to charge that Mulroney was helping out a powerful free trade ally. It would have been just the kind of embarrassing revelation that could have made Canadians even more suspicious of free trade, just as they went to the polls in an election almost solely focussed on the issue. Many observers were left wondering if there hadn't been a promise made to Robinson, and Mulroney had simply had to wait for the last possible moment to deliver on it.

The revelation was so suggestive of a deal that even Amex director David Culver concedes that there is "circumstantial evidence in the extreme," and that the last-minute approval of the licence "couldn't have been worse for feeding the suspicious mind." Culver adds that he knows of no deal and doesn't remember the subject ever coming up at an American Express board meeting. Still, Richard Thomson, chairman of the Toronto Dominion Bank, expressed a sentiment no doubt shared by many in the Canadian banking community when he charged at a press conference that it appeared there had been a deal — a charge he later retracted for lack of proof.

Still, the banks insist that the government has shown favouritism to American Express. Under proposed federal legislation, banks will be able to own insurance companies. With its bank licence, Amex too will be able to sell insurance in the Canadian market. But the Canadian banks insist that Amex will have an advantage in the marketing of insurance policies, because it will be able to use a marketing method that fits its needs, while the banks will not be allowed to use the method that fits theirs. For the banks, the most convenient way to market insurance would be through their branches, which are dotted across the country. But the new legislation prohibits this, and requires that insurance be sold from separate premises. American Express, on the other hand, has no bank branches, and prefers to market everything through its credit card — a method that will be permissible under the new legislation.

"What other bloody country in the world would permit that?" protests Bank of Nova Scotia chairman Cedric Ritchie. "It's bucket shop! . . . We look like a third-rate dummy. . . . As a Canadian, you're ashamed."

But, while it's hard to imagine why the government would give an advantage to a foreign bank over its own banks, it's not clear that there was an actual deal over the licence. In saying that, perhaps I risk sounding naive. Let me clarify that I don't find it hard to believe that the Mulroney government is capable of being less than forthright on occasion. And I acknowledge that to accept the government's assertion that the bank licence approval had nothing to do with free trade is roughly equivalent to investing in swampland in Florida.

Still, I'm not sure I believe there was a deal. Certainly, there was an opportunity for one; the subject of a bank licence could easily have surfaced during Mulroney's late night chat with Robinson at the Washington hotel. But if there was a deal, wouldn't Canada or Mulroney have had to get something in exchange? The deal theory implies that we were rewarding Robinson for something he'd done for us, that he'd put all that effort into promoting the free trade agreement as a *favour to Canada*. But this seems like a serious misreading of what happened. Free trade was far more a favour to Robinson and the U.S. than it was to Canada.

Indeed, as we've seen, Robinson had been pushing for free trade everywhere in the world since the early eighties. And the deal with Canada was so beneficial to American business that the biggest problem U.S. multinationals faced was containing their enthusiasm, lest the Canadian public become suspicious. Furthermore, the Canadian agreement included a comprehensive deal covering services — the first international agreement to do so — just in time to set a precedent for Robinson's coveted goal of getting countries around the world to sign a comprehensive deal on services in the GATT negotiations. Rewarding American Express with a Canadian bank licence for helping win a free trade deal was like a prostitute giving her client a warm pair of pyjamas to thank him for the sex.

So, at the risk of being taken for a dupe of government propaganda, I'm going to argue that there was no deal on the American Express bank licence. Now, I don't mean to suggest that there wasn't a flagrant disregard of Canadian guidelines in order to help out a U.S. friend. Obviously there was. It's just that there seems to have been no quid pro quo. What kind of deal is that? Canada got nothing in exchange. Indeed, we got a worse deal on free trade than the U.S. would probably have been prepared to give us had we handled our cards a little better and looked a little less desperate. In some ways, it's too bad that there wasn't a deal; maybe Canada could have something in exchange for acquiescing so completely to Amex's demands — if not secure access to the U.S. market, perhaps at least a warm pair of pyjamas.

So why did Mulroney give Jim Robinson a bank licence? The answer, I suspect, is that Mulroney ignored his nation's banking rules — just as he knowingly signed a free trade deal stripping his own people of control of their country — for no better reason than that Robinson was an enormously powerful U.S. business leader, someone important enough for Mulroney to meet for a late-night session in a Washington hotel. And Mulroney dealt with him as he'd always dealt with the rich and powerful: he gave them what they wanted.

WHATEVER BENEFITS JIM Robinson may have received from free trade, the benefits to Canadians were less clear. As we've seen, the most significant change was perhaps the transfer of power from public to private hands. Indeed, by stripping government of much of its power, the free trade deal — and the whole Globalization philosophy on which it was based — left Canadians with far less control over their destiny.

Thousands of workers living in small communities along the west coast of British Columbia were to be the first to find out exactly what this meant.

7 • COCKTAILS WITH CARROT TOP: HOW THE SALMON GOT AWAY

The desperate band of B.C. fishworkers had just one goal in mind: to stop the trucks streaming across the border into the U.S. In the backs of those massive transport trucks were thousands of pounds of raw salmon, freshly fished off the British Columbia coast and now heading south for processing in U.S. fish plants. For the fishworkers, who had come by bus to this Canada-U.S. border crossing, those crates of salmon represented everything: their livelihood, their future, the survival of their communities. Every truckload crossing the border seemed like one more devastating blow to a group that felt it had been pummelled enough over the past two years.

Before that, the fishworkers had always felt they had a future, although hardly a glamorous one. Working in a fish plant was a difficult and dirty job, with endless hours spent standing in sweaty, smelly plants slicing off the heads of fish and pulling out their guts. But it was a secure job that paid a decent wage, and in many small communities along the B.C. coast, it was often the only work available, particularly for women, Natives and immigrants. British Columbia had been blessed with some of the finest salmon runs in the world, and its fish processing business had been a thriving, internationally competitive industry for more than a century. But the security of that world had been slowly undermined by the actions of the Canadian government since the mid eighties, and by the summer of '89, when angry fishworkers massed at the border, there was widespread fear for the future.

A group of fishworkers angrily pulled open the back of one of the trucks. There, in plain view, were huge crates of raw salmon on their way to U.S. fish plants. In the past, such a shipment would have been illegal. Canadian federal law had long required that salmon caught off the B.C. coast had to be processed in Canada before export. That law, passed in 1908, had been crucial to the creation of the prosperous B.C. fishery, guaranteeing a secure supply of salmon for the hundreds of canning factories that grew up along the coast. But, in the free trade climate of the eighties, Washington had applied intense pressure on Ottawa to abandon the law. Roughly eighty years after it was first put in place, the law had been removed by the Mulroney government.

For the B.C. fishworkers, the whole saga had been baffling. Why had the Canadian government agreed to abandon a law that had served B.C. so well for decades? Ottawa had said it had done everything it could to resist the U.S. demands, but insisted its hands were tied. Yet somehow the government's explanations sounded as fishy as the cargoes of those trucks heading south.

The reality was that decisions about the fate of the B.C. fishery had been made thousands of miles away in Washington, Geneva and Ottawa, by people whose polished lives would have been barely comprehensible to the workers in the fish plants. The final blow had actually come during a quiet round of cocktails at a Washington reception in January 1989. It was during that cocktail hour — before a luncheon meeting between Canadian and American trade negotiators — that the Canadians had tried one last time to win a reprieve from American demands that we abandon the 1908 law. Howie Wilson, who headed up the Canadian trade delegation, had outlined to the head of the U.S. delegation a proposal to replace the old 1908 Canadian law with a compromise solution that would still provide some protection for the B.C. fishery.

But the head of the U.S. delegation was not a man known for compromise. In fact, he was the scourge of Canadian negotiators, the man who had wreaked havoc months earlier as chief U.S. negotiator in the Canada-U.S. free trade talks: Carrot Top, or Peter Murphy. His presence in these fish talks signalled that the U.S. was planning to put up quite a fight. And this time, Canada hadn't even thrown its top prize fighter — Simon Reisman — into the ring. Carrot Top now faced a far easier opponent in Howie Wilson, a career civil servant who had already developed a reputation in the B.C. fish industry for being a "wimp."

Carrot Top listened as Wilson outlined a Canadian compromise solution at the Washington cocktail reception. Wilson had barely finished when Carrot Top told him to put the plan right out of his mind, not to bother tabling it for discussion: the U.S. would not even consider it. By the time the two men and their delegations headed into lunch in the impressive dining room, Canada's chief negotiator had done just as he'd been told: he'd discarded the idea completely.

For the fishworkers back in B.C., eating lunch out of brown paper bags with fish-drenched hands, it was the end of a dream.

IRONICALLY, AS WASHINGTON officials settled into their free trade negotiations with Canada back in the summer of 1986, the West Coast salmon and herring fishery was not high on their list of priorities. While the fishery was an important aspect of the B.C. economy, ranking as the fifth largest industry in the province, it was of relatively little significance to the American West Coast. Years of poor conservation measures in American rivers had eroded the size of the U.S. catch, and little money had been invested in onshore canning facilities. Traditionally, fishermen on the U.S. West Coast had been content to sell their catch unprocessed to Japan.

Canada, on the other hand, had enjoyed a prosperous West Coast fishery for more than a century, based on the Fraser River's abundant salmon and herring resources, which had been carefully preserved. Even before the turn of the century, Canada had found a booming market for canned fish in

England. Salmon was one of the first high-quality foods that could be effectively preserved and, with growing demand for it among England's working class, canning factories quickly sprang up in B.C. to process the local fish for export. With this kind of virtually guaranteed supply and demand, the West Coast canning sector became highly sophisticated. It was one of the first Canadian industries to adopt assembly-line technology.

The industry increasingly formed itself into a cartel, imposing prices on fishermen and guaranteeing itself security of fish supplies. In response, the fishermen had organized themselves into a union in the late nineteenth century and tried to break the power of the Canadian cartel by selling their catch to American companies whenever they could get a higher price from them. The militant fishermen staged a massive strike in 1901 — one of the first major trade union actions in the country — and enlisted the support of the low-paid workers from the Canadian canning factories.

But, in the years that followed, the powerful canning interests managed to lobby Ottawa to bring in legislation that would prevent these maverick fishermen from selling Canada's fish to higher bidders south of the border. That law, passed in 1908, became the backbone of the B.C. fish processing industry, requiring that all herring as well as sockeye and pink salmon be processed in Canada before export.*

Despite its contentious origins in a dispute between fishermen and the powerful canning interests, the law ushered in relative peace in the fishing industry. The fishermen and the fish processing workers united in the forties to form a powerful union, the United Fishermen and Allied Workers, to balance the power of the plant owners. As a result, the fishermen came to share the fishworkers' interest in preserving fish processing jobs in Canada, dropping their demands to be allowed to sell their catch to Americans.

Although there were strikes over the years, the law worked relatively well for both sides, with B.C. fishermen and fishworkers becoming a well-paid and efficient work-force and

* For a detailed history of the fascinating struggles in the fish industry, see Geoff Meggs's book *Salmon: The Decline of a Fishery*, published by Douglas and McIntyre.

canning companies reaping sizeable profits. By the 1980s, it had developed into a business worth $750 million annually, operating state-of-the-art canning facilities that rivalled those anywhere in the world. Even with its unionized workers, the B.C. industry was competitive in world markets, enjoying an international reputation for quality.

It was this sleepy old 1908 law, which had been more or less gathering dust since it was first put on the books, that suddenly came into the gunsights of the trade officials in Washington. Ironically, it was the actions of a Canadian company that alerted Washington to the situation. In 1984 and 1985, a Canadian fish processor had ventured into Alaskan waters to purchase fish from American fishermen. American processors, led by Seattle-based Icicle Seafoods Inc., filed a grievance under U.S. trade law, complaining that they were not allowed equal access to Canadian fish. The U.S. processors had a legitimate point, but what they really wanted was the same kind of protection that the Canadian canners enjoyed. Icicle president Bob Brophy later indicated that he would be content to see the U.S. protect its own fishery by introducing legislation similar to the 1908 Canadian law. But, as the 1908 law came to the attention of the trade establishment in Washington, a more ambitious plan came into focus.

The Canadian law was really a direct contradiction of the free trade philosophy the U.S. was trying to foster in the world. By insisting that Canadian fish be processed in Canada, Ottawa was imposing rules that interfered with the free functioning of the marketplace. It was protecting Canadian jobs through government intervention. It was allowing national boundaries to intrude into economic activity, ensuring that a Canadian natural resource would be reserved for the benefit of Canadians. In short, it was a violation of the most basic tenets of U.S. trade philosophy.

U.S. officials decided in September '86 to take the complaint to GATT. Although GATT rules generally dealt with removing restrictions on imports, a little-used provision in the GATT code also opposed export restrictions. Canada's 1908 law was in essence an export restriction, in that it allowed fish to be exported only after they were processed in Canada. Under the GATT code, the Americans had a strong case and they made their objections forcefully in Geneva to a three-person GATT panel made up of representatives from Hungary, Czechoslovakia and New Zealand. The Canadian government defended its law largely on the basis that, although the law violated the GATT code, it deserved to be excepted on the grounds that it was necessary for conservation — grounds that GATT permitted for exceptions. But the proposition that fish had to be processed in Canada for purposes of conservation and management was far-fetched and unlikely to convince a panel of trade experts dedicated to the notion of knocking down trade barriers.

While all this was going on, the free trade talks between Canada and the U.S. were reaching a climax. Although the fish dispute was a matter that could have been addressed in the deal, both sides agreed to leave it out and accept whatever GATT ruled in the matter. This was a dangerous course for Canada, since the chances of losing at GATT were fairly high.

What made the Canadian action more bizarre was that Canada insisted on and won special provision in the free trade agreement for the *East* Coast fisheries. As a result, the free trade agreement specifically condoned laws enacted by the maritime provinces requiring that east coast fish be processed before export — even though these provincial laws mirrored the federal law protecting the West Coast fish processing industry. When the terms of the trade deal were released in October '87, the B.C. industry charged that the Conservative government had provided special protection for the east coast only because the Tories had more seats to hold onto there, including that of powerful cabinet minister John Crosbie.

But the free trade deal went further: it ruled out the application of export taxes. This was significant because, in the event of a negative ruling from GATT on the West Coast fish processing law, Canada would still have had the option of imposing an export tax on unprocessed B.C. fish — a measure that would have had the same practical effect as the original law, while not technically violating the GATT code. Indeed, export taxes were sometimes used by countries to get around negative GATT rulings. By agreeing to rule out this option in the free trade agreement, Canada was painting itself into a corner on the fish issue.

Only a month after the conclusion of the free trade agreement, the GATT panel announced that it had decided in favour of the U.S. The decision came as a sharp blow to the West Coast fishing industry, which felt it had barely been consulted by the Canadian government as its fate was pondered in places half-way around the globe. The union and the processing industry, usually at odds across the bargaining table, quickly swung into action in a united campaign to push Canada to fight the GATT ruling.

In fact, there was still time to overturn the ruling. It had only come from a GATT panel, and panel decisions had to be approved by the full GATT Council, of which Canada was a member. Indeed, Canada had a veto at the Council, in much the same way that members of the United Nations Security Council have vetoes over Security Council resolutions. With the B.C. fishing industry in an uproar, the Conservative government moved to quell the anxiety. Two weeks after the GATT decision in November '87, federal Fisheries Minister Tom Siddon told the House of Commons that, "What we have here is a panel recommendation which will, in all likelihood, be overturned by the GATT Council." Siddon even went on to pledge to the House that, "We will be opposing that [panel] recommendation when it reaches the GATT Council."

The next day, U.S. processor Bob Brophy commented to the press that he was not insistent on stripping Canada of its export controls, and would be satisfied if there were similar laws to protect American processors. But the moderate approach of the U.S. fish industry was brushed aside. The dispute was now in the hands of U.S. trade officials, who had no desire to back down in the face of victory. The GATT ruling could set a precedent for other industries based on processing other natural resources. It could serve as a useful U.S. tool in arguing for the elimination of similar laws designed to protect local processing jobs in countries all over the world. With a plump Canadian duck lined up perfectly in its gunsight, the U.S. was hardly going to back off from pulling the trigger now.

The Canadian industry, with the union and processing companies still making common cause, kept up the pressure on

Ottawa. All up and down the B.C. coast, where small communities depended heavily on the local fish processing business, town councils passed resolutions backing the industry's campaign. More than 3,000 fishworkers walked off the job for a day of protest in March '88 in Vancouver, Prince Rupert, Victoria, Ucluelet and Steveston, to urge the government not to knuckle under to the GATT panel ruling.

But Ottawa turned out to be more intimidated by the pressure it was receiving from south of the border. At a meeting in Washington in February, U.S. trade officials insisted that Canada implement the GATT ruling before the two sides decided on any future rules for the West Coast fishery. With mounting U.S. pressure, the Canadian government began to retreat. Its own trade experts urged acceptance of the GATT ruling. One government official involved in the issue, who declined to be identified, defends the government's retreat, noting that generally, "Unless the [panel] report was outrageous, the losing party should not stand in the way of adoption."

But, in fact, there were many instances of other countries — including the U.S. and European countries — not accepting GATT panel rulings. Certainly, if Canada had decided to oppose the ruling, it could have found support among many of the ninety-five countries that belonged to GATT. Many of those countries were also signatories of the international rules drawn up in the seventies under the Law of the Sea. The whole thrust of the Law of the Sea — endorsed by both Canada and the U.S. — had been to ensure that nations received the full benefits of the fish off their coasts. Canada had invoked the spirit of the Law of the Sea when it defended its case before the three-person GATT panel, but abandoned the argument once the panel ruled against it. Had Canada wanted to turn this into an issue on the world stage, it could have fought out the point on the far more important platform of the GATT Council, where most of the world's nations were represented.

Indeed, Canada could have undoubtedly lined up considerable support, had it decided to fight the case. While many nations joined GATT in order to increase the number of their trading partners, there was considerable disaffection within GATT over the kinds of free trade rules the organization had sought to impose on the world. GATT's free trade philosphy had generally been pushed by the industrialized nations, particularly the U.S., and had primarily benefitted those nations. Third World countries had found their hands tied when they attempted to impose restrictions — such as tariffs — to ensure local development. Now, the U.S. was increasingly trying to use GATT to target non-tariff restrictions too, and Third World countries were finding many of their other laws designed to encourage local development under attack as well.

The Canadian fish processing law was a perfect example of the kind of law the U.S. objected to — either in the Third World or in an advanced country like Canada. The law ensured that one of Canada's key natural resources — fish — would be reserved for the benefit of Canadians. Many Third World nations had resorted to similar types of laws to try to prevent their countries from being mere export warehouses for large multinationals, with little of the benefit of their natural resources accruing to their own people.

As the U.S. increasingly targeted these "non-tariff barriers" at the Uruguay Round of the GATT talks in the late eighties, there was strong resistance from many Third World countries. "There's a monumental struggle out there between national sovereignty and the transnational corporations," says Jim Sinclair of the B.C. fishermen's union. Sinclair faults Canada for not seeking supporters more actively among other GATT nations to challenge the assumptions in the panel ruling against Canada. Of course it would have been difficult to do so when Canada had so fully endorsed the concept of free trade. "Once you philosophically buy into free trade, all the rest falls into place," argues Sinclair. Certainly, Ottawa's embrace of the free trade philosophy made it harder to resist the logic of the GATT ruling, which was firmly rooted in free trade ideology.

So, despite his pledge that Canada would veto the GATT ruling, Siddon joined Trade Minister Pat Carney four months later in announcing that Canada would not exercise its veto, paving the way for the GATT Council to adopt the panel report the following day. Siddon and Carney tried to soften the blow to B.C. by pledging to replace Canada's rejected law with a compromise that would require fish be landed and handled in some way in Canada. The compromise enraged both sides: the Americans were angry that Canada had not completely abandoned its protectionist approach in light of the GATT decision, while the B.C. industry was furious that Ottawa had allowed it to be stripped of its protection.

To appease the Canadian industry, Ottawa appointed a committee of union and company representatives to advise it on how to proceed. The committee had little trouble coming up with a compromise solution: a new law requiring that B.C. salmon and herring be landed and eviscerated in Canada before export. Such a law would fall short of the old law requiring full processing before export, but at least it would guarantee that the fish would be cut open in Canada. Once they had gone under the knife here, the theory went, it would make economic sense to process them here as well. This would get around the GATT ruling and, it was hoped, keep the domestic processing industry intact.

So by the time Howie Wilson was set to face off against Carrot Top in Washington, the lines were clearly drawn between U.S. trade officials and the Canadian industry. What was less clear was whose side the Canadian government was on. Mike Hunter, president of the Fisheries Council of B.C., which represents the seven largest Canadian processing companies, says there appeared to be more fighting between Ottawa and its own industry advisory committee than between Ottawa and Washington. In a sense, Ottawa had already gone over to the American side with its decision not to veto the GATT panel ruling and its willingness to give up the possibility of export taxes in the free trade agreement. With these two steps, Canada had essentially accepted the notion that Ottawa no longer had the right to impose controls over the management of its own resources to ensure jobs for Canadians.

Indeed, even before Howie Wilson met Murphy for the lunch-time negotiation session in January '89, Wilson had tried to prepare the members of his industry advisory committee for disappointment. While promising them he would make a pitch for their evisceration proposal, he had warned them that the Americans would never accept it. So when he went off to meet Murphy for lunch on January 17, the industry committee members, waiting in an annex of the Canadian embassy, were already apprehensive about their negotiator's apparent lack of resolve. They ate pizza and waited nervously.

When Wilson mentioned the evisceration proposal to Murphy casually over cocktails before lunch, he was not surprised by the vehemence of Murphy's rejection. And Wilson had little trouble abandoning the idea. After all, it didn't really fit with the new free trade agenda Canada had signed up for. More worrisome to Wilson was Murphy's threat that, if Canada didn't resolve this issue to U.S. satisfaction quickly, the U.S. would launch trade retaliation against Canada. With the evisceration option off the table, or never even on the table, the Canadian negotiating team was reduced to arguing for a simple landing requirement — that fish be landed and counted in B.C. — before export.

Wilson reported back to the advisory committee after lunch that the negotiations now centred on whether or not this simple landing requirement would be acceptable to the Americans. Enraged that the Canadian negotiators had simply abandoned their evisceration proposal, both the union and the company representatives stormed out of the Canadian embassy in protest. Jack Nichol, president of the fishermen's union, recalls the group's utter frustration with the Canadian effort: "The Canadians turn tail and run in the face of any American resistance."

Hunter, from the employers' council, was equally disgusted. Several years earlier, Hunter had served for a while as chief Canadian negotiator during the talks over the Pacific Salmon Treaty, and had become accustomed to American pushiness and threats — threats that the Canadian delegation learned were best ignored. But in these negotiations Canada seemed to be traumatized by the possibility of U.S. retaliation, Hunter recalls. "It seemed to us that every time the U.S. delivered a bluff, Canada jumped to attention. It was almost laughable," he said. "Everyone went back to Ottawa to shake and quiver."

With his own industry advisors walking out in protest, Wilson returned to the bargaining table that afternoon only to discover that the Americans still weren't satisfied with the pound of flesh they'd extracted from Canada. They sensed more weaknesses in the Canadian position. Canada was now arguing that it was necessary to land all fish — for conservation purposes. But this was a far-fetched proposition and Murphy wasn't buying it. With negotiations at a stalemate, both sides agreed to refer the matter to the dispute settlement mechanism of the free trade agreement.

A five-member panel, with three Canadians and two Americans, was set up to resolve the dispute. But its focus was restricted to the narrow question of whether a Canadian landing requirement was necessary for conservation purposes, since Canada had given up fighting for anything more. As far as the union and fish processing companies of B.C. were concerned, this was far from the central issue. Conservation was certainly important, and Canada had a good record for it. But if there was no Canadian industry to protect, what was the point of the Canadian government spending tens of millions of dollars each year — as it did — in fish management and conservation measures? "Why would we produce salmon in B.C. at your expense and mine in order for an American processor to benefit?" asks Hunter.

In the end, the free trade panel ruled that Canada could require that *most* of the fish had to be landed, but not all of them. It said that 10 to 20 percent of the Canadian catch each year could be sold directly off the boats without ever being brought onto Canadian soil. Although the Canadian negotiators were pleased that the panel had largely accepted their conservation argument, the Canadian industry was unimpressed; the ruling would do nothing to keep fish processing in Canada.

But the Americans were still not satisfied, and a further round of negotiations between the two sides followed, once again headed up by Howie Wilson and Peter Murphy. In the final agreement that was reached, Canada's landing requirement was further eroded: 20 percent of the catch could be sold directly off the boats in 1990, and 25 percent in 1991 and each of the next two years. After that, the whole matter would be reviewed again. The Canadian negotiators claimed that this agreement included greater safeguards for conservation, but the Canadian industry was once again left baffled, wondering how the Canadian side had actually managed to give up even more ground after the matter had apparently been settled by the "binding" dispute settlement panel.

FOR WEEKS DURING the summer of 1989, as the two former allies turned into bitter enemies across the bargaining table, the salmon sped relentlessly towards their spawning ground up the Fraser River. The arrival of millions of salmon from the vast stretches of the Pacific Ocean was an event anticipated eagerly each year by thousands who made their living catching, gutting, canning and selling the fish. The fishing season lasted about six weeks, but the optimal fishing period — when the bulk of the salmon was within fishing reach — was really only two weeks. The boats had to be there, ready, or a year's catch would be missed.

For both labour and management, the stakes were high. The fish came only once a year. As July wore on, the processing companies and the workers were deadlocked in what was becoming one of the nastiest disputes in the industry's 100-year history. Both sides waited for the other to blink. But behind the mounting rhetoric and suspicions in the two camps there was the gnawing realization that time was running out. The fish were coming!

After making common cause against the GATT ruling for two years, the industry was now badly split. Although tough negotiations in the B.C. salmon fishery were nothing new, the two sides had reached an impasse this year that seemed insoluble. The companies were demanding dramatic concessions from the union, particularly from the shoreworkers who performed the unglamorous job of pulling out the guts and preparing the fish for canning.

Demands for concessions were familiar fare in the early stages of fish negotiations. The processing companies were fond of pointing to the lower wages paid to shoreworkers south of the border, where non-unionized fish plants kept wages low and offered workers little in the way of benefits or job security. But the Canadian processors traditionally abandoned their demand for concessions in the final stages of bargaining. There was plenty of money to be made in the B.C. fishery, and, as profits in the industry had grown, so had union wages.

But now, suddenly, the rules had changed. The GATT ruling and the free trade agreement had suddenly handed the processors enormous new leverage over their workers. Since Canadian fish could be sold south of the border, fishworkers in B.C. were now in competition with the low-paid U.S. fishworkers. The Canadian workers would have to let their wages drop to American levels or face the prospect of losing their jobs, as fish processing increasingly shifted to the U.S. On the other hand, the Canadian processing companies, many of whom owned fishing fleets, could still benefit from sales made to the U.S. And, as time went on, they could relocate their own production south of the border, as some of them were already doing. The mobility of capital insulated them, to some extent, from the full blow of the changes wrought by free trade. Mike Hunter, from the fisheries council, says that the companies in his organization want to stay in Canada, but "capital will go where the return is greatest."

The companies were up-front about their new offensive. The Fish Processors' Bargaining Association handed out leaflets to workers saying that "significant change must be made if the B.C. fishing industry is going to be able to stay in business." The leaflets argued bluntly, "We have to cut costs. To do that, labour costs must be reduced." And in a letter to its workers, J.S. McMillan Fisheries Ltd., one of the biggest processors, linked the concessions clearly to the new free trade environment: "GATT is going to mean changes. They will not happen overnight, but we must start preparing for the tough competitive battle to come. . . . We are not 'gutting' your contract. Some adjustments, yes. . . . We are attempting to establish the competitive environment that free trade will thrust on this industry in the future."

The leverage of the companies was increased by the eagerness of some counties in Washington state to attract new investment to their depressed regions. Local governments and business associations quickly dispatched information packets to would-be Canadian investors, offering a wide array of tax credits and special programs available to companies interested in investing in their county. "Included is information on Business and Occupational Tax Credits and information on Sales Tax

Deferrals. . . . Additionally, included is information on various public supported funding programs that are available," advised a covering letter from the Economic Development Association of Skagit County in response to a request from one Vancouver processing firm.

For the union, the acceptance of concessions meant a slow and steady trek to a lower standard of living. The hard-fought gains of the fishworkers over the years would be whittled away until their wages matched those south of the border — some $5 below the $13 an hour earned by unionized workers in the B.C. plants. And would it stop there? What was to prevent the companies from then insisting on parity with Mexican fishworkers, who earned a small fraction of even what the American workers earned? If you accepted the need to match American wages, the logic of matching Mexican wages next was irresistible. "We can't make our labour rates the cheapest in the world," says union spokesman Jim Sinclair. "At some point, there is no point in working if you don't make enough to feed your kids."

The union had an added problem to contend with. Although the companies were seeking concessions from all union members — including the fishermen and "tendermen" who worked on the boats — by far the biggest concessions were demanded of the shoreworkers. It was their jobs that were vulnerable, now that there was no longer a law requiring that fish be processed in Canada. As the salmon approached in those hot days of July '89, this disparity created growing tension within the union, which represented both those on the boats and those on the shore.

On July 21, just days before the expected peak of the sockeye run to the Fraser, the union went out on strike, with all sections of the union voting in favour. The situation quickly turned hostile, as companies sought injunctions against picketing and brought in scab crews to man company-owned fishing boats. As companies loaded tonnes of B.C. salmon onto trucks, union pickets rushed to the border. The event, broadcast across the country that night, brought to the public the poignant sight of Canadian workers desperately trying to prevent the flow of an unprocessed natural resource across the border.

Still, the companies had succeeded in exacerbating the tensions between the different sections of the union, by softening still further demands for concessions from the fishermen and convincing Native fishermen to return to their boats. With support for the strike weakening among the fishermen by the early days of August, the union decided to release them to fish before the entire season was lost. Several days later, after seventeen tense days of picketing and occupations in communities all along the B.C. coast, the union settled. The final package, worked out by a mediator, largely referred the issue of concessions to a provincial Industrial Inquiry Commission that would be empowered to resolve the question. The strike — the most bitter fish strike in decades — had ended inconclusively, with the free trade agenda still hanging over the industry.

FOR GLOBALIZATION ENTHUSIASTS, what happened in the B.C. fishery is simply Globalization in action, as the industry is sorted into two camps: the quick and the dead. If the B.C. processors and their workers prove inventive and adaptable, maybe they will be lucky and end up in the quick camp. If not, they may end up dead, like the limp fish in the trucks heading south.

What is remarkable about this is how unnecessary it all seems. Why have we brought this do-or-die scenario upon ourselves? We had a system in place that had worked well for the past hundred years, and indeed was still working well until we tampered with it. And for what? There were no changes that happened in the world compelling us to do this. There was nothing in the new-fangled computer technology and high-tech wizardry that dictated the export of raw Canadian fish. Fish are still just plain fish, as they were a hundred years ago. What dictated such a change was nothing more than a devotion to the Globalization ideology, pitting worker against worker in a deadly struggle for survival.

The Mulroney government's obedient acceptance of this ideology as its guiding philosophy — at the request of the U.S. and the multinational business community — led it to abandon the competitive advantage that Canada had always enjoyed in world fish markets: our fish. It was our abundant supply of fish — and our ability to take full advantage of this natural resource through public policies aimed at economic development and conservation — that made us successful on the world fish front. What's wrong with that? Isn't that just being sensible, making use of our natural endowments, in the same way people strive to make the most of their natural talents? Canada is a country richly blessed with resources. This is clearly one of the reasons we've ended up a rich nation. Why not make use of these resources?

We have abandoned this natural advantage, opting instead to play by the rules of Globalization, where countries slug it out in a desperate bid to attract capital. In this lopsided game, all the cards are in the hands of those with capital and nations are obliged to bid for this capital with low wages and low corporate taxes. Without a law guaranteeing that Canadian fish will be processed in Canada, Canadians must compete by these Globalization rules, offering up lower wages to match those in the U.S. and eventually those in Mexico.

Globalization advocates often argue that we should accept this agenda willingly, since it benefits the low-wage countries by channelling much-needed capital to them. But a drop in Canadian wages would only put further downward pressure on wages in the U.S. and Mexico — or whatever low-wage country we happened to be competing with — as workers in these countries would be obliged to let their wages drop still more to maintain their competitive advantage. The result would be a "race to the bottom," with nations all over the world being played off against each other in a quickening orgy of economic desperation.

Once again, we must ask who the beneficiaries of all this are. Clearly, not those competing in the race to the bottom. The beneficiaries are rather those with capital, who sit on the sidelines and cheer. Indeed, the B.C. fish processing companies showed a real keenness for having their workers join in the race towards lower wages. Throughout the battle with the U.S., the Canadian companies fought stalwartly alongside the union, in the interests of preserving a nationalist system that had served them well. But once the battle was lost, the future prospects for the companies and the union were clearly different. The companies moved quickly to take advantage of the opportunities available to them, wielding their new-found power over their workers unabashedly. There was nothing particularly insidious about their behaviour. Indeed, they were doing exactly what companies are supposed to do: maximize profits — and ignore any borders that get in the way of that goal.

But the situation is worrisome to anyone concerned about preserving the industry in Canada, particularly now, with the B.C. fishery at something of a crossroads. The future salmon markets lie not so much in traditional canning, but in freeze-and-microwave dinner packages. A great deal of money has to be spent in adapting the fish plants for this new production. The question is: Where will it be spent? The lure of low American wages and taxes has already attracted B.C. fish companies, according to Mike Hunter. Three of the four largest fish processors have invested in U.S. plants. And while the companies are not dismantling their large Canadian operations, in which they have invested hundreds of millions of dollars over the years, Hunter notes that "virtually all new investment by Canadian firms is going into Washington and Alaska."

Joe Weiler, a law professor at the University of British Columbia who specializes in labour law, argues that the new situation in the B.C. fishery could lead to greater efficiencies and an improved new relationship between workers and employers. As companies win concessions that undermine union power, the union bureaucracy will be weakened, leading to a new arrangement in which more decision making is vested with workers on the plant floor, according to Weiler.

But, like many Globalization enthusiasts, Weiler appears to be indulging in a little wishful thinking. What clearly *is* happening is a transfer of power from workers to companies, as companies now have the clout to demand concessions from their workers and back up those demands with the real threat of moving operations elsewhere. The delicate balance of power that existed over the years between the companies and the workers — and that kept labour strife in the industry at a relatively low level — is now gone, as power has shifted dramatically to the corporate side. "The whole social equation of the industry has been altered," says Rob Morley, the chief negotiator for the companies in the 1989 strike.

Weiler's idyllic vision of a more harmonious labour-management situation can happen only if employers prove to be benevolent with their new-found power. Weiler's scenario calls for employers to think of creative new ways to increase the power of individual workers and, presumably, forgo the temptation to increase their profits at the workers' expense. While this sounds nice, there have been few signs of such employer benevolence so far. Certainly the kinds of "creative" solutions that employers showed an interest in during the 1989 strike were such time-honoured favourites as paying the work-force less and trying to break the power of the union. The cutting edge of Globalization has shown a strong attraction to the strong-armed solutions of centuries past.

Some supporters of the new Globalization agenda for the B.C. fisheries — including the *Globe and Mail* editorial board in faraway Toronto — see exciting new competitive opportunities for independent B.C. fishermen. These fishermen, who do not work for the big processing companies, "will be able to sell their catch to the highest bidder," instead of being restricted to bidders in their own country, said the *Globe* in an October 1989 editorial. The fishermen will be free from the "profitable monopoly" long enjoyed by the large Canadian companies, the *Globe* contended. While the *Globe* has a point about this monopoly power of the companies, it is naive to assume that this monopoly power will end at the border. Indeed, free trade paves the way for growing integration of the industry, with monopoly power concentrated in a few hands spanning the border.

Furthermore, with or without free trade, the independent fishermen have little real hope of gaining much bargaining power over the giant processing companies, according to Don Cruickshank, former president of Seafood Products Ltd., a successful B.C. processor. "Are there still red-necks who think that they will receive higher fish prices as a result of the GATT ruling? Give your head a shake," says Cruickshank, who has more than thirty years' experience in the B.C. industry. "Fishmongers, on either side of the border, have never been noted for their benevolence. You will get exactly what the buyers feel they must pay while maximizing their profits, and not one penny more."

Certainly, for the fishworkers and their families living on the B.C. coast, the changes are potentially devastating. Ironically, their case has been championed by Cruickshank, a prosperous employer until his retirement in 1988. A resident of the resource town of Port Hardy, B.C., Cruickshank notes that fishworkers are paid roughly the same as workers in other B.C. resource industries. "My neighbours and friends are loggers, miners, fishermen and fishworkers, and their life-style is not particularly one of affluence," he says. "They are simply workers who meet their mortgage payments, pay their taxes, feed their kids, and hopefully have enough left over for a beer on Saturday night." In other words, they are ordinary people leading ordinary lives — not the lazy, spoiled Canadians often conjured up by Globalization buffs.

But their world has been jeopardized, for no other reason than that Ottawa decided to accept an ideology that calls for government to surrender its power to shape the economy. In embracing this business agenda, the Mulroney government has decided that the West Coast fishery — and the thousands of Canadians who depend on it for survival — can be sacrificed on the altar of Globalization.

8 • TEQUILAS AND GROUP SEX: WHO'S REALLY RUNNING THE COUNTRY?

The show-down over the Goods and Services Tax in the fall of 1990 was one of the most dramatic political confrontations in recent Canadian history. Opposed to the Mulroney government's new sales tax was virtually the entire country — consumers, labour, small business, the right-wing National Citizens' Coalition, the nationalist Pro-Canada Network, and just about anyone else who bothered to express an opinion. With the government turning a deaf ear to their protests, the anti-GST cause was taken up by the Liberal majority in the Senate with Liberal leader Allan MacEachen leading the charge. MacEachen was branded by many commentators as a dictatorial figure who had usurped the role of the democratically elected government and made himself the supreme power in the land.

There is tremendous irony in these accusations. Not only was MacEachen championing a popular cause in holding up passage of the GST — perhaps the most unpopular piece of legislation in decades — but he was taking on a government that had been anything but democratic in its handling of the new tax, to the point of making a mockery of the very notion of elections and public accountability.

The GST in many ways became the flash-point of confrontation between the Canadian public and those pushing the new business agenda. Although the tax was only one item on the agenda, it was a key one for business and one that also hit the public very directly. The GST example illustrates how dramatically out of sync the forces pushing the new agenda were with the Canadian public — and also how determined they were to put the agenda in place anyway.

Although the Tories had vaguely outlined plans for the GST before the November '88 election — in dull government tax documents — they had avoided like the plague any mention of the proposed tax during the election campaign. Indeed, the tax had only surfaced by accident in the campaign, and the government had moved quickly to quash any kind of public debate on the issue. The problems began when Tory MP Don Blenkarn, Chairman of the House of Commons Finance Committee, made some remarks about the revenue-raising potential of the tax to a conference of tax specialists — an event that would normally have passed unnoticed. But when his comments were reported the next day on the front page of the *Globe and Mail,* the issue was suddenly thrust before the public in the midst of an election campaign. Terrified by the prospect of public awareness of the tax, Mulroney and Michael Wilson both vehemently denied Blenkarn's reported statements that the tax would raise billions of dollars in extra revenue. They insisted that the new sales tax would simply replace an existing tax and would be "revenue-neutral"; that is, it would raise no additional revenue — a claim they abandoned once the election was over.

With the government's assurances in the heat of the election campaign, the issue faded into oblivion. Only after the election, as the government proceeded almost immediately to introduce the sweeping new tax, did Canadians come to see what Blenkarn had inadvertently made public months earlier: they were about to be gouged. Wilson began openly speaking about the extra revenues from the tax as a tool of deficit reduction. By this point, of course, it was too late for Canadians to lodge their democratic protest at the election polls. All they could do was rage against the tax and pray that Allan

MacEachen and the unelected Senate would stop it. So much for democracy.

There was a deeper irony in all this. While commentators, particularly in the business press, fumed at the notion that MacEachen was now running the country, the real truth was quite different. MacEachen was simply using the constitutional powers of the Senate to hold up passage of a bill that was almost universally hated and that few Canadians had even been aware of until after the election. In the end he lost, when the Mulroney government simply appointed an extra batch of senators to give the Tories a majority in the upper chamber. The real power in the country clearly lay elsewhere — in the hands of whoever was pushing the government to persevere with the GST, despite overwhelming public opposition.

As the controversy dragged on for months, with opposition to the tax growing and the Mulroney government sinking lower and lower in the polls, the fascinating question — one that the commentators never asked — was: What enormously powerful force was behind this loathsome tax anyway? Who was so powerful that he or she could keep this tax on the government's agenda, month after month, against the will of virtually an entire country? Now that's power! Forget Allan MacEachen! If we could just unmask these individuals surely we would know who was *really* running the country.

This then is our quest — to find out who these people are and what they want with our country. Michael Wilson himself provided an important clue in our search for the real power behind the Mulroney throne. In his February '90 budget — which introduced a number of changes amounting to a serious assault on Canada's social programs — Wilson pointed out that his stringent measures were simply another step in the government's "broad plan that we set out in November 1984." He was referring to the government's *Agenda for Economic Renewal.* As we saw in Chapter 4, this document was a blueprint for changing the country, above all for transferring power from the democratically elected government to the private sector — a domain the public has almost no power to control. Wilson returned to this theme in his 1990 budget with a reminder that the government was trying to bolster the private sector and prod Canadians "to change their ways of doing things."

Wilson went on in his budget speech to give us a clue as to who the people behind the broad plan might be: ". . . let's be clear about the real source of pressure for change. It is not the government." Then Wilson, as he came to the point of identifying the real source of power, alluded vaguely to the mysterious powers of the new global marketplace. "It is the rapidly evolving and increasingly competitive world in which we must earn our way," he said.

Once we sift through pious expressions like "we must earn our way," we can zero in on the key phrase, "increasingly competitive world." Wilson shied away from telling us who the forces were behind this "increasingly competitive world." It was enough for us to know that there were anonymous forces out there demanding that we redesign Canada in order to make it more "competitive." But business commentators who interpreted Wilson's remarks for us came closer to identifying these forces, explaining that Canada must be redesigned in order to satisfy disgruntled "international investors."

Dunnery Best, commenting on the budget in the *Globe and Mail's Report on Business* several days later, noted that the real audience Wilson was performing for was those who handle investments in the international money market centres. "When they speak, Canadians must jump," wrote Best, who was director of research in the treasury department of First City Trust. "They are the managers of the vast ocean of international capital, which flows unimpeded by political boundaries, seeking the highest yields and the greatest security. And their priorities don't necessarily coincide with those of Canada."

These international investors, then, are presumably the ones who are the "real source of pressure for change." Their power lies in the fact that they hold some 20 percent of the country's debt, and that we need their money to keep paying the interest we owe on the debt. Government and business leaders tell us that this gives them enormous power over government policies, that we must make Canada acceptable to them or they'll take their money elsewhere. These must be the people, then, who are really running the country.

But who are they, and what do they want? The concept of "international investors" conjures up images of jet setters lounging around indulging themselves. So are we to believe that the crucial decisions about Canada's future are being made wherever these international jet setters congregate — on the beaches of southern France, the night-clubs of Rome, the discos of Rio — in between tequilas and group sex parties? To uncover the whims of these elusive international investors, we must talk to someone who handles their money.

THE SHIMMERING GOLD exterior of the Royal Bank Tower in Toronto suggests the kind of place where you'd expect to find the truly powerful. Up on the seventeenth floor of the bank's north tower, it seems that we are hot on the trail. The entire floor is occupied by the Toronto branch of something called the BT Bank of Canada, a wholly owned subsidiary of Bankers Trust Company of New York. In the fast-paced world of round-the-world, round-the-clock commercial banking, Bankers Trust is on the cutting edge. With large operations in Tokyo, Bonn, London and more than twenty other world financial centres, Bankers Trust was a pioneer throughout the eighties in developing exotic new financial instruments for sophisticated investors. Indeed, among the thousands of commercial banks that came to prominence in the eighties, Bankers Trust ranked among the top three — along with Citibank and Manufacturers Hanover Trust — in the lucrative takeover-financing business. When American Express's subsidiary, Shearson Lehman, was trying to line up about $25 billion to finance the takeover of RJR Nabisco, the chairman of Bankers Trust was one of the first people to be called.

I am sitting in the well-appointed lobby of BT Bank's Toronto office, contemplating the power that must be wielded by this institution that few Canadians have ever even heard of. Jerry Del Missier, the bank's vice-president of capital markets, has agreed to see me, and I am quietly bracing myself to meet an immensely powerful individual. When he comes out, he looks disappointingly normal. I can't even say that he quietly exudes power. Mostly, he exudes youth and a pleasant aftershave. He is clean-cut and fashionably dressed, in shirt-sleeves with suspenders. When I ask him how old he is, he informs me that he is twenty-eight — *and a half.*

I am struck by this description, which he gives quite naturally. It's a while since I've heard anyone give their age in fractions, except perhaps for children desperate to sound older than they are, in order to convince adults that they should be allowed to stay up late or go somewhere without a chaperon. But then it occurs to me that this is a young man in a hurry, much like the money that his bank hurriedly shuffles all over the world. If millions of dollars can flit from Tokyo to Bonn or New York to Hong Kong in a fraction of a second, surely measuring one's age in whole years does seem a trifle slow. When I seem surprised by his youth, Del Missier informs me that the past president of BT Bank of Canada was only twenty-nine before he was transferred to higher things in London, and that the chairman of BT International Capital Markets, with world-wide responsibilities, is only thirty-five. At the ripe old age of twenty-eight and a half, Del Missier, who was born in Sudbury, Ontario, the son of a blue-collar immigrant from Italy, better hurry if he wants to keep up in this lightning-paced world of global finance.

For all his youth, Del Missier seems to have a good understanding of the wants and needs of the international investor. I can envision him visiting such a mogul on the beaches of St. Tropez: Del Missier's lean, moistened body glistening in the sun as he lays out the differentials between yen, pounds, marks or dollars to the corpulent investor sprawled comfortably beneath the shade of an umbrella. "And how is the money to be invested this week?" Del Missier asks. "Will it be spread-locks, forward start swaps, yield curve spread plays, look-back options or super-floaters? And would you like a little more suntan lotion on your back, sir?"

In fact, Del Missier quickly destroys my illusions, explaining that the elusive investor is rarely the exotic jet setter lying on a beach or draped over a casino table. Rather, he or she is someone much duller — usually an executive in a dark suit working for a large multinational insurance company, financial institution or pension fund. Some of the big investors in Canada's debt, for instance, include Canadian insurance companies like London Life, Confederation Life, Manufacturers Life, as well as the Japanese firms Asahi Mutual Life and Nippon Life.

Every Thursday the government of Canada tries to borrow somewhere between $4 billion and $6 billion to cover the interest costs it constantly owes on its $400 billion debt. In order to raise the money, it auctions short-term Canadian treasury bills — typically, three-month, six-month or one-year bills. At the auctions, the treasury bills are sold to bidders from banks and brokerage houses, which each may buy as much as $300 million worth. These institutions then turn around and, for a commission, sell the treasury bills they have just bought to investors all over the world, often through their overseas offices.

Even as I sit talking to Del Missier, there is a flurry of excitement in the BT Canada office. We are sitting in a meeting room with a large window that looks into a room full of computers where traders are hunched over their screens watching for developments in money centres around the world. A group of traders gathers around a computer at one end of the room and Del Missier says that there seems to be a sudden rally of interest in bond markets in Hong Kong. At this point, it's not clear what's going on. Every now and then he is called out of the room briefly for consultation. It is all very important.

Del Missier explains that international investors can be picky, particularly since there are so many countries, as well as individual companies, keen to borrow their money. Above all, investors want to put their funds somewhere where they will be safe. There is no point in lending money to a borrower who cannot repay it when the loan is due. Beyond this, investors buying government bonds or treasury bills are largely looking for two things: high interest rates and a stable or appreciating currency.

The value of high interest rates is obvious: the higher the interest, the better the return for the investor. Since the interest rate is fixed at the time of purchase, investors want to be sure that they are locking in their money at a favourable rate. The stability of the currency is also crucial. Investors buying six-month Canadian treasury bills, for instance, are gambling on the fate of the Canadian dollar, since their loans will be repaid, with interest, in Canadian dollars.

Abruptly, the door flings open and a young trader beckons to Del Missier to come quickly. "Everything's falling apart," the trader says. I ponder the possibilities: the Tokyo stock exchange has been bombed, Nippon Life has pulled its investments from Canada, the Hong Kong bond traders have all gone fishing. As I think of other things that could cause alarm in the fragile world of finance, a smile cracks over the face of the young trader in the doorway; he's only kidding, just playing a joke on his young boss. A brief moment of levity in the corridors of power? It's nice to know that the kids running the country have a sense of humour.

We resume our discussion. So when international investors try to decide where to put their money, these are the factors that they look at: is the borrower sufficiently solvent to repay the loan as agreed, is the interest rate good, and is the currency strong? What they are really looking for is a certain pattern of government policies that will ensure these conditions. And the pattern they are looking for is largely the same all over the world. International investors have no national loyalty; they simply want the best return on their investments. So whether they put their money in Canada or Colombia or Ghana or Switzerland is determined by how these countries measure up on the criteria investors deem important.

But what foreign investors deem to be important is, needless to say, often very different from what a country's population considers important. A low infant mortality rate, a clean environment or an equitable distribution of the country's resources may be pleasing to the bulk of the population, but does little to boost a country's rating in the eyes of international investors. On the other hand, high interest rates and low government spending might bring hardship for the majority of the population, while attracting foreign investors in droves.

Basically, international investors are looking for a set of government policies that include high interest rates, tight control of credit, cuts to government spending, removal of trade barriers, export promotion and deregulation and privatization. Indeed, this is the agenda countries must adopt in order to receive loans from the International Monetary Fund (IMF) and the World Bank, the powerful international credit agencies set up by the U.S. after World War II to rebuild the international economy along lines favoured by private western capital. Both these institutions use largely the same criteria as private international investors for determining which countries will qualify for their loans. Both the IMF and the World Bank routinely demand the agenda outlined above as a condition of their loans.

Indeed, this agenda amounts to what the Ecumenical Coalition for Economic Justice calls the "standard menu" insisted on by the IMF and World Bank. In a perceptive book on the world debt crisis called *Recolonization or Liberation,* this Canadian church-sponsored group has outlined how the demands in the "standard menu" have become more rigid since 1985. Whereas their loan requirements were once confined to economic stabilization measures, these powerful agencies now routinely impose a "structural adjustment program" on borrowing countries that often amounts to a complete overhaul of the economic structure and priorities of these nations. A statement by the Institute for African Alternatives following a 1987 conference in London, England on the impact of the IMF and the World Bank put it this way: "Under structural adjustment [the IMF and the World Bank] do not merely supervise individual sectors of the economy as in the past. . . . They now manage each country entirely. . . . This is the recolonization of Africa."

The result is to drive these countries deeper into poverty. As high interest rates are imposed and credit tightened, domestic industries and farmers are driven out of business, destroying the local supply of food and basic items. Under the IMF regimen, the focus is placed on developing crops for export. But the key export commodities — such as sugar, coffee, bananas, oil, copper and bauxite — are each controlled by a handful of multinational corporations, leaving Third World countries with little bargaining power over the price they receive for their commodities.*

---

* Statistics prepared by the United Nations Conference on Trade and Development (UNCTAD) show that the vast majority of world trade in the following exports is controlled, in each case, by fewer than six large corporations: 85 to 90 percent of the world's wheat, 60 percent of sugar, 85 to 90 percent of coffee, 70 to 75 percent of bananas, 90 percent of forest products, 75 percent of crude oil, 80 to 85 percent of copper, 90 to 95 percent of iron ore, 75 to 80 percent of tin and 80 to 85 percent of bauxite.

With powerful corporations driving down the commodity prices paid to producing nations, the Third World countries are left unable to meet their debts and obliged to accept even more stringent terms in the next round of borrowing. In its 1990 annual report *The State of the World's Children,* UNICEF minces few words about this vicious circle of debt in which the Third World is trapped: "It is essential to strip away the niceties of economic parlance and say that . . . the developing world's debt, both in the manner in which it was incurred and in the manner in which it is being 'adjusted to' . . . is simply an outrage against a large section of humanity."

While this restructuring amounts to an outrage against humanity in the eyes of the UN, it is viewed as an essential part of the new world economic order by the international business and investment community. That's why the Third World debt situation has been of interest to those, like Jim Robinson, who are keen to tear down national barriers and create safe harbours for U.S. investment. As we've seen Robinson proposed a complex scheme to restructure the world's debt in a way that would deliver ever greater power over Third World economies to the U.S. In a detailed speech to the Overseas Development Council in Washington in February '88, Robinson made it clear that he didn't think the existing powers of the IMF and World Bank went far enough in obliging Third World countries to accept the "market-oriented policies" favoured by the West.

Robinson proposed to set up an "Institute of International Debt and Development," which, as a joint venture of the IMF and the World Bank, would buy up some $250 billion worth of Third World debt at discounted rates. The Institute would have even greater powers than the IMF and the World Bank as it "establishes ongoing discipline" over debtor countries needing "structural adjustments." As Robinson told his audience, ". . . the scope of incentives and the mechanisms for discipline are well beyond anything presently available" — an astonishing claim considering that the mechanisms for discipline already used by the IMF and World Bank amount to virtual control over national economies. Robinson noted that his institute would have the beneficial effect of ensuring that debtor countries would become a " 'safe harbour' attraction for direct foreign investment." In short, the institute would have the power to force desperate nations to redesign their entire economies so that companies — such as American Express, for instance — would feel safe investing there.

In the end, the U.S. opted for a similar debt restructuring plan initiated by U.S. Treasury Secretary Nicholas Brady. Launched in March '89, the Brady Plan includes the same basic features as the Robinson Plan — debt relief in exchange for compulsory structural adjustment in Third World countries. And in June 1990 U.S. President George Bush contributed his own initiative called "Enterprise for the Americas." Amid rhetoric about the glories of a free trade zone "stretching from the Port of Anchorage to Tierra del Fuego," Bush announced a plan that amounted to further measures to push the major debtor nations of Latin America into structural adjustments long desired by the U.S. business community.

What is particularly interesting for Canadians is the striking similarity between these "structural adjustment programs" imposed on the Third World by the IMF, the World Bank and the U.S. government, and the "broad plan" imposed on Canada by the Mulroney government. Indeed, with only slight variations, the IMF's "standard menu" has been imposed on Canada. Our government's compliance with this agenda is all the more noteworthy since it has been essentially voluntary; Canada does not borrow from the IMF or the World Bank. Ottawa is taking its marching orders not from these powerful agencies, but from the international business and investment community.

But then the IMF and the World Bank are largely agencies of the international business and investment community. The two organizations were structured so that they are essentially controlled by the U.S., and the U.S. government generally takes its cues on such matters from its own large corporations. It is not surprising, then, that the course of action promoted by the IMF and the World Bank broadly reflects the same business agenda that we've seen promoted in Canada by the business community, which of course includes Canadian-owned as well as foreign-controlled corporations.

Indeed, the international investor whose psyche we are trying to explore is not really such a mysterious specimen. He or she is much like investors everywhere. Whether they put their money in government bonds or corporate stocks, in Canada or in another country, they are simply seeking a safe place for it, where it will earn the maximum rate of return. This too is the prime concern of the businessperson who manages the capital of a corporation on behalf of the owners of the corporation.

So, while all these people play different roles in the world of international business and investment, they also share common interests as the holders or managers of capital, and their interests are different, say, than the wage-earners who are employed by that capital.* For simplicity, then, we will sometimes refer to these members of the business and investment community as "business" or occasionally even "the rich," even though they perform different tasks and have dramatically different incomes. The point is that they share a common interest in maximizing the return on their capital or the capital they manage and, therefore, tend to promote a particular agenda that they believe will achieve that.

So when Canadian business leaders stress the need for policies that satisfy international investors, they are, in effect, stressing the need for policies that satisfy themselves. Of course, it sounds considerably less self-serving for the Canadian business community to argue that Canada should implement certain policies, not because it wants these policies for its own benefit, but because other people insist on them — anonymous people who are important players in the global marketplace. Suddenly, the demands appear to be coming from the mysterious global forces of international competition. They can thus be presented as simply part of the new set of rules Canada must play by to compete effectively in the world, rather than sounding like the self-interested requests of one group in Canadian society trying to get a better deal for itself.

* The owners of small businesses also primarily see their function as protecting their small holdings and aspiring to turn them into larger holdings. While they tend to side with the owners and managers of larger businesses on most policy issues, there are important exceptions. When I refer to "business" in this book, I generally mean larger businesses.

Thus, the Canadian Manufacturers' Association, in a 1989 brief called "The Aggressive Economy," attached considerable importance to an IMF recommendation that Canada cut $9 billion from its federal deficit. Referring to the IMF as "the authoritative watchdog of government finances," the brief went on to argue that the actions recommended by the IMF were "necessary" and "warranted." By puffing up the IMF into an "authoritative watchdog," the CMA was trying to lend credibility to its own familiar demands for deficit reduction, suggesting that a respected international body was urging this course of action as a way to gear Canada up for competitive world challenges. In fact, the IMF broadly represents the same narrow interests of investors and holders of capital that the CMA does. No wonder the CMA found such merit in the actions recommended by its soul mates at the IMF.

We should not be particularly surprised, then, that there is general agreement about economic policies among those in the IMF, the Canadian and international business community and the Mulroney government. The IMF, for instance, praised Canada in September 1990 for its tough anti-inflation policy, and also for the GST, which it said "should significantly improve the efficiency of the economy and enhance growth prospects." This assessment was echoed on the pages of *Euromoney,* a magazine geared to the international investment community, which enthusiastically endorsed the GST as "much-needed" and indicative of Michael Wilson's "determination to restructure further the Canadian economy." Both the IMF and *Euromoney* also wanted to see far more action on reducing the Canadian deficit — a position shared by the Mulroney government as well as those at the BCNI and the Canadian Manufacturers' Association.

But while business and investors everywhere are largely united behind an agenda, that agenda offers few benefits to the broad base of Canadians. In championing the agenda, Canadian business and government leaders have tried to disguise this simple fact, implying that we are all potential beneficiaries.

The Canadian government's plan to enter into a free trade deal with Mexico provides a revealing illustration of this. Trade Minister Michael Wilson noted in a speech in Ottawa at the end of May 1991 that Canadian companies will have to take advantage of Mexico's low-wage labour pool if they are to compete effectively with American firms. "If Mexico is going to provide those inputs into the U.S., and we didn't have access to those inputs for Canadian companies, we would be in a competitive disadvantage," he said. Wilson was effectively endorsing the relocation of at least part of the operations of Canadian companies to Mexico — relocations that would help Canadian companies remain competitive, but would clearly have disastrous implications for the Canadian workers in those companies.

In an insightful column in the *Financial Post* in April 1990, Vancouver businessman Gordon Gibson nicely exposed the fallacy of portraying the government's economic policies as equally beneficial to all. Gibson asked readers to imagine the government calling a press conference and announcing that it had decided to correct the nation's economic ills by causing "a very substantial rise in the incomes of the wealthy." In Gibson's imaginary scenario, the government would go on to explain that it planned to impose a high interest rate policy that would throw people out of work, create particular hardship for the poor and less developed parts of the country, drive up the deficit and ultimately undermine our international competitiveness. Gibson wryly noted, "Nobody issued such a press release last year, but that is exactly what is going on."

In fact, what is going on is nothing short of recutting the national pie, and giving a larger slice to those with capital. A senior Finance department official admitted as much in an attempt to defend the Mulroney government's claim in the May '91 Throne Speech that its economic policies would raise the real incomes of Canadians by 25 percent by the year 2000. The exaggerated claim, which economist Michael McCracken joked could only be dreamed up if someone were to "smoke something," didn't mean that real salaries and wages would rise by 25 percent, explained Don Drummond, Finance's Director of Fiscal Policy. Rather, he said, they would rise by only about 16 percent, but the overall increase would amount to 25 percent once corporate profits, interest income and profits from unincorporated businesses were factored into the equation. While the government's numbers seem unduly optimistic, the point is that even the Department of Finance was acknowledging that government policies were going to result in a much higher rate of growth in business and investment income than in wage income.

Business commentators consistently deny that business is trying to cut itself a larger share of the pie. They insist that what business wants is not a bigger share of the pie, but a larger overall pie, with more for everyone. But, while business would no doubt like to see a larger overall pie, this has not been the case. The model of continuing growth, with more for everyone, was the pattern in North America up until the early seventies. But that came to a halt with the oil crisis and the onset of stagflation. With lower growth and less to be divided, business and labour struggled to protect their positions, like kids scrambling for the few remaining seats in a game of musical chairs.

For business, the reality of slower growth was a reduced rate of return on investment. And it didn't have to look far for the culprits — workers, whose standard of living had risen throughout the post-war boom years. Suddenly that improved living standard seemed, to the holders of capital at least, to have been achieved at their expense. While this is a debatable point, it is interesting to note that businesspeople and investors believed it to be true. Jacques de Larosiere, former managing director of the IMF, expressed the resentment of the international business community against the rising wages of workers in a major policy address in 1984:

> Over the last four years, the rate of return on capital investment in manufacturing in the six largest industrial countries averaged only about half the rate earned during the late 1960s . . . even allowing for cyclical factors, a clear pattern emerges of a substantial and progressive long-term decline in rates of return on capital. There may be many reasons for this. But there is no doubt that an important contributing factor is to be found in the significant increase over the past twenty years or so in the share of income being absorbed by employees. . . . This points to the need for a gradual reduction in the rate of increase in real wages

over the medium term if we are to restore adequate investment incentives.

Indeed, with the pie no longer growing at such a fast rate, a
key focus of business became making the employees' slice
smaller. Despite rhetoric claiming that its sole interest was in
enlarging the overall pie, business became increasingly interested in protecting and enlarging the size of its own slice, at the
expense of others if necessary. Indeed, business grew more and
more determined to drive wages down and also to shift the tax
burden off its own back and further onto the backs of the middle
and working classes. For a group that preached the bigger-pie-
for-all approach, business leaders spent a surprising amount of
their time devising ways to reduce the share for others.

And, to the extent that business and the rich did attempt to
make a bigger overall pie, the solutions they proposed to achieve
it had the effect of first ensuring a larger slice for themselves.
They argued, for instance, that the way to get the economy
growing was to provide more tax breaks for savings and investment, since this would encourage well-to-do individuals first to
accumulate more savings and then to invest more. If they
invested more, this might lead to economic growth, and therefore to more jobs for everyone. In other words, the benefits
might "trickle down" to the general public. (On the other hand,
they might not.)

But notice that, even in this scenario, once again the rich are
taking no chances. The first step in the scenario involves them
enlarging their own slice of the pie; the next step is (we hope) for
them to invest this larger slice in a way that will enlarge the
whole pie. Whether or not the second step is ever achieved is, of
course, a matter of chance, since there would be no method of
enforcing it. (That would make the rich nervous, and inclined to
move their capital somewhere else.) Thus, both the solutions
advocated by the rich — for making the pie bigger and for
giving others a smaller slice — have a common bottom line: the
rich would be sure to get more, while the fate of the rest of the
population would be less certain.

In its desire to appease the international business community,
the Mulroney government has imposed on Canada a variation

of the IMF's "standard menu," a menu that has turned out to be no more popular here than anywhere else in the world. A number of the government's policy initiatives — from privatization of the public sector to deregulation of key sectors of the economy — are all part of the standard menu. But three of these new initiatives have been particularly important and controversial in the Canadian context: high interest rates, tax reform and social spending cuts. Let's take a closer look, then, at the key items in the standard menu, Canadian style.

As WE'VE SEEN, Ottawa's policy of keeping interest rates high has been helpful to investors with money to buy treasury bills, bonds or any investment where interest rates apply. It would be wrong, however, to characterize all those in the Canadian business and investment community as beneficiaries of the high interest rate policy. Many businesses — including smaller businesses that rely heavily on credit — have been badly bruised by the policy. But, while the impact of high interest rates has affected members of Canada's elite differently — largely depending on whether they are primarily borrowers or lenders — it has spelt only hardship for those without capital to invest.

In fact, the Mulroney government has used high interest rates as a deliberate club to keep wages down. Stanley Hartt, Mulroney's former chief of staff, indicates that the government sees the high interest rate policy as part of a plan to break the power of unions to push for higher wages. In an interview, Hartt said that high interest rates have the same effect as the wage and price controls and the "6 and 5" policy of voluntary wage restraint introduced by the Trudeau government in the seventies as a way to control galloping inflation.

Hartt says that Trudeau's Anti-Inflation Board, which had the power to roll back wage settlements, "broke the back of union power." He argues that the Mulroney government's high interest rate policy will have the same effect over time, as the government maintains high interest rates until wage settlements decline. Eventually workers will learn that they are no further ahead by seeking large settlements, since they will simply be squeezed by the higher interest rates that lead to unemployment as the credit crunch forces businesses to lay off more workers. "It will teach unions that, if they make a demand for a net shift in the distribution of the pie, they will not gain," says Hartt. "It will constrain those who attempt to increase their share."

For Hartt, the interest rate policy is a key part of the "competitiveness agenda." He talks about it as "all part of the same thing — the idea that there's no free lunch. If you want to eat, you've got to work." This kind of rhetoric suggests that workers bargaining for wage increases are somehow lazy and expecting hand-outs. It echoes the sentiments of David Culver, the former Alcan chairman and free trade activist who heads up the BCNI's task force on the global economy: "Canadians know they have to earn their own way. Nobody's going to give us a good life for free." But who are these Canadians who allegedly keep suggesting that there *is* a free lunch, that someone is going to give them a good life for nothing? I certainly haven't run into any. The implication is that Canadian workers feel this way. And yet it is labour, above all, that is pushing government for more jobs, so they can get back to work. They want a decent life, but they clearly expect to work for it.

It is also interesting to note that what Hartt and the Mulroney government are trying to accomplish is not the control of runaway inflation. In the mid seventies and the early eighties inflation was running well above 10 percent, but it had dropped to a moderate level — hovering about 4 or 5 percent a year — by the time the Conservative government came to power in 1984, and has stayed close to there since. (The only significant jump came with the imposition of the GST in January 1991.) In such periods of relatively low inflation, the high interest rate policy takes on a whole different character. What Hartt is talking about is not preventing wages from sky-rocketing, but driving wages *down*. Hartt in fact notes that the process the government has in mind "may be painful. There may be wage *concessions*." What the government clearly wants is more than simply to use high interest rates to prevent workers from going on a greedy binge. Rather, it sees high rates as a way of keeping unemployment high, thereby making those with jobs nervous about keeping them and inclined to make concessions. Thus, high interest rates become a weapon for driving unions back from the ground they have already taken, for breaking their power, for recutting the pie and serving workers a smaller slice.

Economist Mel Watkins has nicely exposed the double standard in the high interest rate policy when he notes that those lending their money expect to receive a return that more than compensates for inflation. "But workers, well, they're supposed to keep right on working, and working harder (or starve if they can't find a job) while getting paid not more, not even the same, but less."

Of course it is difficult to mention the government's attempt to drive down wages without at least a passing comment on the hypocrisy of some of the players involved. John Crow, who was appointed governor of the Bank of Canada by the Mulroney government in 1987, kept interest rates high through 1990 in the name of dampening inflation and curbing excessive wage demands. Yet the salaries of the more than 2,000 non-unionized employees of the Bank of Canada rose by far more than the salary of the typical Canadian worker. And Crow's own salary range — the exact amount is not disclosed to Canadians even though they are paying it — jumped by a massive 35 percent over the same period, bringing his pay to somewhere between $162,000 and $243,000 in 1989. So we have the spectacle of someone comfortably in the top one percent of the nation's income earners lecturing those much further down the ladder on the need to do with less, while quietly doing with more himself.

And not only do Canadian workers face downward pressure on their wages as a result of the new business agenda, they are also being called upon to shoulder a larger share of the tax burden. Indeed, the key function of the GST is not simply to raise more revenue, but to shift the burden of paying all those extra taxes from business to the ordinary consumer. Tax expert Neil Brooks has pointed out that the move to the GST from the Manufacturers' Sales Tax (MST) shifts about $4 billion of the tax burden each year from corporations to consumers.* This shift in the tax burden from corporations to consumers will inevitably become more pronounced as the government raises more and more of its revenue from the GST in the future. This perhaps explains the enthusiasm of the BCNI for the GST — it allows a large and growing chunk of the burden of deficit reduction to be transferred to the masses of Canadians.

The GST is just one element — although a key one — in a wider tax reform under which the Mulroney government has shifted the tax burden more and more off the backs of business and the well-to-do, and onto the middle class. One of the major thrusts of Michael Wilson's 1987 tax reform has been to move away from Canada's long-established principle of progressivity, under which tax rates rise as incomes rise. By flattening the rate structure considerably, Wilson has greatly eroded the principle of progressivity, so that the rates faced by the highest income earners are not significantly higher than the rates faced by many middle-income people. He has compounded this favouritism to the rich by putting in place a lifetime tax exemption for capital gains of up to $100,000 — a measure whose benefits go exclusively to those receiving capital gains, primarily high-income stockholders. And Wilson has also enriched the tax benefits of retirement savings plans, allowing much larger annual contributions — another measure that primarily benefits those with excess cash.

The business and investment community often argues that tax benefits for the rich are necessary to encourage savings and investment. They tend to shrug off the importance of the fact that the benefits of these measures go disproportionately to the rich, arguing that the key thing is to ensure that the national savings rate is high so that the economy will grow. But these

---

* Unlike the GST, which is paid by consumers at the point of purchase, at least part of the MST appears to have been paid by corporations out of their profits. The MST was applied at the manufacturer's level and, while most of it was likely passed on to consumers, tax experts agree that at least $4 billion of it — largely the portion that was charged on exports and on the purchase of business equipment — was paid out of corporate profits. Under the GST, this $4 billion will be collected at the retail level, directly from consumers.

business advocates ignore the fact that, with or without tax relief, Canada's savings rate has always been relatively high (9.7 percent of national net income from 1980 to 1987, compared with 6.2 percent in the U.S. and 8.9 percent in West Germany). Indeed, the evidence suggests that tax breaks actually do little to encourage savings and investment. Even the IMF, which is certainly sympathetic to the interests of investors, notes in a recent study of countries that offer tax breaks for saving that, "the effect of taxes on the level of private saving has been relatively small."

There are more reasons to question this alleged need for tax breaks for saving. Personal savings, at which these measures are aimed, are actually a relatively small part of the nation's overall savings rate. Besides, there is no guarantee of how the rich will invest their windfall. In the U.S., where the Reagan administration dramatically reduced taxes for the rich in 1981 with the stated goal of boosting the national savings rate, the savings rate actually declined in the following years, dropping from 7.5 percent of disposable income in 1981 to 3.2 percent in 1987. The rich, it seemed, had better things to do with their new-found cash than save and invest it; there was also the option of travelling, or splurging on yachts and fur coats. Even when they did invest it, they generally put it into investments that did little to help the economy: real estate ventures, junk bonds and stock speculations.

Despite their lacklustre record in stimulating the economy, tax breaks continue to be popular with the rich. Indeed, while business vociferously demands cut-backs in government spending, it has little to say about the "spending" governments do through the tax system, which largely goes to business and high-income groups.

Neil Brooks has identified some $8 billion worth of what he considers unnecessary tax breaks favouring business and the rich, including breaks for real estate developers, for Canadian multinationals investing abroad, and for those indulging in business meals and entertainment. Yet, despite its apparent keenness to reduce the deficit, business has not suggested cutting any of these measures. Asked about this apparent contradiction, d'Aquino said that the BCNI was studying Brooks's list and preparing a response. That was in February '91. The BCNI's response has yet to be released.

It's not surprising that business likes to receive benefits through the tax system. Unlike direct government spending, tax breaks are largely invisible. This allows the business community the luxury of ranting against government spending (on things like social programs), while turning a blind eye to government largesse in the form of tax subsidies. And so David Culver can unabashedly declare, "I'm not in favour of subsidies to industry. I don't think you'll find the BCNI advocating hand-outs." Culver apparently doesn't count in his calculations the $8 billion a year in tax breaks identified by Brooks or the $4 billion a year in tax savings that Ottawa handed the manufacturing sector with the move to the GST, even though these measures provide just as much money to business and the rich as if the government had simply written a cheque for the same amount. These tax benefits remain conveniently off-stage, out of sight, where the rich can feast on them quietly.

As Michael Wilson's reforms have continued to shift the tax burden off business and the rich, there has been a tremendous sense of overload on financially strapped middle income Canadians. This growing resentment against taxes is a potent political force, as was illustrated by the strength of the opposition to the GST, as well as by the angry protests of heavily taxed truckers in May 1991. But, while this resentment is at least partly responsible for the Conservative government's low standing in the polls, it has another important political dimension that is undoubtedly pleasing to advocates of the new agenda.

The sense of tax overload among Canadians has greatly assisted the government and the business community in their efforts to sell the message that Canada can no longer afford its social programs. As the tax burden grows heavier and is linked to frightening stories about the size of our debt, we are far more likely to accept business-government lectures that our social spending is out of control and is at the root of our economic problems. Over time, the rock-hard resistance of Canadians to any tampering with Ottawa's social spending is slowly beginning to crumble. This brings us to the third and what has proved to be the most controversial item on the Canadian business agenda: cutting social programs.

IN MANY WAYS, cutting social spending goes to the heart of the business agenda. Social programs represent an egalitarian, community-oriented approach to society that has no place in the new global marketplace. If Canada is to become truly lean and world-competitive, it will have to shed the notion of itself as a society with high uniform standards guaranteeing equality in some of the most crucial areas of life — health care, education, social security. Such a system is costly to maintain: it drives our taxes up and makes business uncompetitive. Besides, in this every-man-for-himself world, don't Canadians have to learn to do with less? As long as such a comfortable system is in place, will Canadians ever really accept the need to compete in the global marketplace, to go head-to-head against the workers in Hong Kong, Singapore and Mexico?

So, for those embracing the new business agenda, scaling down Canada's social programs is a top priority. But this poses considerable political problems. As the BCNI noted in its August 1984 paper, there is a "broad consensus" among Canadians in favour of retaining high social spending. Thus, the BCNI has always approached the question with kid gloves, stressing it was not advocating changes that would hurt the most disadvantaged members of society.

But it is hard to imagine the kinds of cuts advocated by business groups, including the BCNI, not hurting both the poor and the middle class. The BCNI joined the Canadian Manufacturers' Association and the Canadian Chamber of Commerce in October 1990 in calling for a two-year freeze on increases in federal program spending, the main component of which is funding for social programs. This amounts to a serious cut, since the programs would be unable to keep pace with inflation. The government apparently listened to the business community's advice, and in its 1991 budget imposed a three-year freeze on increases in the money it pays the provinces for social programs — primarily health care and education. It is hard to imagine that the provinces, the other major contributors to these social programs, can possibly make up for the billions of dollars of lost federal funds. And if they don't, serious cut-backs of some sort seem inevitable. Just how this can be done without hurting the disadvantaged — and just about everyone else — is not clear.

The cut-backs will almost inevitably lead to a breakdown of the high standards to which Canadians have become accustomed. Health economist Dr Michael Rachlis says that, under the scheduled cuts, Ottawa will stop transferring cash to any of the provinces by the year 2002. This will not only leave provinces badly strapped for funds, but will remove Ottawa's clout in enforcing national standards, he argues. Provinces will be increasingly tempted to make up for lost revenue with user fees, ushering in a two-tier system where doctors offer special services for well-to-do patients making extra payments. Canada will risk becoming like England, where cuts in public health care spending under Margaret Thatcher led the elite to retreat to expensive private medical clinics. The rest of the population was left in the under-funded public system, with overworked doctors and run-down facilities.

In education, too, there are pressures to abandon the long-established egalitarian principles of our public system. The Canadian Manufacturers' Association has argued for the need to stress quality over accessibility. In a 1987 report by a special task force of corporate executives, the CMA argued that Canadian universities should be remodelled along the lines of the top U.S. universities, which specialize in quality research at the graduate level and "a small, select undergraduate body." Task force chairman David Vice, the vice-chairman of Northern Telecom, noted that Canada has traditionally emphasized accessibility by keeping tuition fees low. This open-door policy has, indeed, been a key aspect of our relatively egalitarian society, allowing kids from even fairly low-income families to go to university and gain a more equal chance of achieving financial success later in life.

Vice and his task force wanted to see Canada move towards a deregulated system, under which tuition fees would no longer be controlled but would better reflect what the market would bear. The result would be higher tuition, a more "select" group at universities, and less emphasis on ensuring that as many Canadians as possible receive the benefits of higher education. When questioned on this stance by CBC radio broadcaster Stuart McLean, Vice rejected the notion that this system would necessarily be elitist, noting that bursaries could be made available for very bright students from disadvantaged backgrounds.

But, bursaries or no bursaries, such a system would clearly lead to elitism. The occasional bursary would do nothing to compensate for the exclusion of tens of thousands of low-income students who would fall into the middle range of intelligence — bright enough to have received a university education in the past and bright enough to receive one under this new system, if they happen to come from a family with money. Our education system, the great leveller in Canadian society, would be transformed to resemble the system south of the border, where higher education and all its rewards have long been the preserve of the rich. For poor Americans who want to pull themselves up to a higher station in life there has traditionally been only the army.

With strong popular support for egalitarian programs in Canada, business and government have trod softly in proposing these sorts of changes. Rather than a frontal assault against the egalitarian principle of accessibility, business leaders have emphasized instead the argument that we simply can't afford the luxury of such programs, that they have become too generous. What business leaders never mention, however, is that, compared with other western industrialized countries, our social spending is not particularly generous. Indeed, it is rather modest.

Canada's social spending is 21.5 percent of its Gross Domestic Product (GDP), compared with an average of 25.6 percent for all the other industrialized countries in the Organization of Economic Co-operation and Development (OECD), according to the latest OECD statistics. Many of the European countries, which have enviable standards of living and successful economies, spend considerably larger percentages of their GDPs on social programs: Belgium, 37.6 percent of GDP; the Netherlands, 36.1 percent; West Germany, 31.5 percent; France, 29.5 percent. The only major industrialized countries where social spending is lower than Canada's are the United States, which spends 20.8 percent of GDP on social programs, and Japan, which spends 17.5 percent. Clearly, the portrait of Canadian social programs as wildly out of line with other nations is accurate only if we compare Canada with countries like Haiti or Bangladesh.

But, of course, it is with the U.S. that we are constantly being compared. The BCNI made this clear back in August 1984 when it compared Canadian and U.S. social spending levels and then noted that Canada would have difficulty competing "if the private sector has to support a government sector which has been allowed to get too far out of line." It is this kind of statement that has led to speculation about whether free trade, by tying us in more tightly with the Americans, endangers our social programs.

The debate over this question was one of the fiercest of the 1988 election campaign, cutting to the heart of what Canadians feared most about free trade. In dismissing the charge, government and business leaders were being somewhat disingenuous. They kept insisting that nothing in the free trade agreement called for the dismantling of social programs. While this was true, the denial side-stepped the more interesting question of whether free trade would create a situation in which social programs were more likely to be dismantled.

Here the issue became more murky. In a perceptive column on the subject in the *Financial Post,* Arthur Drache drew a comparison with the impact the Charter of Rights has had on Canada. Drache noted that nowhere in the Charter is there any mention of increasing the power of judges, yet the Charter has very definitely had this effect. Similarly, Drache argued, social programs could be in some way jeopardized by free trade even if the free trade agreement made no specific mention of them.

Certainly, once the free trade agreement was in place, business began calling unabashedly for cut-backs in government spending. And, as we've seen, these calls became quite shrill by the fall of 1990, with demands for a two-year freeze on increases in federal program spending. Business could argue, perhaps, that all this had nothing to do with free trade. This is true in a sense: even if business had failed to secure a free trade agreement, it would have no doubt called for cut-backs in social programs. Indeed, the BCNI was calling for cut-backs in social spending back in 1984 as part of its deficit-reduction package, long before Jim Robinson had likely even located Canada on a map. Clearly free trade did not create the business community's desire to cut back social programs. Rather, free trade and social spending cuts are parallel prongs, two parts of the same agenda, two essential elements in the same "broad plan." They both go to the heart of remaking Canada, in the name of Globalization. But once the free trade deal was signed, there was added fuel for the business argument that Canada had to cut back its social programs in order to become more competitive with the U.S.

One revealing indication of the business attitude towards social programs is the fact that the free trade agreement makes no provision for incorporating the protection of social welfare that the Europeans have built into their plans for a common market in 1992. While North American business and government commentators often point to Europe as the model of the free trade world to come, they rarely mention the fact that the European countries have built very specific safeguards into their trading agreement to prevent just the sort of "race to the bottom" of ever-lower standards for working people. These safeguards ensure the preservation of labour and social standards — already far higher in Europe than North America — to prevent footloose capital from doing the kind of shopping-for-the-country-with-the-lowest-standards that we are seeing develop in the North American market.

Nor has there been any mention of incorporating such requirements into a trade deal with Mexico, even though such a move could help raise labour and welfare standards in that very poor country. Business commentators frequently try to portray their interest in investing in the Third World as partly driven by a desire to help these less developed countries. Yet, surely business could help them more directly by instituting just the kind of minimum standards that Europe has opted for as part of its common market. Mexico would still enjoy a competitive advantage, since Canadian and American standards would inevitably remain considerably higher, given their far greater wealth. But business has shown no interest in this approach, revealing that its true interest in countries like Mexico is nothing more than interest in a source of cheap labour.

The desire of business to reduce social spending in Canada is also evident in its characterization of social programs as hand-outs, or a "free lunch." This kind of attitude was evident in a *Globe and Mail* editorial endorsing the federal spending cut-backs in Wilson's '91 budget. The *Globe* presented the situation as a fable, in which "every family in Canada had a rich uncle in Ottawa," and praised Wilson for showing Canadians that the answer to the country's fiscal problems did not lie in "a few more billions on the credit card of a rich uncle in Ottawa."

But this ignored the fact that Canadians do not receive their social programs free, from a "rich uncle" so to speak, but rather pay for them out of their tax dollars. Whether they pay for these services privately or collectively through the tax system, they still end up paying for them. Moreover, a system of pooled resources has the potential to be — and generally is — far more efficient. In the U.S., for instance, the private health care system has left Americans paying, on average, twice as much for health care as people in other industrial nations, including Canada, Japan, West Germany, and France, according to a May 1990 report by the U.S. public interest group Citizen Action. And, even with the high levels of spending on health care in the U.S., some 37 percent of Americans still have no coverage. Indeed, the only way we might save money by privatizing health services is if we followed the American example and stopped providing them altogether to many people who are now receiving them. By collectively pooling their resources, Canadians are able to set high collective standards and to achieve real economies of scale.

And all this is well within Canada's means! While business points to the deficit as evidence that we are overspending, this picture is somewhat misleading, as we saw in Chapter 1. Canadians are, in fact, paying more in taxes than the government is spending — if the interest payments on the national debt are excluded from the calculation. The interest payments on the debt have grown wildly because of the government's high interest rate policy. Even so, the deficit has in fact been declining in real terms since 1984, largely because of inflation and the growth of the economy, Neil Brooks has shown. Although the deficit was roughly $38 billion a year in 1984 and is about $30 billion now, these numbers take no account of inflation. Translated into 1991 dollars, the 1984 deficit was equivalent to about $52 billion today. In shrinking to $30 billion a year from $52 billion, the deficit now represents about 4.5 percent of the country's Gross Domestic Product, down from 8.7 percent in 1984. Thus, contrary to the alarmist statements of business, there has been a real decline in the size of the annual deficit. Over time, this will also result in a decline in the country's $400 billion accumulated debt, as the annual cost of servicing this debt declines.

Furthermore, the size of the deficit would shrink considerably if governments used the same method of accounting that businesses use. While businesses account for their investments over time, governments treat all expenses as one-time costs. If a company buys a truck, for instance, it considers that it is paying for the vehicle over a number of years, reflecting the fact that it plans to use the truck for that time. This reduces the cost of the truck per year. Yet, if the government builds a bridge, it considers that it has incurred the whole cost that year, even though the bridge may last for decades. This method of accounting seems particularly inappropriate for items like bridges, but it also is arguably inappropriate as a way to account for the costs of, say, education, where the value of the service provided will presumably benefit the student — and the country — over long periods of time.

Indeed, cut-backs in spending on long-term needs, such as bridges and education, can be as detrimental to future generations as the debt itself. In the U.S., where government spending — apart from that on the military — has been dramatically reduced in the eighties and nineties, public transportation facilities and education systems have deteriorated significantly. In response to what many perceive as a crisis, more than three hundred U.S. economists, including Robert Reich, Lester Thurow, John Kenneth Galbraith and Paul Krugman, have signed a petition calling for an increase in spending on services and facilities they consider "vital to the nation's future."

Although Canadians are deeply attached to their social programs and are able to pay for them, the Mulroney government has strongly committed itself to further serious cuts, in the name of deficit reduction. This brings us back to the question of who's really running the country.

IT MIGHT BE useful to imagine a referendum. All Canadians are given the right to check one box on a ballot. The question is simple: who should run Canada? Possible candidates might include organized labour, Conrad Black, the Boy Scouts, the Kiwanis Club, Saddam Hussein, the international investment community, or the people of Canada.

Apart from a few spoiled ballots, it is hard to imagine anything other than an overwhelming vote for the last choice: the people of Canada. Probably nothing is more basic to our political culture than the notion that we are a democracy, that we collectively determine our own destiny. Yet if we really examine what is going on in some crucial areas of our national life, this is becoming less and less true. Increasingly, we are abdicating control over our country in favour of the international investment community, who, in our imaginary referendum, would have undoubtedly beat out Saddam Hussein but probably attracted no more votes than the Boy Scouts.

But is it really necessary for us to hand over the keys to the country so easily, without even putting up a fight? Business wants to encourage us to think that we have no choice, that we must cater to these unnamed international investors because otherwise they will withdraw their money. "When they speak, Canadians must jump," as Dunnery Best put it. But is it possible we're getting a little spooked by all this, that we don't really have to jump? Surely we should keep in mind that those most vehemently advocating that we jump are business leaders who subscribe to the same agenda, and have had trouble convincing us to jump when they say so. They are clearly hoping that if the command appears to be coming from a more authoritative source — "international investors" who are portrayed as some mysterious global force — we will be traumatized into thinking we must obey.

Yet even BT Bank's Jerry Del Missier concedes that international investors, for all the behavioural patterns he attributes to them, are an unpredictable lot. He notes that when Canadian interest rates dropped below German interest rates in the spring of 1991, there wasn't a return flight of capital that had come from Germany, as would be expected. Del Missier believes German investors decided to leave their money in Canadian treasury bills because they seemed safer. Similarly, he notes, despite the hue and cry from the business community over the large deficit predicted in Ontario's April '91 budget, investors did not pull their money from Ontario bonds. "You have to step back and look at the whole world," he says. With so many factors at play, it is perhaps simplistic to assume investors will pull their money every time a country deviates from their agenda. Although high interest rates and an appreciating currency are important, perhaps the most important thing is to have a healthy economy that employs people.

Indeed, if the Canadian government would put more emphasis on creating employment, we wouldn't need to borrow so much money from foreign investors in the first place. To a large extent, the deficit is a function of unemployment. With so many Canadians out of work, there is far less money collected in tax revenues and far more government money paid out in social services for these people and their families. Yet reducing the deficit by creating employment — which would put more money in the hands of Canadians — is not a priority on the business agenda, perhaps because it does little to help business increase its slice of the national pie.

Business pays lip service to the goal of creating more jobs. But it places its top priority on controlling inflation — a policy that leads to high interest rates and spending cuts and therefore has the effect of eliminating jobs. Business leaders insist that, in the long run, their prescription will create a healthier economy and more jobs. But the future always seems to be well around the corner.

Globalization enthusiasts are constantly encouraging us to think that international capital holds all the cards. They have helped us lose sight of the fact that we hold some of the cards, that we have more leverage than we realize. While we want their capital, we have something they want: our markets. Without markets to sell to, business is in trouble. This is why powerful businessmen like Jim Robinson devote so much of their time to finding ways to knock down trade barriers. And Canada, although not a large country by international standards, is a rich one. "The Toronto and Ontario markets are some of the wealthiest in the world," said Ron Pump, the Washington lobbyist for AT & T, explaining why the telecommunications giant was so keen on a free trade deal with Canada. "Everybody wants to sell in Ontario."

And yet this is a card that Ottawa refuses to play. It refuses to try to win concessions from business in exchange for access to our rich market. As we have seen, this principle worked successfully with the auto pact, which gave the large U.S. automakers access to our market, in exchange for guarantees that, for every car sold here, one would be produced here. Business doesn't like these "performance requirements," but would undoubtedly put up with them in order to gain access to markets that AT & T considers among the "wealthiest in the world." Yet the free trade deal with the U.S. took us in exactly the opposite direction. Canada offered up full access to the Canadian market without insisting on the slightest requirement of local production.

By acquiescing to the business agenda, the Mulroney government has stripped Canada of much of its power to control its economic future. The slavish devotion to a borderless world where goods and services flit easily across national boundaries has blocked a whole range of government initiatives. This attack on government has all but ruled out a positive role for government in building a stronger economy.

And yet a positive role for government is perhaps needed now more than ever. If the business community's hype about Globalization is even partly true, then Canadians are more vulnerable than ever in the world marketplace and more in need of a strong force to represent their interests. Business is telling us to strip government of its power and hand that power over to business, and yet at the same time business makes clear that it is not willing to commit itself to Canada or to Canadians. Why should we hand over power to a group that prides itself on being fully mobile, able to move its capital and its operations out from under us to another corner of the world, simply because the deal offered there is sweeter?

Business argues that we have no choice; that this is part of an inevitable set of developments taking place all over the world. But it is important to separate out what is inevitable from what isn't. For instance, the breakthrough in computer technology and the resulting transformation of business may indeed be inevitable. But how we respond to this mini-revolution is not inevitable. We can, as we have, follow the business agenda and fling our borders open, allowing data — and jobs — to flow freely out of the country, thereby helping foreign firms to centralize their operations back home. Alternatively, we could listen to the kind of sage advice that came from the Clyne Committee and use the power of government to prevent this kind of needless job drain, by insisting that Canadian data be processed in Canada.

An acceptance of a positive role for government would also have led us to take a different course in such diverse examples as the West Coast fish dispute and the drug legislation fight. In both cases, the federal government backed off from Canadian laws that had been implemented to ensure benefits for Canadians — jobs in the fish industry in the first case, and reasonable drug prices as well as a boost to the Canadian drug manufacturing industry in the second. The Mulroney government's rigid adherence to the free market ideology — under pressure from the U.S. — caused it to abandon these sound policies that had served Canadian interests well for decades, even though the policies really had nothing to do with changes in the world marketplace.

Business would like us to believe that its agenda is the only realistic response to the changes going on in the world. And it is easy to fall into this kind of thinking, with the media so heavily dominated by commentators who support the business agenda. Any deviation from that agenda is almost never given serious consideration. To suggest that business be made more responsible to the communities it operates in, or to advocate a redistribution of the tax burden onto the shoulders of those with capital is to be badly out of sync with the current obsession with making Canada more globally competitive. We are being led to believe that a kind of economic free-for-all is now the way of the world.

Rarely do the media give us any glimpse of the strong resistance to the business agenda in the developing world, where countries such as Brazil, Argentina, India and Pakistan have banded together to propose different solutions to the new agenda advanced by the U.S. at GATT — solutions that would allow them to impose laws to ensure they are the beneficiaries of development in their own countries. Nor are we often reminded that many of the Far Eastern countries, including highly successful Japan, have relied on nationalistic measures and a strong role for government in achieving their phenomenal rates of growth.

Even European countries, about which we are better informed, are generally portrayed as supportive of the business agenda, with their common market held up as evidence of the inevitability of free trade agreements. The media are less inclined to report the nationalistic policies of many European countries, such as in the key area of telecommunications, or the fact that their common market has built-in safeguards to protect the erosion of social programs. When resistance to the business agenda became so strong in Europe that it was difficult to ignore — such as in the winter of 1990, when some European countries vigorously resisted U.S. efforts to force them to cut back farm subsidies — there was little sympathy in the media for the resisters. The protesting farmers were portrayed as misguided throwbacks to another age, rather than people legitimately trying to prevent their way of life from disappearing, just as the family farm was long ago replaced by powerful agribusiness interests in the U.S.

While business would have us believe that our only hope lies in implementing its agenda, in fact some of the most successful economies in recent years — Japan and the west European countries, particularly Germany — have followed a different course, mixing a strong role for government with a vigorous private sector. The irony of this, as political scientist James Laxer has noted, is that this public-private mix is the same model that Canada had used successfully throughout its past and that the Mulroney government has so abruptly abandoned.

It is beyond the scope of this book to propose a detailed alternative agenda for Canada. Others have already done so.* My point is simply to remind Canadians that there is another way, which involves a positive role for government and limitations on the operation of the free market. Despite the sermons emanating from the business community and the Mulroney government, their views represent only one model — a model that serves the interests of a particular group and has so far provided little evidence that it has much to offer the rest of Canadians.

Unfortunately, by opting for a free trade deal with the U.S. we have locked ourselves in to this U.S.-style free-market model, just as the U.S. is losing ground to Japan and Europe in the world economy. And, with a three-way deal with Mexico now in the works, we are locking ourselves in deeper. As Mexico suddenly embraces the business agenda in a desperate attempt to sign a trade deal with the U.S., the pressure on Canada to go along with its two trading partners in further reducing the role of government will only increase. And the presence of a massive pool of cheap Mexican labour right within the trading bloc will supply business with a ready threat for Canadian workers during wage negotiations.

Ironically, Canada would have been far better off to fight U.S. protectionism by banding together with other countries whose interests were also threatened by U.S. measures. By making common cause like this against the massive power of the U.S., we would have actually had more leverage. The U.S. chose to get into bed alone with Canada — and now has chosen to invite an even weaker power to join in — precisely because, as we have seen, Washington was not getting its way in multilateral talks in the early eighties. Canada and Mexico have proved far more pliant.

Indeed, Canada has shown itself to be embarrassingly acquiescent to the demands of international business. But it is important to see that Canada is putting the business agenda in place,

---

* For more detailed proposals, see the work of academics such as Laxer, Daniel Drache and Mel Watkins, as well as the Council of Canadians, the Canadian Centre for Policy Alternatives and the Ecumenical Task Force on Economic Justice.

not because it is inevitable or even desirable for the majority of Canadians but because business leaders have indicated that they want it in place. The Mulroney government has simply knuckled under, even though there is no clear evidence that we would suffer if we steered a more independent course, as we did in the past and as many countries continue to do. As Herb Gray noted, France has traditionally been highly nationalistic, refusing to give in to American demands. Yet the U.S. still does business with France. Canada, on the other hand, by showing itself quick to acquiesce, has perhaps only encouraged the U.S. to become more demanding.

U.S. trade officials provided a revealing glimpse of their low opinion of Canadian negotiating resolve during the GATT talks in Brussels in December 1990. While the U.S. is evidently happy to face off against a compliant Canada when the two are opponents at the bargaining table, it is clearly less happy with a weak-kneed Canada when the two countries are making common cause together, as they were against European farm subsidies in the GATT talks. *Financial Post* reporter Peter Morton wrote in a dispatch from Brussels that the Americans privately accused the Canadians of being "spineless" and like "Jell-O" over their unwillingness to push hard enough on the farm support issue. With such a view of Canadians, it is easy to see why the U.S. was anxious to bring Canada back to the bargaining table in the negotiations for a free trade deal with Mexico — to win even more concessions from a neighbour it clearly regards as gelatinous.

While business leaders have generally tried to sell us their agenda by suggesting that the free-market model is inevitable and in our own best interests, they are not above resorting to threats to reinforce their argument. Ultimately, we should accept their agenda, they say, because if we don't, capital will flee the country. How are we supposed to respond to such threats? Most governments — including even the Mulroney government — usually make a point of refusing to deal with threats or ultimatums. In the midst of one of the heated moments in the constitutional crisis with Quebec, Mulroney told a Toronto audience in February '91 that Quebec could not expect Canada to bargain with a gun to its head. Imagine if he stood up with equal vigor to those trying to dictate how our economy should be run!

Besides, the threatened capital flight might be less serious than it seems. To be sure, a few high-profile types would head out amid great fanfare, huffing and puffing in rage as they went, with the business press loudly lamenting their departure. This is similar to what happened in the doctors' strike in Ontario in 1986. Doctors pointed out that their skills made them highly mobile, and they threatened to leave if they were denied the right to extra-bill. And, after they lost the strike, a few did leave, kicking and screaming as they headed to the warmer climes and higher pay of private U.S. clinics. But the vast majority of doctors stayed on, and the health care system continued to function.

Similarly, the departure of a few Robert Campeaus or Conrad Blacks, for instance, would be unlikely to destroy the fabric of the nation. Life would go on more or less as it has. While departing business barons would of course take their capital with them, they could never take with them what really makes this country rich: our natural resources. And Canada would still be an affluent market, with many ready to serve it. If our cable TV companies, our retail chains, our media outlets all packed up and left, would others not step quickly and willingly into the breach, thrilled by the opportunity?

The point is not that the rich should leave. Let's hope they don't. The point is that no one — not even the rich — should get away with holding a gun to Canada's head. That's no way to run a country. We might be better off with the Boy Scouts.

9 • THE SEDUCTION OF CANADA

In the stately, historic cemetery in Kingston, Ontario, Brian Mulroney placed a wreath on the gravestone of Canada's first prime minister and enjoyed his first good photo opportunity in weeks.

The one-hundredth anniversary of the death of Sir John A. Macdonald could not have come at a better time. It was June 6, 1991, and the prime minister had just returned from a trip to the Far East — a trip that should have provided little more than a host of photos of Mulroney looking statesmanlike. Instead, his decision to attack the budget of Ontario's NDP government at a luncheon of Japanese businessmen left him looking like a traitor to his own country, attacking one of its provinces in front of a foreign audience. A week later, Mulroney had largely put that embarrassing gaffe behind him, and, as he appeared at Macdonald's gravesite, managed to strike a statesmanlike pose for the reporters and TV cameras recording the event.

"It matters not who wins the next election. The only thing that matters is the unity of the nation," he told the crowd.

Mulroney went on to draw an implicit comparison between himself and Canada's first prime minister: "Some days I think I know in some very small degree what Sir John A. felt. Being prime minister of Canada is no picnic, even in the best of times."

It was a clever bit of speech-writing that cloaked Mulroney in the mantle of the respected first Prime Minister. And, with no hecklers or opposition members to contradict him, his message was largely transmitted unchallenged that night to living rooms across the nation.

A year earlier, the scene at Macdonald's gravesite had been very different. Without the special one-hundredth anniversary occasion to draw politicians and the media, the annual celebration was a far more modest event. In place of the Prime Minister, a tall, slightly gangly young man had walked uncertainly up to Macdonald's grave and placed the wreath in the wrong place. The wreath was quickly moved to its proper spot in front of the gravestone by a watchful guard dressed in a bright red nineteenth-century soldier's uniform.

Nobody from Mulroney's Conservative government had come to the Cataraqui cemetery for the ninety-ninth anniversary that afternoon, even though Macdonald was the patriarch of the Conservative Party, as well as of Canada. Instead, the local Member of Parliament, Liberal Peter Miliken, had sent his riding association president to lay the wreath for Canada. The Meech Lake negotiations were in the process of breaking down even as the ceremony progressed. It seemed oddly appropriate that Mulroney's Conservative regime was too busy presiding over the dismantling of the country to send one of its own to honour the Conservative who had united the country in the first place.

But then, despite Mulroney's attempt to identify himself with Macdonald, his brand of conservativism derived little inspiration from Macdonald. Indeed, almost everything Mulroney had done since taking office would have been anathema to Macdonald and to many Conservatives who followed in his footsteps. Above all, Macdonald had stood for a strong central government as a bulwark against the economic and military might of the United States, and as a positive, interventionist force within the country.

To Macdonald, the American empire was a real threat. Only half a century earlier, before Confederation, the United States had invaded Canada in a bold attempt to annex by force the

British North American colonies strung across its northern border. Defence of the colonies from possible U.S. aggression remained a driving motivation behind the push for Confederation in the 1860s. As late as 1866, the colonies were still forced to call up volunteers by the thousands to fend off attacks by free-wheeling adventurers known as the Fenians, who made frightening raids over the border shouting for the capture of Canada. One such raid across the Niagara River in June 1866 left nine Canadians dead and thirty wounded. That same month, the people of New Brunswick elected a pro-Confederation government, and many attributed the victory at least in part to the anti-American sentiment unleashed by the Fenian bloodshed.

But there was more than simple fear of American aggression behind Macdonald's desire for a strong bulwark against the U.S. He also disliked and distrusted many basic aspects of the American republic. He saw that the American reverence for rugged individualism and unrestrained liberty had led to an acceptance of a lawless western frontier and an unbridled free market. Instead, Macdonald envisioned for Canada a strong role for government in preserving order. And preserving order meant much more than simply keeping criminals in line. It meant creating an ordered society in which government used its collective power to intervene to protect the weak from the strong. That included protecting minorities from tyrannical majorities and protecting the general public from the sometimes rapacious urges of powerful private interests.

At Macdonald's graveside Kenneth McNaught, a tall, soft-spoken historian from the University of Toronto, was delivering a tribute to Canada's first prime minister at the ninety-ninth anniversary of his death, portraying him as a leader, a great humanist — and a great conservative. Even if the Conservative government in Ottawa had little time to honour its patriarch in the absence of TV cameras, other Canadians hadn't forgotten his role. Indeed, McNaught injected a sharp note into the low-key graveyard tribute, amidst people dressed in nineteenth-century costumes, when he ended his remarks about Macdonald with a reference to the present: "We are, I think, in sore need of his conservatism today."

IN THE QUIET afternoon atmosphere of a restaurant in Ottawa's Royal Bank Plaza, Eugene Forsey was holding forth about the conservative tradition in Canada. It was not long before his death in 1991, but, despite a triple heart bypass, the eighty-six-year-old retired senator and Canadian icon was still going strong. Upstairs on the eighth floor of the same building was the headquarters of the BCNI — a representative of the corporate power that seemed to hold so much sway over the Conservative government of Brian Mulroney. But down here on the main floor, the charming octogenarian sipping tea spoke of a different sort of conservatism.

Forsey's conservatism was rooted deep in Canadian history. His ancestors had come north to Nova Scotia in 1783 as part of the Loyalist migration that was hostile to the new American republic and looked to England for its political inspiration. Forsey himself was born in Grand Bank, Newfoundland, but, after his father's death when Eugene was still a young child, the family moved to Ottawa. There, Eugene was powerfully influenced by his mother's father, William Bowles, who was Chief Clerk of the House of Commons and a die-hard John A. Macdonald conservative.

Forsey grew up steeped in the traditions of British and Canadian parliamentary democracy, and a devotee of Macdonald-style conservatism himself. Central to that was a loyalty to Britain, and sense of old-world propriety and order. Forsey recalled a strong religious bent and primness in his upbringing, certainly when it came to things like sex. "You didn't say 'legs'; you said 'lower limbs,'" he noted with an impish smile. Indeed, he remembered that in the family home a crinoline was draped around the piano to conceal its "lower limbs."

But the conservatism that inspired Forsey and others of his generation was based on far more than simple modesty and old-fashioned values. It was a belief in a strong central government that would preserve and protect the traditions and independence of the community against international encroachment — particularly, in Canada's case, encroachment by the U.S. As journalist Charles Taylor wrote in his book *Radical Tories*, on the conservative tradition in Canada, "A conservative . . . [is] . . . concerned to protect his traditions against continental and international forces which threaten [his] particularity." The emphasis on the British connection for conservatives was partly an attachment to Canada's roots and partly protection against the powerful drift of continentalist forces that always threatened to draw Canada into the American orb. Forsey fiercely opposed any moves to decentralize power in Canada, whether to the provinces or to the private sector. The central government, he felt, must remain strong, and the House of Commons must be the base of that power.

But for all his old-world conservatism, Forsey had a strong radical streak in him. Indeed, his life was in some ways a mixture of conservative and left-wing politics. Despite his reverence for John A. Macdonald as well as Conservative prime ministers Arthur Meighen and John Diefenbaker, both of whom he knew personally, Forsey was a strong advocate of progressive reform. He helped in the formation of the Co-operative Commonwealth Federation (CCF), the forerunner of the NDP, and spent twenty-five years as the research director of the Canadian Congress of Labour, which later became the Canadian Labour Congress. But for Forsey the two divergent political strains didn't seem to be an awkward fit. For all their differences, both Conservatives and the left in Canada believed in a strong central government and the need for some protection for the public against unrestrained private freedom.

Indeed, this notion of a centralized power that places limits on private freedom is central to the political consensus that has developed in Canada over the years. While the U.S. has enshrined above all else the rights of individual freedom — including the freedom of limitless accumulation — Canada, following the British tradition, has been more collectivist, recognizing the need, at times, to curb individual greed in the name of the public good. This is evident in the far greater role Canadians have assigned to their government, through public ownership of major enterprises, greater regulation of private industry and a more extensive publicly supported social welfare system.

American commentators have tended to explain our willingness to accept this bigger role for government as an indication of our greater deference to authority — a favourite theme of

Americans who can see no other explanation for the fact that Canada doesn't allow everyone to carry a gun. In fact, our support for big government may not indicate a deference for authority at all, but just the opposite. It may reflect our desire to have greater control ourselves as a community, rather than to allow control to rest in the hands of some powerful private interests.

Indeed, the American notion that the greatest threat to freedom lies with big government is a curious one. Enormous concentration of wealth and corporate ownership provides tremendous clout to a small but powerful elite. While government determines the political rights of citizens — that is, what rights they have if they're charged with a criminal offence or want to march in a political demonstration — private corporate interests often determine things that are at least as important and basic to the lives of ordinary citizens, such as whether they are able to feed themselves. The sustained attack on the evils of big government, perpetrated most often by the owners and supporters of big business, obscures the key source of the powerlessness most people feel — that is, lack of economic control over their lives.

The evils of big government and the glories of the private marketplace are familiar business refrains that are basic to the American political tradition. And they have not been entirely absent in Canada. Clearly, both the Conservative and Liberal Parties in Canada have derived the bulk of their support over the years from business, and have put in place policies that have benefitted business, just as the Republican and Democratic Parties have in the U.S. But, as Canadian political scientist Gad Horowitz has suggested, what is most interesting is perhaps not how much we are like the U.S. in this respect, but how we are different. One difference Horowitz examines is the degree to which Canada has endorsed a greater role for government in managing the economy.

And Conservatives in Canada — unlike their Republican counterparts in the U.S. — have traditionally been part of this consensus. There are many possible explanations for this phenomenon. One of the most common is that Canada derives this attitude from Britain, where traditional pre-capitalist conservatism saw the community as a group of interrelated individuals who each had a place in a hierarchy and whose interests were each subservient to the larger good of the whole community. Another possible explanation is the much greater presence in Canada of socialist or left-wing movements that have sought to limit the power of private interests and have kept up the political pressure for government intervention in the marketplace. On the other hand, the explanation could be something as banal as the weather: it is so cold in Canada and conditions so harsh that we have had to band together more to survive.

Whatever the explanation, a consensus for greater government involvement evolved in Canada, generally with the support of members of the Conservative Party. In some cases, Conservative prime ministers have actively furthered the cause, even when it meant directly antagonizing business interests. Certainly Macdonald supported the idea of a strong government with powers to regulate the marketplace, and his government was the first to pass laws giving rights to trade unions. R. B. Bennett established the CBC explicitly for the purpose of maintaining national control over broadcasting rather than allowing such an important public forum to be exclusively in the hands of private corporations. Arthur Meighen nationalized three railways over the protesting howls of powerful railway interests in Montreal. And John Diefenbaker, who was frequently at odds with the country's powerful business elite, championed a kind of prairie populism that included more generous social welfare benefits and government aid to outlying regions.

This collectivist strain in our Conservative tradition is what allows Canadian conservatism to co-exist peacefully with many progressive ideals. It explains the existence in Canada of a strong current of conservatism known as "red Toryism," exemplified by people like Forsey, who are a mixture of conservatism and radicalism. This combination can also be found in a writer like Stephen Leacock, the Canadian humourist and political philosopher. A devout Conservative in the pro-British tradition, Leacock was also a progressive committed to the notion that the state had a responsibility to care for members of society, to ensure them employment and a decent way of life. He was a fan of the progressive income tax and even the inheritance tax — measures conspicuously absent from the current Conservative government's agenda. In *Arcadian Adventures of the Idle Rich*,

Leacock ridiculed a set of fictional robber barons who were indifferent to the plight of the poor and who could usually be found dreaming up ways to enrich themselves as they sat around the lavish "Mausoleum Club."

The Canadian philosopher George Grant was another important Canadian political thinker firmly in the red Tory camp. Grant was deeply suspicious of the liberal, technocratic ideology of the U.S., which he believed threatened to absorb Canada and the rest of the world into a uniform American-dominated empire. Grant saw conservatism, with its emphasis on tradition and order, as a means of preserving distinctive communities against this soulless, commercial encroachment from the south. His strong support for Diefenbaker sprang from his conviction that Dief was mounting the best defence against the continentalist thrust of the U.S. government and its sympathizers in Canada.

Even in real-world Canadian politics, this red Tory tradition has been a force. David Crombie, who served as a Conservative cabinet minister under both Joe Clark and Brian Mulroney, nicely exemplifies this. Growing up in a CCF household in Toronto, the son of a rubber salesman who had also been a milk-delivery man, Crombie developed a healthy respect for craft unions, the social gospel and the temperance movement. It was all part of a world, he recalls, that focussed on God, the community and one's personal responsibility. Crombie says that craft unions were an integral part of this sense of community, in that they allowed workers to "deal with life in a way that made them feel good about themselves" before the emergence of the big industrial unions destroyed their sense of pride in what they produced and turned work into a mere hourly grind to win a paycheque.

But, while the Crombie family had a strong tie to the working class, it also felt comfortable in the world of Canadian conservatism. While Crombie's grandfather had been a member of the United Farmers of Ontario, a populist agrarian reform movement of the 1920s, his grandfather had also supported the Conservative Party federally. And when Crombie entered municipal politics in Toronto, he won enormous support, eventually becoming mayor, on the conservative appeal of preserving the integrity of city neighbourhoods against the encroachment of developers. This was very much in the tradition of collectivist conservatism; it involved championing the rights of communities even when it meant ruffling the feathers of powerful monied interests.

Another intriguing example of this conservative-radical hybrid that haunts Canadian politics is Kenneth McNaught, the historian who paid tribute to John A. Macdonald at the cemetery. McNaught is the grandson of W. K. McNaught, a Toronto industrialist who headed the Canadian Manufacturers' Association and whom his grandson fondly remembers as something of a "minor robber baron". As a Conservative member of the Ontario legislature, McNaught's grandfather helped Conservative Premier Adam Beck develop a public sector solution to the province's energy needs with the creation of the crown corporation Ontario Hydro. McNaught's father, however, joined the CCF, as did Ken.

But the conservative and radical traditions seemed to co-exist comfortably in the McNaught family and among the broader Canadian establishment. Young Ken was sent to Upper Canada College, the private boys' school for the sons of the Toronto elite. There he and the other scions of the establishment were exposed to heavy doses of CCF thinking by the masters who ran the school, including principal "Choppy" Grant, father of George Grant. McNaught went on to become chairman of the CCF Club at Upper Canada College — an amazing concept in itself — and won a school prize for writing a history of the left-wing party. Years later, McNaught still sees himself as a progressive, yet is comfortable praising Canada's first prime minister and calling for a return to traditional conservatism.

Certainly, the conservatism of John A. Macdonald and his successors bears little resemblance to the conservatism of Brian Mulroney. Indeed, Macdonald's commitment to a strong central government and independence from the U.S. — principles that had been preserved in the political traditions of both his party and the country for nine decades after his departure — were quickly and easily abandoned by Mulroney's government, which brought Canada closer to the edge of the American orb and handed much of the traditional power of the central government to the private sector. What was going on wasn't conservatism at all, in the sense that Canadians understood the term. It was a foreign import — a version of the "neoconservatism" that Ronald Reagan had brought to the U.S. and Margaret Thatcher had brought to Britain. It was, in the words of Forsey, "just a fancy name for the biggest international romp ever mounted by the rich for skinning the poor."

Indeed, the new conservatism was really just an assortment of policies aimed at further enriching the rich and increasing their power. To be sure, it was dressed up in sophisticated lingo and philosophical trappings aimed at making it sound like a convincing political theory. But the bottom line was that all its policies first and foremost aided those with money, while making vague promises to help everyone else in due course. Whether the policy was high interest rates, free trade, tax reform or cut-backs in social programs, the rich were always the prime beneficiaries and the ones urging everyone else to take their harsh medicine stoically. The new conservatism was really nothing more than the self-interested conservatism of the business establishment. Canada was being wooed by a suitor whose intentions were all self-interested, who whispered gently in her ear, "Make me richer and you'll be richer too. . . . Someday. . . . Really. . . . You can trust me. . . . Honest."

Not surprisingly, many Canadians found themselves suspicious of this new conservatism, particularly as time went on and things only became bleaker. As the economy deteriorated badly in 1990 and 1991, the Mulroney government continued bull-headedly down the path it had set out on, despite widespread evidence of suffering. With the recession in full swing by the winter of '91, the government proceeded to introduce the regressive GST and to bring down a cut-and-slash budget that offered only more restraint and austerity. The government seemed to be stuck well below 20 percent in the polls, despite the massive public relations machine at its command — millions of dollars of taxpayers' money spent selling Tory policies to the public, a sympathetic business press and the endless resources of the BCNI promoting the new agenda.

The new conservatives were having little success selling their ideology, largely because, for most Canadians, it was clearly unpalatable. But they had a trump card up their sleeve: Globalization. Where lectures failed to win converts to the new agenda, the suggestion that Canada was in the grip of powerful global forces could be used. If Canadians were reluctant to agree to austerity measures, they could be half-coaxed, half-intimidated into accepting them on the grounds that they had no choice, that unstoppable forces in the world marketplace were forcing them to accept change.

As we have seen, the concept of Globalization was a particularly important strategy in Canada, where there was really little else to help in selling the public on the changes business wanted. Unlike the U.S., where there was a long-standing political culture based on the importance of the free market, Canada had little of this free-market mentality in its traditions. By invoking Globalization, the new conservatives could attempt to do an end-run around Canadian tradition.

The other thing the government tried was simple sneakiness. Although it prattled on endlessly in vague terms about global competitiveness, it was less than forthcoming when spelling out specifics — at least before elections. It tried its best to convince the public that the GST would be revenue-neutral when the tax briefly surfaced as a volatile issue during the '88 election campaign. It certainly never let on that the GST would result in $4 billion of the tax burden being transferred from the backs of corporations to the backs of consumers — something voters might have found to be of passing interest. Such sneakiness and hypocrisy were evident, too, in its implementation of a tough regimen of tax hikes and spending cuts in the name of deficit reduction, while quietly letting the rich off the hook with stealthy changes to the rules governing family trusts, saving some of the richest families in the country billions of dollars.

But perhaps nowhere has the government's lack of truthfulness been more evident than in its dismantling of social programs. From the beginning, there was suspicion in some quarters about Mulroney's commitment to these basic Canadian programs. So, from the beginning, Mulroney went out of his way to dispel these suspicions with promises that social programs were nothing short of a "sacred trust." Is there any language that could be stronger than this? According to the *Oxford Paperback Dictionary,* "sacred" means "associated with or dedicated to God" and a "trust" is a "firm belief in the reliability or truth or strength, etc. of a person or thing." Are there any words that could convey a firmer commitment? Mulroney hadn't just casually mentioned to Canadians that he would maintain social programs; he had presented this commitment to them as a higher order of duty, as a pledge connected with God. Is it any wonder that many Canadians were taken in by these solemn vows?

When they first caught him breaking that pledge — in his plan to remove the full indexation of old age pensions in his May '85 budget — they reacted with outrage, creating the first crisis of his leadership. Mulroney quickly retreated, reinstating full indexation. The public was satisfied. When the issue of social programs surfaced again during the '88 election campaign over free trade, Mulroney once again went out of his way to assure Canadians that free trade would in no way lead to the dismantling of social programs.

He specifically assured them, for instance, that there would be no changes in the unemployment insurance program. Yet, with the election won, the Conservatives moved quickly to begin seriously cutting back unemployment insurance. When asked about what happened to the government's commitment to leave the program untouched, Employment Minister Barbara McDougall told reporters that the government wasn't changing the program, it was improving it. What can be said about such a disingenuous response? Do we demand no higher level of truthfulness and forthrightness from our politicians?

And by 1990, the Mulroney government was blatantly cutting back on all social programs — with drastic cut-backs in payments to the provinces to cover the costs of welfare, of health and education, and of social housing. Perhaps Mulroney has satisfied himself that he never misled the Canadian public during the '88 election campaign because he only addressed the question of whether *free trade* would lead to the dismantling of these social programs. Perhaps he feels he can wipe his hands of the whole matter, confident in the belief that the dismantling of social programs has nothing to do with free trade; it was something that the government wanted to do anyway. But wouldn't an honest politician have said up-front during the campaign, "Look, free trade or no free trade, there may have to be some cuts in social programs"? Then Canadians could have demanded to know why, and there could have been a debate on the subject — and an opportunity for voters to decide the issue. But Canadians were kept in the dark. They never saw the changes coming.

Following in the footsteps of Reagan and Thatcher, Mulroney has thrust a new pro-business conservatism on Canada. But, unlike Reagan and Thatcher, who were up-front about their plans, Mulroney has been sneaky, like a man trying to seduce a woman he has no real interest in. Knowing he risked enormous opposition if he was honest with Canadians, Mulroney has brought the new conservatism to Canada stealthily.

BACK AT THE Cataraqui cemetery, the ceremony commemorating the ninety-ninth anniversary of Macdonald's death was over and the small collection of local townsfolk and members of the historical society gathered under an awning for tea and cookies. A local children's choir that had sung some old Canadian songs during the ceremony now munched on cookies and delighted in having the afternoon off school. As I mingled with the crowd, it occurred to me that I was lucky to be seeing this event before it was marred the following year by the inevitable government cavalcade that would attend the one-hundredth anniversary. The presence of dignitaries making puffed-up speeches to television cameras would surely spoil the simple beauty of this Canadian tribute.

As it was, there seemed to be something uniquely Canadian about this event and this place. Macdonald's desire to be free of the American empire was nicely symbolized here by this humble ceremony and unassuming gravesite, so lacking in American bravado. As I walked around the little hills of the cemetery, I was struck by how discreet Macdonald's grave was, tucked away among the stately old trees.

Certainly the Americans do things differently. Macdonald's simple grave — in a public cemetery full of the bodies of other, ordinary Canadians — is a far cry from the grandeur with which the U.S. pays homage to its first president. Indeed, the Americans have commemorated George Washington with a huge phallic tower that thrusts 170 metres into the air in their capital city, in line with the city's two most prestigious sites — the White House and the Capitol building. Tourists line up all day and late into the evening to ride the elevator to the top of the Washington Monument — the tallest masonry structure in the world, the brochures boast — where a snack bar and look-out spot provide the best view of the U.S. capital, which of course is also named after the founding president.

But at the Cataraqui cemetery, there are neither towering monuments nor snack bars, and from Sir John A.'s gravesite you can't even get a view of the rest of the cemetery. His gravestone, which rises a modest few feet off the ground, stands on a little crest partway up a small hill. Oddly, another more impressive gravestone belonging to a much lesser-known Canadian stands at the top of the hill. Macdonald is buried just below, along with other members of his family. And, even within the family plot, Sir John A.'s monument is relatively humble, and is dwarfed by that of his brother-in-law, the Reverend James Williamson. Macdonald's grave was even more modest before 1982, when a historical foundation managed, after some difficulty, to scrape together enough cash to refurbish it. Still, the site is so unpretentious, it is hard to find. A small black wrought-iron marker with the words "Sir John A. Macdonald" points the way to the grave, which otherwise simply blends into the rolling hills of the shady cemetery.

So, while the Americans build towering monuments to celebrate their political heroes with stately grandeur, we put ours to rest in simple burial grounds and have trouble scraping together the funds to upgrade the site. But then, unlike the Americans, we are not an imperial people. That's one of our charms. It's also one of the reasons the new conservatism — with its emphasis on individual greed and the survival of the strongest — has little resonance here.

But the new conservatism has been quietly imposed upon Canadians, without their support and largely without their knowledge. And it fits no better with the Canadian landscape than a soaring monument — complete with look-out spot and fast-food stand — would fit into the gentle hills of the Cataraqui cemetery.

INDEX

INDEX